Border Politics

Cengiz Günay • Nina Witjes
Editors

Border Politics

Defining Spaces of Governance and Forms of Transgressions

Springer

Editors
Cengiz Günay
oiip
Austrian Institute of International Affairs
Vienna, Austria

Nina Witjes
Munich Center for Technology in Society
Technical University of Munich
Munich, Germany

ISBN 978-3-319-46854-9 ISBN 978-3-319-46855-6 (eBook)
DOI 10.1007/978-3-319-46855-6

Library of Congress Control Number: 2016959615

Printed on acid-free paper

This Springer imprint is published by Springer Nature
The registered company is Springer International Publishing AG
The registered company address is: Gewerbestrasse 11, 6330 Cham, Switzerland

Add-On, Yearbook of the Austrian Institute for International Affairs (oiip), Berggasse 7, 1090 Vienna

Acknowledgements

We would like to thank the authors of this volume for their inspiring and insightful contributions and for their dedication in the various steps of this project.

The discussions we had during international conferences and workshops with many of our colleagues have been a huge motivation to pursue this book project. We are particularly glad that the volume includes different theoretic approaches, perspectives and views from scholars with different geographic and academic backgrounds. The variety of the topics addressed in the volume highlights the diverse shapes and expressions of the reconfigurations of power, politics and identities which take place at the various borders and borderlands. We hope that this volume adds new perspectives to a much needed interdisciplinary dialogue in the field of border studies and beyond.

We would also like to thank our colleagues at the Austrian Institute for International Affairs (oiip). This fifth volume of the institute's Add-On Yearbook series would not have been possible without their involvement and active support at the different stages of the project. The thought-provoking discussions have added valuable perspectives and ideas. Our special thanks go to those colleagues who have also been part of the institute's review committee. We would also like to thank the scientific advisory board of the Austrian Institute for International Affairs (oiip) for their support in putting this volume together.

Our special thanks also go to Chris Heather who has done a brilliant job on proofreading and formatting the chapters.

As in the past years, the City of Vienna has been an important and valuable partner in producing the Add-On Yearbook series of the Austrian Institute for International Affairs.

We would like to thank Springer Publishing for the kind support and assistance with this book project.

Last but not least, we are indebted to our families and friends for their support during this exciting and time-intensive intellectual journey.

Contents

Editors and Contributors

About the Editors

Cengiz Günay is a Senior Researcher at the Austrian Institute for International Affairs (oiip) and lecturer at the University of Vienna. He specializes in the transformation of statehood, the role of non-state actors and Euro-Mediterranean relations. His regional areas of expertise are the Mediterranean and specifically Turkey, Egypt and Tunisia. Cengiz Günay has published a wide range of articles, two monographs, policy analyses and policy briefs on these questions. He has initiated and co-authored the Add-On—Yearbook of the oiip series.

Nina Witjes is a Research Associate at the Research Group "Innovation, Society and Public Policy", Munich Center for Technology in Society (MCTS), Technical University Munich. Until May 2016, she was a researcher at the Austrian Institute for International Affairs, heading the research group on Science, Technology and Foreign Policy. She holds an MA in Development Studies from Vienna University and is currently pursuing her dissertation on Science, Technology and International Relations. Her main areas of interest are satellite imagery analysis and visual securizitation, geospatial big data and crisis response, geopolitical infrastructures as well as conceptual intersections of Science Technology Studies (STS) and Security Studies.

Contributors

Reem Ahmed Institute for Peace and Security Research, University of Hamburg, Hamburg, Germany

Clemens Binder Austrian Institute for International Affairs (oiip), Vienna, Austria

Maren Borkert Centre for Entrepreneurship, School of Economics and Management, Technical University Berlin, Berlin, Germany

Alexander C. Diener Department of Geography and Atmospheric Science, University of Kansas, Lawrence, KS, USA

Vedran Dzihic Austrian Institute for International Affairs (oiip), Vienna, Austria

Cengiz Günay Austrian Institute for International Affairs (oiip), Vienna, Austria

Joshua Hagen College of Arts and Sciences, Northern State University, Aberdeen, SD, USA

Marko Lovec Centre of International Relations (CIR), University of Ljubljana, Ljubljana, Slovenia

Nicholas Natividad Criminal Justice Department, New Mexico State University, Las Cruces, NM, USA

Polly Pallister-Wilkins Department of Political Science, University of Amsterdam, Amsterdam, The Netherlands

Daniela Pisoiu Austrian Institute for International Affairs (oiip), Vienna, Austria

Sybille Reinke de Buitrago Institute for Peace Research and Security Policy, University of Hamburg, Hamburg, Germany

Helena Rytövuori-Apunen Tampere Peach Research Institute, University of Tampere, Tampere, Finland

Gabriella Sanchez National Security Studies Institute, University of Texas at El Paso, El Paso, TX, USA

Paul Trauttmansdorff Austrian Institute for International Affairs (oiip), Vienna, Austria

Nina Witjes Munich Center for Technology in Society (MCTS), Technical University Munich, Munich, Germany

Introduction

Cengiz Günay and Nina Witjes

The fall of the Iron Curtain in 1989, was heralded by many authors (Ohmae 1995; Shapiro and Alker 1996 and others) as the beginning of a new borderless age. Impressed by the speed of economic globalization, the rapid spread of communication networks, and the increase of affordable international mass transportation, they assumed the end of the world as we knew it and the beginning of a global liberal era. However, despite the proliferation of international institutions and organizations as well as transnational networks of non-state actors, borders remain a prominent fixture of the post Cold War era. Borders have not disappeared, they are still a reality on maps and a physical experience at security checks and passport controls (Rumford 2006: 156), but they have become more diffuse, turning whole territories into borderlands (Balibar in Rumford 2006). While globalization might have seriously changed the consciousness of borders in the global North, where 'borders are being both multiplied and reduced in their localization and their function, they are being thinned out and doubled' (Ibid.: 156); in many parts of the South borders have always held a different meaning. In many regions state borders have reflected European powers' attempts to transform and organize the world by exporting their own conceptions of state and borders. Balibar and Williams (2002) speak of the construction of 'another Europe' which was never really achieved. Most of the territories that gained independence and became sovereign states, represented in the international arena, were hardly unified or homogeneous nation states (Balibar and Williams 2002: 75). In most cases the entities that gained independence were traditional units, created and constructed by their colonizers,

C. Günay (✉)
Austrian Institute for International Affairs (oiip), Vienna, Austria
e-mail: Cengiz.gunay@oiip.ac.at

N. Witjes
Munich Center for Technology in Society (MCTS), Technical University Munich, Munich, Germany
e-mail: Nina.witjes@tum.de

C. Günay, N. Witjes (eds.), *Border Politics*, DOI 10.1007/978-3-319-46855-6_1

some with scant regard to realities on the ground, often driving extended families and ethnicities apart. In many parts of the South, cross-border migration and movements are an everyday practice of people living in borderlands, reducing the meaning of borders to little more than demarcation lines on maps.

While our understanding of borders has deepened to encompass disciplines beyond international relations, the idea of sovereign nation states as the primary actors of international affairs has proved to be resilient and is still well rooted in the international system (see chapter "Changing Modalities of Power in the Twenty-First Century" by Diener and Hagen). The modern world order might have experienced various political changes, but recognized state borders have proved to be rather stable. Since World War II, only a few conventional symmetric wars have redrawn international borders and hardly any of these have been recognized by the international community (e.g. Turkey's invasion of Northern Cyprus, USSR's invasion of Afghanistan, Argentina's invasion of the Falkland Islands etc). One can hold that 70 years of a relatively stable international state system have supported the idea that the world has moved beyond conventional wars and that borders have become regarded as fixed territorial lines and demarcations, which organize the world, and that no one would dare to redraw. In recent years however, a series of developments have profoundly challenged the notion of state borders as fixed and irreversible realities of the international system. Russia's annexation of the Crimea in 2014 and the ensuing war in Eastern Ukraine are events which highlighted that borders are not only still heavily contested, but that the limits of sovereign nation states are currently also challenged and redefined by non-state actors such as para-military groups. The war in Syria, the threat of Iraq falling apart, the rise of the so-called Islamic State (IS) and terrorist attacks around the world are other examples for the reconfiguration of power, the redefinition of nation, identity and sovereignty.

In different ways, these developments have called borders and border politics into question, and challenged peace, stability and security in the world. In many countries of the global North disappointment with the economic outcomes of globalization and a growing feeling of insecurity and unease have triggered more rigorous approaches to border politics. Growing calls for safeguarding sovereignty and control through the deployment of more military, police, fortification and more surveillance technologies along borders have been heard in Europe and the US.

Europe's so called 'refugee crisis' in the summer of 2015, when thousands of people marched across the continent without being checked and controlled, first triggered a wave of solidarity that was soon replaced by intense debates on border security, the nature of border regimes, and integration with implications that reach far beyond Europe. The inability of the European Union to develop a common European strategy, and the lack of solidarity among EU member states, have called the whole union into question. The partial suspension of the Schengen regime—characterized by the hardening of surveillance and control at the external borders and the removal of physical obstacles to the free movement of persons and goods inside—revealed the difficulties the idea of a world without borders faced even in an already highly integrated European context. The EU's ideal of a borderless single market for the free flow of goods and persons is now counteracted by the resurrection of walls, barbwire fences, and military and police patrols along national borders within the Schengen area. In view of the EU and its member states' inability to respond to people's fears and concerns, nationalist, anti-immigration, EU-critical forces have dominated public discourse. Migrants have been largely represented as a threat to national security (Huysmans 2000; Guild 2006 and others) and the nexus established between immigration and security (van Munster 2009) has supported seclusionist, isolationist and in some cases xenophobic voices. The concern for national sovereignty, and discontent with the scale of migration, played an important role in the Vote Leave campaign in the UK. The Leave camp initially focused on the economy and British sovereignty, but soon discovered that 'taking back control' over migration provided a stronger message (Mason 2016). The rhetoric of the leave campaign suggested that things were out of control and that continued EU membership would stop British people from controlling who comes into their country; that it would be impossible to stop criminals and low-skilled migrants from entering while potential job creators from non-European countries would be blocked (Vote Leave 2016). While this book was in its final preparation stage, the future direction of the European Union was called into question by Britain's decision to leave an act that poses a severe challenge to the illusion of a borderless Europe.

In the US, the question of migration as a threat to the survival of the nation has been exploited in a highly populist fashion by presidential candidate Donald Trump who claimed that 'a nation without borders is not a nation' and, therefore, that a wall needs to be built across the southern border of the US (Trump 2016). Trump's argument entails the idea that irregular migration from South American countries is undermining the sovereignty of the American nation, indirectly defined as being primarily white in contrast to Mexican Latinos (see also chapter "Reframing Migrant Smuggling as a Form of Knowledge: A View from the US-Mexico Border" by Sanchez and Natividad).

Recurrent calls for more border security in order to protect the nation have been as much a reaction to a feeling of insecurity and fear caused by terrorism and crime, as they have been to increasing social insecurity. Migrants have often been blamed as the source of both. Didier Bigo (2002) calls attention to the fact that securitization is not just a common response to a rise in the feeling of insecurity caused by crime, terrorism or the negative effects of globalization, but it is also a transversal political technology which has been used and misused by various institutions as a mode of governmentality. In the context of securitization, Bigo (2002: 65) sees in migration the creation of a 'truth' about the link between crime, unemployment, migration, terrorism and other security threats.

Through border controls states have aimed to maintain state sovereignty over an exclusive territory. The control of the movement of people and goods has entailed categorization and identification and thereby strengthened the state's monopoly to define what are the legitimate means of movement and terms of trade. Apart from providing an instrument of sovereignty, control and governance, ordering space, delimiting legal and political authority, regulating entry and access to the community of the 'nation' and managing trade, from a constructivist perspective borders determine the imagined community that a person belongs to, and which shapes mindsets and influences perspectives (Anderson 1983). In other words, borders not only define interactions in the international sphere, they also create and limit the space for the 'exercise of intellect, imagination, and political will' (Agnew 2008: 2).

Border studies are a broad discipline that has undergone various shifts. While early works on border politics in the 1960s (Minghi 1963; Prescott 1965 and others), mainly dealt with borders as the demarcation of boundaries and almost exclusively focused on political geography, more recent studies have shifted their focus to human practices which 'constitute and represent differences in space. In other words, the border is now understood as a verb in the sense of bordering' (van Houtum 2005: 672). This new focus, certainly accelerated by globalization, entailed further opening up towards different disciplines such as anthropology, sociology, history, political sciences, economics and others as well as the inclusion of different perspectives and approaches (i.e. state-centric, geopolitical, law-based, performative and many others).

A change also occurred in the understanding and conceptualization of 'the role and meaning of a state's territoriality and of its sovereignty' (Paasi 2005: 665). Badie (1996), Mansbach (1989), Ruggie (1993) and others have studied the changing territorial dimension of states and its repercussions on sovereignty and international relations. Agnew warned not to fall into the 'territorial trap' as 'social, economic, and political life cannot be ontologically contained within the territorial boundaries of states' and that an 'idealization of the territorial state would hinder the perception of changes in its meaning and its role' (Agnew 1994: 77).

Rumford (2006: 156) highlights that under the influence of globalization theory borders have been either contextualized by networks where the 'space of places (the territorial nation-state) is being replaced by a space of flows' or theorized 'in the context of societal transformations and a new spatiality of politics'. Among others, authors such as Andreas (2003) and Torpey (2000) have studied through whom, and by which means, borders have been controlled.

From the beginning of the 2000s border studies have increasingly explored the biopolitical dimension of border governance (Bigo 2002; Dillon 2007). Induced by a significant growth in international travel and migration as well as new surveillance technologies, the focus shifted from the study of traditional territorially-based forms of border control to mobility management, where the bodies of people have become the sites of border policing (see chapter "Humanitarian Borderwork" by Pallister-Wilkins).

Although, recent inter-state territorial disputes have supported the resurgence of classical or traditional border studies that explore borders as physical lines of separation and political demarcations from a geopolitical perspective, the majority of studies in this volume have applied a post-modern or critical approach. These studies can be roughly divided into two different lines of enquiry; those that deal with the effects of bordering on space and territories as borderlands, on identities and the everyday liminal practices which perform, reshape, reinterpret, reframe and transgress the border and have the potential to challenge and undermine sovereignty and authority (e.g. Anzaldúa 1987). Other studies are more concerned with the spaces of governance created by border politics. Here again one can identify different interests; those studies that have dealt in a de-territorialized perspective of digital border governance often with a focus on the professionals in charge of the management of risk and fear (e.g. Bigo 2002), and those which have rather stuck to a conception of power rooted in territory.

This edited volume does not claim to capture the whole breadth of the field of border studies. Rather, it aims to instigate dialogue among different disciplines, approaches, scientific backgrounds, schools, and geographical perspectives. Contributions to this volume vary from the study of borders in a geopolitical sense to their role in the context of social inequality, othering and different identity constructions. They deal with border politics and their effects on the international system, geography, international law, how they shape governmentality, everyday practices, forms of transgressions, discourses, identities and forms of humanitarian aid.

The volume is divided into the following four parts: First, borders as lines of conflict and identity formation; second, practices of border crossing and border making; third, European border politics; and fourth, borders beyond the nation state.

The first stream of work addresses the geographies of borders, approaching them as contested and contingent delineations between nation states, as visible and dominant features of geopolitical constellations. Here, Alexander Diener and Joshua Hagen argue that visions of a borderless world have recently been questioned by a resurgence of an international system, still deeply rooted in the ideal of nation-states and their efforts to constitute distinct sovereign territories. By pointing to such recent crises as the Ukrainian-Russian conflict, the emergence and spread of ISIS, and the territorial dispute taking place in the South China Sea, the authors contest the ideal of a borderless world. Hagen and Diener contend that borders are, and have always been, far more than lines on a map or locations of demarcation. Rather than eliding their role, the authors find that an ever increasing interaction and interdependence between different places around the world emphasizes the significance of borders and the ways they are shaping and transforming societies, economies, and also ecosystems. From the perspective of critical geography, Diener and Hagen understand the variability of porousness and the breadth of the borderlands as constituting not only central themes of geopolitical research but also vigorous forces affecting people around the world.

Remarkably, the absence of borders makes them no less of a dominant feature of current geopolitical struggles, as Clemens Binder argues in his contribution. In the same vein as Diener and Hagen, he sees borders as a means of territorial demarcation vital to states' foreign and security policies. Binder argues that border disputes are often more complex on the sea where a clear definition of borders is lacking. From a realist perspective, this chapter analyses the United Nations Convention of the Law of the Seas (UNCLOS), which attempts to offer a maritime border regime.

UNCLOS fails to regulate conflicting claims and border disputes on the sea as it lacks the necessary mechanisms that a completely functional border regime would require. Exploring the two examples of the Arctic Sea and the South China Sea as security dilemmas, the author finds that these represent areas where the lack of defined borders causes conflicting interests, especially economic ones, and where tensions are increasing.

Also from a political science perspective, Vedran Dzihic analyses the rebirth of border (power) politics during the Syrian refugee crisis in 2015 and early 2016, in the context of a re-emergence of nationalism Serbia and Croatia. Here, the so-called 'Western Balkans-Route' became a major arterial road for refugees on their way to Germany and other Western European countries. Drawing on Rogers Brubaker's relational approach, this contribution first establishes a conceptual model to explain the continued importance of nationalism and consequently of border (power) politics in the region. It then explores the conflict over refugees between Croatia and Serbia in Fall 2015, and shows how newly emerging political battles and identity discourses surround the concept of borders and demarcations in the Balkans. According to Dzihic, the refugee crisis has re-opened and re-fuelled old identity conflict lines and contributed to an increase in nationalist rhetoric and behavior, and thus to a reaffirmation of national borders in the Balkans.

The next part of this volume applies a slightly different empirical and analytical approach to borders in that it mainly focuses on the various processes of transcending borders, be it illegalized border crossings or cross-border Humanitarian movements. In their chapter on 'Reframing Migrant Smuggling as a Form of Knowledge' Gabriella Sanchez and Nicholas Natividad provide the reader with a view from the US-Mexico Border and propose a critical revision to mainstream engagements with the practice of migrant smuggling from an ethnographical inspired perspective on border and security studies. Drawing on extensive fieldwork data on human smuggling, Sanchez and Natividad reframe migrant smuggling as a component of community-originated forms of protection that aim at reducing the vulnerability inherent in clandestine journeys, rather than being a criminal practice alone. In their view, these 'coyote-led journeys' can also be understood as a form of human security from below that carries deep epistemological roots. Inspired by postcolonial approaches and methodologies, this chapter critically analyzes the frameworks present in academic engagements with migrant smuggling. It thus contributes to the field of border studies by articulating solutions for moving beyond oversimplified accounts of victimized migrants and inhumane smugglers.

Focussing on a different part of the world, the following chapter is concerned with the practices that lie at the 'inbetween', addressing recent changes in the constellations of actors in border (making) practices. In her contribution to this volume, Polly Pallister-Wilkins addresses the changing practices employed by European member states and supranational EU actors such as Frontex in the field of border politics. Based on extensive fieldwork carried out at border sites during the height of the refugee crisis in Greece, she argues that these have increasingly taken account of humanitarian concerns and actively pursued humanitarian practices concerned with saving lives. These changes are understood as being driven by the reduction in safe and legal routes for those fleeing conflict, abuses of their human rights and poverty. Referring to concepts such as biopolitics and intervention, this chapter argues that these restrictions produce increasingly violent border spaces, which result in the need for humanitarian, lifesaving interventions to relieve the effects of such violence. Pallister-Wilkins establishes the notion of 'humanitarian borderwork' as a concept that considers two different but interrelated areas: while one concerns the ways in which demands to save lives in border contexts impacts on the practices and performances of those engaged in border policing; the other addresses the ways that humanitarian actors have entered this field of border performance to save lives and alleviate suffering while also influencing the making of borders. The chapter concludes by finding that the enactment of humanitarian principles is currently changing older forms of borderwork that were concerned with stopping, defending and securing territory to an approach that is increasingly concerned with securing lives.

The following part of this volume addresses border and migration politics through different empirical and disciplinary lenses that all touch upon highly relevant questions at the nexus of borders, authority and identity. Furthermore, contributions to this part share a focus on the recent developments that take place on the level of European Union border politics and the Schengen regime, analyzing a broad variety of issues. These reach from technology-based border management and the pooling of information via its related databases, to analysis of the complex decision-making processes developed in the context of the Dublin agreement. They contribute to an enhanced understanding of the ways that policy makers are attempting to deal with the current refugee crisis and the changing role of transnational border practices. The first of these chapters analyzes the 'Politics of Digital Borders' uncovering how digital systems are deployed and enacted in the processes of identification, data collection and categorization of migrating persons. Paul Trautmannsdorf sees Information and Communication Technologies (ICTs) and large-scale digital databases as playing a crucial role in the European management of borders and mobility governance. Since the 1990 Schengen Agreement, three large-scale IT systems and a number of information sharing mechanisms have emerged. One of the most important agencies here is EU-LISA (responsible for the continuous exchange of data between national authorities). Drawing on Science and Technology Studies (STS) and political sociology, the chapter examines the ways in which digital technologies are deployed for the governance of cross-border mobility. Based on an in-depth analysis of policy documents issued by the European Commission and the European Council, it highlights the de-territorializing effects of digital border governance and the key role of the human body in identification and categorization processes. Trautmannsdorf argues that digital borders are co-produced (Jasanoff 2004) by the interaction and interplay of human actors and technological systems at the various border sites. In doing so, this chapter also contributes to an overdue engagement with digital border politics from the perspective of STS as well as to the emerging intersections between STS and international relations (see for instance Weiss 2015; Witjes and Olbrich forthcoming).

Marko Lovec's chapter investigates the interaction between issues, positions, decision-making rules and rhetoric applied on the EU level during the European migrant and refugee crisis of 2015. Lovec argues that the Schengen/Dublin system (which requires that the first EU member state of entry takes full legal responsibility for migrants and applicants for asylum), has placed an asymmetrical burden on EU border states, resulting in an over-emphasis on the fight against illegal migration and the reduction of protections for refugees. The chapter argues that the Schengen system has been primarily analyzed through the lens of intergovernmental decision-making processes and that the dominance of security discourses has enabled member states to block the sharing of burdens. Grounded in mid-range theory, the author argues against such an approach and finds that the regulatory framework is not due to a particular institutional-discursive setting as such but rather due to deeper causes such as the absence of community policies in areas relevant to migrations and asylum. Furthermore, Lovec concludes, firstly, that the sharing of burdens as such was in fact not a disputed issue, secondly, that there is broad support for the existing policy among member states, and thirdly, that departure from a veto setting triggered a nationalist security rhetoric that deepened the crisis, suggesting the role of deeper level causes.

While these chapters address borders as having been constructed by social actors as well as technologies, the following chapter applies more conceptual approaches to the role of borders and the making of (trans)national identities under the Schengen Regime. In her contribution on the 'Meaning of Borders for National Identity and State Authority', Sybille Reinke de Buitrago asks if, and how, borders can be effectively maintained in times of massive humanitarian crises and refugee influx, and what such mass movements of people imply for both the authority and sovereignty of states with regard to issues of national identity. Premised on the perspectives of critical geopolitics and post-structuralism, the chapter enquires into concepts of bordering, ordering and othering. Reinke de Buitrago understands national borders as a function to distinguish, demarcate and divide, to protect and maintain a particular socio-political system with specific norms, but also as contact points. The chapter argues that in a globalized and more populous world, with the possibility of masses of people moving more readily between countries, new processes of identification with, and differentiation from, an 'other' are likely to emerge. Here, the national sense of belonging may be both diluted and enlarged. In light of the European Union's Schengen regime with its strong external, but soft internal borders, this chapter contributes to a more nuanced understanding of processes of othering, ordering and bordering in the context of the current refugee crisis.

The final part of this volume addresses the changing role of borders beyond the nation state level, or in transnational settings like European border management. Here, contributions reach from a focus on subcultures and jihadi radicalization, to epistemic challenges in the conceptualization of borders, to the different forms of inclusion and exclusion of migrants in knowledge societies. The chapter contributed by Reem Ahmed and Daniela Pisoiu, for instance, illustrates how a jihadi subculture is driven by the need to resist the Western mainstream and the perceived notion that the West is attempting to manage the conduct of Muslims. Offering an overview on recent developments in research on jihadi radicalization, the authors argue that contemporary discourse on terrorism has largely evolved in terms of its unit of analysis from organizations and networks to include 'movements', 'communities', 'milieus', or indeed 'subcultures'. In general, they see subcultures as having been considered for a long time as economically and politically marginal, emerging out of frustration with the impossibility to adapt to mainstream standards and to more generally be successful. In line with recent scholarship on jihadism, the authors acknowledge the autonomous rather than deterministic nature of the jihadi subculture, and their increasingly strong political involvement, as drawing on a transnational identity. Here, individuals living in various European countries seem to have become less related to their national or ethnic identity and to see themselves more as part of a global community of believers.

In her chapter on the analytical, normative and epistemic challenges of studying borders beyond the state, Helena Rytövuori-Apunen sees borders, with reference to the dividing lines between different states, as one of the most heavily institutionalized concepts in the practice of international relations. Addressing the examples of the European Union, Russia, and the breakaway regions of Nagorno-Karabakh, Transnistria, and Gagauzia, she argues that a whole range of other borders escape our attention when applying conceptual *a priori* such as the state-centred view of the world and its normative parallels in the b/ordering principles of sovereignty and territorial integrity. She reflects on three interrelated aspects of this problem. First, the analytical perspectives for examining how the bordering practices of non-state actors, such as internationally unrecognized but internally functioning *de facto* states as well as state agencies, challenge and consolidate internationally recognized borders. Second, the chapter argues that the erosion of international law relating to state borders has made these principles susceptible to political use, and that these discussions have left in their shadow the dynamic social processes in which borders are contested, created and confirmed in international relations. Lastly, inquiries into the reality of borders, in relation to the concepts that define them and their practical implications, must have a place in research in order to address this problem and proactively contribute to the prevention of destructive outbursts of border-related conflicts. Therefore, this paper proposes a pragmatist interpretation of reality to uncover the depth of borders beyond the state.

In the last chapter Maren Borkert addresses the importance of science and knowledge as crucial elements in integration policy making. While European countries differ in terms of their migration histories and policies, this chapter shows a common trend in recent migration policy making to link control with integration. The introduction of *compulsory integration courses for newcomers* before and after entry marks a clear shift from principally exercising territorial control to more complex forms of regulating access to, and participation in, society. This establishment of '*a border within*' is accompanied by the re-definition of European territory along cultural-social lines (*Europeanism*), which translates into exclusionary mechanisms for specific groups of migrants, particularly women from Arab/Islamic societies. Using Austria as a case study this chapter illustrates how migrants are exempted from dialogue structures, even in migration matters, highlighting mechanisms of *exclusion* in the *European knowledge society*. Empirically based on two European comparative research projects conducted between 2009 and 2013, Borkert concludes that the area of 'integration' can be seen as Europe's new frontier in which related policies function as lines of demarcation and separation for what is deemed Europe's distinct 'spiritual-religious and moral heritage' (Charter of Fundamental Rights of the European Union 2007).

References

Agnew, J. (1994). The territorial trap: The geographical assumptions of international relations theory. *Review of International Political Economy, 1*(1), 53–80.

Agnew, J. (2008). Borders on the mind: Re-framing border thinking. *Ethics & Global Politics*. Retrieved from http://www.ethicsandglobalpolitics.net/index.php/egp/article/view/1892

Anderson, B. (1983). *Imagined communities: Reflections on the origins and spread of nationalism*. New York: Verso.

Andreas, P. (2003). Redrawing the line: Borders and security in the twenty-first century. *International Security, 28*(2), 78–111.

Anzaldúa, G. (1987). *Borderlands/La Frontera: The new Mestiza*. San Francisco, CA: Aunt Lute Book.

Badie, B. (1996). La fin des territoires. Essai sur le désordre international et l'utilité sociale du respect. *Politique étrangère, 61*(1), 220–221.

Balibar, E., & Williams, E. M. (2002). World borders, political borders. *PMLA, Special Topic: Mobile Citizens, Media States, 117*(1), 71–78.

Bigo, D. (2002). Security and immigration: Toward a critique of the governmentality of unease. *Alternatives, 27*(Special Issue), 63–92.

Charter of Fundamental Rights of the European Union. EC, (2007/C 303/01). Retrieved from https://fra.europa.eu/sites/default/files/charter-of-fundamental-rights-of-the-european-union-2007-c_303-01_en.pdf

Dillon, M. (2007). Governing terror: The state of emergency of biopolitical emergence. *International Political Sociology, 1*(1), 7–28.

Guild, E. (2006). The Europeanisation of Europe's asylum policy. *International Journal of Refugee Law, 18*(34), 630–651.

Huysmans, J. (2000). The European Union and the securitization of migration. *Journal of Common Market Studies, 38*(5), 751–777.

Jasanoff, S. (Ed.). (2004). *States of knowledge. The co-production of science and social order*. London: Routledge.

Mansbach, R. (1989). *The state, conceptual chaos, and the future of international relations theory*. Boulder, CO: Lynne Rienner.

Mason, R. (2016, June 24). How did UK end up voting to leave the European Union? *The Guardian*. Retrieved from http://www.theguardian.com/politics/2016/jun/24/how-did-uk-end-up-voting-leave-european-union

Minghi, J. (1963). Boundary studies in political geography. *Annals of the Association of American Geographers, 53*, 407–428.

Ohmae, K. (1995). *The end of the nation-state*. New York: Free Press.

Paasi, A. (2005). Generations and the 'development' of border studies. *Geopolitics, 10*(4), 663–671.

Prescott, V. (1965). *The geography of frontiers and boundaries*. London: Hutchinson.

Ruggie, J. G. (1993). Territoriality and beyond: Problematizing modernity in international relations. *International Organization, 47*(1), 139–174.
Rumford, C. (2006). Theorizing borders. *European Journal of Social Theory, 9*(2), 155–169.
Shapiro, M., & Alker, H. (Eds.). (1996). *Challenging boundaries: Global flows, territorial identities*. Minneapolis, MN: University of Minnesota Press.
Torpey, J. (2000). *The invention of the passport: Surveillance, citizenship and the state*. Cambridge: Cambridge University Press.
Trump, D. (2016). Immigration reform that will make America great again. *Donaldjtrump.com*. Retrieved from https://www.donaldjtrump.com/positions/immigration-reform
Van Houtum, H. (2005). The geopolitics of borders and boundaries. *Geopolitics, 10*, 672–679.
Van Munster, R. (2009). *Securitizing immigration. The politics of risk in the EU*. London: Palgrave Macmillan.
Vote Leave. (2016). Briefing: The EU immigration system is immoral and unfair. *Vote Leave*. Retrieved from http://www.voteleavetakecontrol.org/briefing_immigration
Weiss, C. (2015). How do science and technology affect international affairs? *Minerva, 53*(4), 411–430.
Witjes, N., & Olbrich, P. (forthcoming). Fragile transparency: Satellite imagery and the making of international security issues. *Science and Public Policy*.

Part I
Borders: Lines of Conflict and Identity Formation

Changing Modalities of Power in the Twenty-First Century

Alexander C. Diener and Joshua Hagen

Abstract Once fashionable predictions of an imminent borderless world have been questioned by recent headlines that suggest an international system very much rooted in the ideal of nation-states and their efforts to constitute distinct sovereign territories. State borders remain among the most visible features of geopolitics and useful political modalities for managing trans-border dynamics of environmental change, migration, and trade, among other issues. Rather than eliding their role, the growing interaction and interdependence between different places around the world emphasizes their significance and the way they shape, divide, and unite the world's societies, economies, and ecosystems. Borders have never constituted absolute demarcations of group identities or unambiguously reflected spatialities of power. Their material and cartographic production nevertheless afforded them an idealized gravitas among many theorists and the general public. This chapter joins a growing literature challenging this idealization by contending that borders are, and have always been, far more than lines on a map or locations of demarcation. Their variability of porousness and the breadth of the borderlands they engender constitute not only central themes of geopolitical research but also active forces affecting people around the world. This chapter examines current international crises to explore specific lines of inquiry, research, and theory within this growing, multidisciplinary field of border studies.

Keywords Borders • China • Iraq • Islamic State • Refugees • Russia • South China Sea • Syria • Terrorism • Turkey • Ukraine • Sovereignty • Nationalism

A.C. Diener (✉)
Department of Geography and Atmospheric Science, University of Kansas, Lawrence, KS, USA
e-mail: diener@ku.edu

J. Hagen
College of Arts and Sciences, Northern State University, Aberdeen, SD, USA
e-mail: Joshua.Hagen@northern.edu

C. Günay, N. Witjes (eds.), *Border Politics*, DOI 10.1007/978-3-319-46855-6_2

1 Introduction

Since the Age of Exploration and the dawn of modern cartography, people have grown accustomed to visualizing the world as a mosaic of sovereign territorial states demarcated by clearly defined and ideally mutually-affirmed borders. The number of states and the courses of their borders may fluctuate through successive waves of colonization and decolonization, conquest and revolution, coercion and negotiation, but the notion of a state-based world order remained the dominant and often unquestioned paradigm. The end of the Cold War, the birth of the internet age, and the proliferation of myriad transnational corporations, non-governmental organizations, and inter-governmental agencies, to name a few examples, were taken by many as harbingers of an imminent borderless world (Ohmae 1995; O'Brien 1992). At the turn of this century, state-centric thinking seemed obsolete as societies grappled with an array of new challenges, including climate change, economic inequality, environmental sustainability, terrorism, and undocumented migration. Some hypothesized that a new world framed around networks of nodes and flows would transcend and largely erase state borders and territorial-based identities (Castells 1997).

It was against this backdrop that world leaders like American President George H. W. Bush spoke of 'a new world order' in which a justice-based ideal of multilateral, global governance would replace the rivalry-based bipolarity that dominated the twentieth century. Academics such as Kenichi Ohmae (1995) followed suit with best-selling books proclaiming that neoliberal economic linkages, and the rise of global corporate management, would supersede the bordered state-system and give rise to a 'borderless world.' Soon, a broad consensus emerged among many leading figures in economics, business, information technology, and the media around the idea of globalization as an irresistible process of de-territorialization in which the significance of borders would precipitously decline (see Caney 2005; Friedman 2005; Fukayama 1991; Kuper 2004; O'Brien 1992; Ohmae 1990, 1995). Humanity seemed to have entered an age of 'end-ism', such as the end of the state, the end of history, the end of geography, etc. The excitement spilled over into popular culture with high-tech corporations like Microsoft promoting ubiquitous slogans asking 'where do you want to go today?' implying that overcoming distance was merely a matter of desire.

In retrospect, these prognostications seem rather exaggerated and a bit naïve. They underestimated the continuing power of ethno-territorial attachment, notions of place-based belonging, and aspirations for sovereign control (Murphy 2012; Agnew 2009; Diener and Hagen 2009). Advances in technology (air travel, containerization, internet, cell phones, etc.) have certainly opened unprecedented avenues for mobility and communication, but people remain organizers of spaces and makers of places in a fundamental sense (Sack 1997). The creation and maintenance of borders are intrinsic to those processes, whether they are the highly visible borders dividing sovereign states or the less visible borders that demarcate places of work, leisure, public, and private in our daily lives.[1] Yet if expectations of an imminent borderless world are simplistic, it is important to acknowledge that borders and the processes of bordering (i.e. means by which space is divided, organized, and controlled) are evolving in often-contradictory ways over time and in different parts of the world. While acknowledging that new spatialities are forming at different scales, for the sake of brevity, this chapter will illuminate how borders remain a key political modality for enacting state power through an examination of four contemporary crises.

The first case focuses on the conflict between Russia and Ukraine over rightful possession of the Crimean and Donbass regions. Officially considered part of Ukraine's sovereign territory, these regions host large ethnic Russian populations. Clear majorities of Russians in some localities enjoined with specific geographic imaginaries of the *Ruskiy Mir* (Russian World) and discourses of ill-treatment by the Ukrainian-government to constitute a public rationalization for Moscow's annexation of Crimea and a mixture of overt and covert support for secessionist movements in other regions. This case highlights the evolution of 'traditional' border disputes between sovereign states to encompass state militaries disguised as non-state actors (e.g. 'Little Green Men' or the masked, insignia-less troops that crossed the border from Russia into Ukraine) and novel attempts to both reinforce and undermine the ideal of state sovereignty and by extension the notion of territorial inviolability as a foundational principle of international law (Agnew 2009).

The second case investigates the tangled web of territorial claims over the islands, reefs, shoals, and assorted maritime features scattered across the South China Sea. The central dispute revolves around the Chinese government's assertion that its sovereignty extends southward to encompass practically every conceivable piece of land between it and the northern coast of Borneo. To outside observers, these features seem little more than worthless rocks, but they possess strategic value far beyond their diminutive size because ownership confers sovereignty and exclusive economic rights over the surrounding waters. In addition to sitting astride some of the world's busiest shipping lanes, these waters have long supported productive fisheries and contain significant oil and natural gas deposits. The acrimony between the states surrounding the South China Sea illustrates the increasing stakes concerning claims of territorial waters and maritime sovereignty by way of seemingly innocuous and often overlooked land features.

The third case examines the emergence of the so-called Islamic State (IS) and its proclamation of a universal caliphate demanding the allegiance of all Muslims and subjugation of non-Muslims. IS has literally erased the border between its Syrian and Iraqi territories and, with declarations of allegiance from other extremist

[1]Despite operating at multiple scales and with varied levels of formal delineation, these different manifestations of borders are all intrinsic to the human propensity 'to draw lines that divide the world into specific places, territories, and categories.' As such, borders fulfill a variety of functions as 'dividers of space, symbolic markers of control, and social processes of daily life' (Diener and Hagen 2012: 1–2).

groups, now exercises effective control over parts of Afghanistan, Libya, and Yemen, as well as a lesser presence in Egypt, Nigeria, and several other countries. Yet IS employs many of the same basic territorial strategies and assumptions of the state-based system upon which it has effectively declared war. This is most clearly evident in its attempts to export its brand of illiberal cosmopolitanism while morphing from non-state terrorist organization to something resembling a traditional territorial state.

The fourth case, namely the surge in migration to Europe, has been catalyzed, at least in part, by the growth of IS and more generally structural factors such as global economic inequality, foreign interventions (and the lack thereof), and the failure of governments across the greater Middle East to enact political/social reforms, alleviate poverty, and consequently impede upheaval and violence (Khouri 2015). The European Union's model of supranational governance has faltered in response to this humanitarian crisis, so much so that several member states, as well as neighboring states in the Balkan region, have reinstated border controls and erected new border fences to block the arrival of migrants. Large-scale population movements are hardly unprecedented, even in Europe's relatively recent history, but this most recent immigration surge raises divergent views of the priority afforded considerations of refugee status and human rights versus resurgent notions of territorial-based identity, citizenship, and governance.

Taken together, these four crises lay bare the continued and evolving importance of borders and territory in shaping international affairs in our globalized world. These cases also expose how 'traditional' border disputes, such as those involving competing territorial claims or disagreements concerning migration regulation, are evolving to encompass new modalities and spatialities of power. Yet borders continue to provide a dominant, perhaps even predominant, spatial framework for filtering people, resources, commerce, and ideas entering/exiting a given territory and as an instrument of projecting power across the international system and within state territories.

2 Borders, Nationalism, and the Political Modalities of Sovereignty

Before turning to our case studies, it is useful to review some recent themes of border research. A key premise of current scholarship emanating from a variety of disciplines is that borders are social constructs and the processes of bordering occur at multiple scales and sites, not just at the margins of the state (Paasi 1998: 76). This stands in stark contrast to the long-running refrains of Westphalian ideology that naturalize borders as rigid lines dividing nation-states. John Agnew (2009) refers to the effect of this naturalization as the 'territorial trap' which stems from three interrelated and flawed assumptions. First, states are regarded as possessing absolute sovereignty of their territories. Second, domestic, internal affairs and foreign, external affairs are assumed to be separate spheres of activity with their own distinct standards of conduct. Third, state borders are assumed to correspond to the borders of society and thereby divide the globe into discrete nation-states and their corresponding societies.

Over the course of recent history, these three assumptions proved mutually reinforcing and, when combined with the fervor of mass nationalism, projected an aura of legitimacy and permanence for a state-centric worldview and the corresponding partitioning of territory. This appeal became hegemonic during the nineteenth century as practitioners of the new social sciences, especially sociology, political science, and economics, set out to prove that their objects of study were best understood and organized through state-centric perspectives. The territorial trap's reification and naturalization of the state scale was intensified by the mobilization of mass nationalism during the World Wars and the Cold War, ultimately leading to a broad-based consensus that local communities and ethnic groups would eventually be subsumed within national identities and state-based societies. Such a process may be termed 'modernization erasure' and speaks to an assumption of 'development' eliding historical and cultural patterns of identity and territoriality (Herz 1957; Deutsch 1966). Evidence from the latter half of the twentieth century and first decades of the twenty-first century belie its success and highlight the significance of international boundaries for nationalism (Adamson 2016).

Borders continue to mark the formal extent of units within the international state system and have, with the advent of new technologies of mobility and resource extraction, come to require conceptualization as invisible vertical planes extending upwards into the airspace and downwards into the subsoil (Glassner and Fahrer 2004: 73–74). Moreover, borders constitute unique spatio-legal entities that have multiplied over time (Diener and Hagen 2012). Despite their ubiquity, and the prodigious efforts of scholars from a variety of disciplines seeking to ascertain laws that govern their genesis and evolution, offering taxonomies and typologies pertaining to their development, and constructing models and theories explicating their societal significance,[2] borders remain only limitedly understood.

Recent theorization conceptualizes borders as social processes and by consequence opens productive engagement with studies of nationalism (Paasi 1998; Diener and Hagen 2009, 2010; Jones 2012). Although physically at the margins of a state, boundaries commonly occupy the core of national imaginations (Sahlins 1998; Nevins 2002; Popescu 2012). But rather than forming an immutable ideal, borders evolve over time and in relation to a variety of contingencies. In short, they materialize, re-materialize, and de-materialize—sometimes overtly and sometimes in subtle ways (Megoran 2012). What remains consistent is their role as a mechanism of political communication (domestic and international), technique of power (domestic and international), and filter of mobilities (domestic and international).

[2]See Ratzel (1969); Semple (1907a, b); Hartshorne (1936); Martinez (1994); Paasi (1998); Newman (2003); Diener and Hagen (2012); Jones (2012); Popescu (2012); Megoran (2012); Sidaway (2015).

A variety of actors including those from fields of religion, business, ethnic groups, civil society, and most prominently politicians use borders as tools to frame visions of their communities within states, and also as an international mechanism locating their communities within regional and international systems of geopolitics and geo-economics. Such a statement aligns with Critical International Relations theory's suggestion that protection of homelands from external threat (a process inherently linked to borders) is a core principle of international relations (Ashley 1989; Krause and Williams 1997; Weldes et al. 1999; Pain and Smith 2008). Through critical explorations of how space is 'labeled' (Agnew 2003), political geographers reveal the discursive practices by which international politics is spatialized and characterized, or perhaps caricaturized, by selective typologies of peoples, places, events, and actions (Ó Tuathail and Agnew 1992: 192).

One may argue that the very acts of policing borders and delimiting boundaries extend from particular visions of regional and global space. Such visions are also commensurately constitutive of group identity and the political processes of determining the criteria of 'belonging' within a given territory. Borders can thus be examined as a way to understand the links between nation building, state ideology, regime consolidation, and foreign policies. This requires consideration of border management and territorial practices not strictly in terms of the rational pursuit of interests, such as filtering licit from illicit mobilities or garnering customs income, but also as an inherent component of the process of creating/re-creating political identities and state ideologies (Gavrilis 2010).

The targeted 'scripting of places' (e.g. good/bad, friend/foe, safe/dangerous, rich/poor, etc.) is among the most powerful tools available to governing elites. While this process is far from hegemonic, being negotiated on a daily basis within borderlands (Megoran 2010, 2012; Martinez 1994; Diener and Hagen 2010; Anzaldua 2012; Donnan and Wilson 1999), the map of international politics nevertheless manifests through the construction of discursive and material geographical boundaries. These boundaries mark the division between the idealized self and the demonized other, the domain of freedom and the domain of danger, the inside realm of community and the outside realm of anarchy (Ó Tuathail 1996: 10; Megoran 2008: 29). Peter Andreas suggests, 'there is a powerful political and bureaucratic imperative to at least project an impression of territorial control and to symbolically signal official commitment to maintaining such control' (2000: 5). Assertions of legitimacy or authentic leadership may therefore become inexorably bound up with elites' geopolitical visions of the relationship between state, nation, and territory. By consequence, border disputes resulting therefrom are commonly the product of ideologically charged domestic power struggles to signal the extent of formal sovereignty and affirm regime legitimacy. Differences between national cultures can become amplified in such circumstances but may also reveal hybrid identities that undermine the very ideal of divided space that borders symbolize.

'The geography of the world is not a product of nature,' as Gearóid Ó Tuathail notes, 'but a product of histories of struggle between competing authorities over the power to organize, occupy, and administer space' (1996: 1). The cases below demonstrate that borders remain essential components in these evolving modalities and spatialities of power. Specific points of focus include the (1) advent of strategies to redefine the limits of territorial sovereignty through the use of pseudo-non-state actors, (2) a unique attempt to reset a maritime border and extend sovereignty through land-reclamation, (3) an ideological-movement's complex negotiation of both de-territorialized and territorialized strategies of power in the formation of a de-facto state, and (4) the reversal of de-territorializing trends within the archetype supra-national organization once thought to have transcended the pejorative aspects of state territoriality and pejorative nationalism. Collectively, these cases reveal adaptations by states and a range of other actors to harness borders and bordering processes as mechanisms to project power within evolving domestic and international contexts.

3 Russia and Ukraine

On 27 February 2014, unidentified soldiers dubbed 'little green men' seized the regional parliament, airport, and other strategic locations across the Crimean peninsula in Ukraine. This dramatic turn of events followed weeks of political upheaval in Ukrainian politics that pitted Ukrainian nationalist groups wanting closer ties with the European Union against those who favored maintaining traditional ties with Russia, including much of Ukraine's ethnic Russian minority population concentrated in the Crimean and Dombass regions. As the former groups gained the upper hand, ethnic Russian areas seemed on the verge of open revolt. It was at this critical juncture that the 'little green men' appeared (see Shevchenko 2014). They helped pave the way for the local Crimean government, dominated by ethnic Russians, to declare its independence from Ukraine and then successfully petition to join Russia. The Ukrainian government denounced the move but was effectively forced to cede Crimea to Russia.

The origins of the little green men remain a matter of contention. The soldiers spoke Russian but wore masks and lacked any identifying insignias, flags, or other markings. Russia claimed they were local militiamen, but the fact that they were equipped with advanced weaponry used by the Russian military gives credence to the claim by Ukraine and many outside observers that the little green men were in fact Russia special forces troops acting under orders from the Russian government to occupy Crimea. Similar groups of disguised soldiers soon appeared in the Donbass region, lending support to the formation of two breakaway republics: the Donetsk People's Republic and the Luhansk People's Republic. A recent tacit admission from Russian President Putin means that there is little doubt now that Russian forces have been actively engaged in fighting in eastern Ukraine in cooperation with ethnic Russian secessionist militias and contributed to the downing a civilian airliner and the deaths of the nearly 300 people on board. The conflict has since evolved into another 'frozen' conflict that has come to mark many territories of the former Soviet Union.

The case of Russian involvement in Ukraine looks like a 'traditional' border dispute between sovereign states but in fact constitutes rather novel strategies to redefine the limits of territorial sovereignty through the use of pseudo-non-state actors (i.e. Russian soldiers disguised as domestic militiamen), thereby blurring the lines between irredentism and secessionism, invasion and insurrection, foreign and domestic. This case also emphasizes that borders and territoriality remain useful instruments of power projection in the post-modern world (Murphy 2012). 'A crisis of the hyphen' (questioning of identity primacy; ethnic-national) served as precursor to Russia's actions in Ukraine, as well as in Georgia in 2008 (Antonsich 2009). It also serves as a warning to other states with Russian minority populations, such as Kazakhstan and the Baltic states. The existence of a 'threatened' or in other discourses 'non-integrated' or 'resistant/defiant' minority of Russian speaking peoples in both cases provided the rationalization for Moscow's actions. These began with 'passportization'—the extension of citizenship rights into the territory of a neighboring state—and culminated in the annexation of territory in the case of Crimea (Artman 2013; Biersack and O'Lear 2014; Clem 2014). Russia's actions are also to be understood within the context of broader geopolitical realities (Biersack and O'Lear 2014; Walt 2015; Diener 2014). In this case, NATO's consideration of Ukrainian and Georgian membership, EU expansion into Eastern Europe, proposed missile defense systems in Eastern and Central Europe, and Western policy toward Syria helped catalyze Moscow's international projection of power. Moreover, a nationalistic turn among political elites in both Russia and Ukraine fueled efforts to strengthen internal control amidst demographic and economic challenges. Similar efforts to 'project' and 'protect' are evident in recent controversies in the South China Sea.

4 The South China Sea

In October 2015, the American navy destroyer USS Lassen sailed in the vicinity of Subi Reef.[3] The remote reef, which normally just barely peaks above water at low tide, is an unassuming feature with no indigenous inhabitants, not unlike thousands of other reefs, shoals, and sandbars in the surrounding waters. Yet the Lassen's proximity to Subi Reef triggered a sharp denunciation from China that characterized its course as being a deliberate provocation and warned others to stay clear. Subi Reef would seem an otherwise unlikely source for international controversy if not for the fact that it is a part of the Spratly Islands archipelago in the southern stretches of the South China Sea. The Spratlys are the center of perhaps the world's most convoluted border dispute, since the archipelago is claimed entirely by China and in part by Brunei, Malaysia, the Philippines, Taiwan, and Vietnam. All of the

[3]Other American vessels and aircraft have subsequently made similar forays across these disputed areas, indicating they are likely to be recurring events.

countries, except Brunei, have reinforced their claims by occupying as many locations as possible with permanent military garrisons. The situation concerning the Paracel Islands to the north is similar but a little less complicated with only China, Taiwan, and Vietnam claiming rightful ownership, but China exercising de facto control over the entire archipelago (Huang and Billo 2015). The US officially takes no side in these disputes, but the route of the Lassen was specifically planned to demonstrate America's insistence that freedom of maritime and aerial navigation be maintained throughout the region. The affair would seem much ado about nothing if not for the fact that some of the world's busiest shipping lanes crisscross the South China Sea. In addition to possessing several productive fisheries, there are widespread expectations that the region contains large undersea deposits of oil and natural gas, although the extent of the deposits remains unknown.

These disputes lingered in relative obscurity but have been brought to the fore recently after China launched a sustained campaign to bolster its physical presence, much to the alarm of its neighbors and other world powers. Beginning in 2014, China launched a systematic land reclamation program across the Paracels and Spratlys. The program focuses on large-scale dredging operations at around a half dozen features that are only intermittently above water like Subi Reef. The goal appears twofold. First, the dredging has deepened channels and harbors making these features more accessible to naval vessels. Second, the dredged material has been accumulated and consolidated within reinforced seawalls, in effect turning these semi-submerged reefs and shoals into artificial islets. On these reclaimed lands, China is in the process of constructing a growing number of airfields, port facilities, air defenses, supply depots, barracks, and other military infrastructures as it converts the new artificial islets into military bases (Nakamura and Lamothe 2016). The construction of this so-called 'Great Wall of Sand' is obviously meant to buttress Chinese claims over the South China Sea. It represents a novel attempt whereby land reclamation constitutes a bordering modality to claim and re-claim maritime sovereignty, much to the chagrin of the other littoral states.

Much like Russia's claims against Ukraine, China's actions are linked to broader geopolitical realties. In this case, long standing disputes concerning the sovereignty of Taiwan, and geopolitical influence in the Pacific, couple with a recent economic downturn to prompt China's projection and performance of power. The political modality brought to bear in this case links to the complex engineering of new territory. More than planting a flag and thereby symbolically asserting territorial claim, the introduction of infrastructure and personnel on the new islets gives material form to China's claims of sovereignty.[4] Moreover, the permanent Chinese presence on the islets buttresses their claim to surrounding territorial waters (Roszko 2015). China's maritime boundary, by consequence, reaches ever further into the South China Sea and carries with it the prospect of limiting mobility (by air

[4]One might look to state-sponsored irrigation projects in desert or grassland regions for agriculture and the settlement of people in frontier areas as similar efforts to demonstrate effective use of land and symbolize its incorporation into national territory (Schechla 1993).

and sea) of other states and actors, as well as control over resource extraction (e.g. oil, natural gas, fish).

Although not directly mentioning China, President Obama's (2016) remarks in February, calling for 'tangible steps in the South China Sea to lower tensions, including a halt to further reclamation, new construction and militarization of disputed areas,' were clearly meant for Beijing. The Lassen's route was intended to reinforce the principle that the legitimacy of any claims to sovereignty rested upon the recognition and agreement by other states. Mobility—whether corporeal (movement by human beings or unmanned physical entities) or ideational (projection of ideas, music, imagery, etc.)—through space expresses power and communicates an alternative geopolitical imaginary. Such is the case with any illicit border crossing as it constitutes a violation of 'sovereignty.' Such actions implicitly reject the spatiality of the current state-based system in favor of new conceptions of rights, authority, and/or belonging (Dodds 1994: 199–202). A similar though far more dramatic rejection of this system is evident in actions by the Islamic State.

5 Islamic State

In June 2014, Islamic State forces bulldozed through the earthen berm that marked the border between Iraq and Syria. Running through rather barren stretches of desert, the border and its breeching seemed of little practical consequence, but the action held great significance for IS. Carried out amid much fanfare, the demolition of the border and its markers symbolized IS's desire to overturn the Sykes-Picot Agreement, named after the British and French diplomats who secretly negotiated the partition of the Ottoman Empire between their respective countries in 1916. For IS followers, and even many mainstream Muslims, Sykes-Picot has come to represent Western/Christian meddling in the Middle East and efforts to divide and subjugate Muslims (see Black 2014). The erasure of the region's current borders, not just the Iraqi-Syrian border, was co-requisite for IS's claim to have founded a greater caliphate owed allegiance by all Muslims. The caliphate declaration went further in asserting that existing forms of government would be regarded as null and void as soon as IS forces arrived in that area.

IS originated as a branch of the al-Qaeda terrorist organization. Based in Afghanistan and Pakistan, al-Qaeda's leadership enjoyed the protection of the largely ethnic Pashtun Taliban guerilla movement, which controlled much of the region. From there, al-Qaeda sponsored terrorist attacks against Western targets, culminating in the 9/11 attacks in New York and Washington D.C. in 2001. After the US invasion of Iraq, al-Qaeda established a branch there to resist American occupation. This branch suffered a series of setbacks but managed to find safe haven in neighboring Syria, which since 2011 had descended into a vicious civil war along ethno-religious lines. Over time, most al-Qaeda forces in Syria and Iraq split with central al-Qaeda to form the Islamic State. Unlike its forerunner, which shunned claiming territorial control, the Islamic State's claims of caliphate status require the claiming, holding, and administration of land (Hashim 2014; Lister 2015). IS has also assumed many of the other characteristics of a sovereign state (i.e. a central executive, a cabinet of ministers, courts, bureaucracies, a capital city, etc.). IS has even organized its territory into provinces (*wilayah*), each with its own governor responsible for carrying out the central government's edicts and supervising mundane matters such as public utilities, road work, and social services (Zelin 2015). Although denied legitimacy by the international community, the Islamic State functions as a de facto state exercising operational governance over large swaths of Iraq and Syria. Yet IS also remains committed to promoting terrorism beyond its borders, most dramatically illustrated by the terrorist attacks that struck in Paris, Beirut, Ankara, California, Brussels, and over Sinai in late 2015 and early 2016. Its calls for violent jihad have prompted thousands of Muslims from around the world to fight under its banner, while inspiring others to act on its behalf abroad. It is not uncommon for terrorist groups to operate with some level of state sponsorship, but the Islamic State may be the first terrorist group to become its own state sponsor.

One may argue that the Islamic State is at its core a reaction against (1) the stilted political, social, and economic realities of the majority of Arab peoples in the Middle East and (2) the seeming futility of one civilizational base to resist the hegemony of another (Khouri 2015). In the first case, the borders created in the aftermath of World War I have a great capacity to be regarded as artificial and flawed. The family-based autocracies that developed within them through the sanction and support of Western powers have offered little opportunity for social mobility for a majority of their populations. IS counters this reality with not only promises of a 'purified' society but appeals to disenfranchised people by offering social services previously absent (Khouri 2015: 17). The added element of IS's territoriality is its seizure of valuable resources (oil and natural gas), its disruption of status quo relations between states of the region, and increasingly its projection of power from a base of relative security into a world system that it purportedly seeks to overturn.

Ideological cloistering or quarantine is not new. The Iron Curtain constituted a monumental effort to keep the West out and the populations under communist rule in. So too, the Islamic State is enacting territoriality and forming new borders in an effort to both 'protect' and confine those that have come under its authority. By forging a haven for similarly minded people replete with a resource/territorial base, the margins of IS control constitute borders that project power into the world. This takes place both through the de-territorialized non-state network that boasts cells throughout the world but also as a territorialized claimant to a portion of global space. One might draw a limited parallel to the affective manifestation of Fortress Europe as an effort to retain a place of cultural uniqueness, while simultaneously projecting Western values through globalized media, economics, and politics. Like the Soviet Union's efforts of the past, the Islamic State has both its committed adherents, as well as its involuntarily integrated, de facto citizenry. For those lucky enough to escape the borders of the Islamic State, prospects of freedom and opportunity are far from assured. The category of 'refugee' and the responsibility of societies at whose borders and on whose territories they arrive have become hotly debated.

6 The Refugee Crisis in Europe

In early September 2015, the world grappled with shocking images of a 2-year-old boy lying dead face down on a shoreline in Turkey. The boy, Alan Kurdi, had drown, along with his brother, mother, and at least nine other people, when their overloaded dingy capsized while trying to cross clandestinely from Turkey to Greece. Alan was part of an ethnic Kurdish family that had fled to Turkey after their hometown in Syria was bombarded by IS forces. After struggling to make a living in Turkey for over a year, the family decided to undertake the dangerous crossing to Greece with the intention of eventually joining relatives in Canada. Alan's story would have likely gone unnoticed if a press photographer had not happened to be present when a Turkish police officer discovered and removed the boy's corpse from the scene. Otherwise, Alan would have just been another of the approximately 7500 people who have died, mostly at sea, while trying to make their way to Europe from North Africa and the Middle East from January 2014 to March 2016, according to information compiled by the Missing Migrants Project of the International Organization for Migration (2016).

These deaths illustrate how the tragic consequences of the ethno-religious conflict roiling the greater Middle East have wide implications beyond the region, most notably helping fuel a migration crisis in Europe. The fighting in Iraq, Syria, Libya, and Afghanistan, as well as endemic poverty and instability across the region and beyond into Sub-Saharan Africa and South Asia, has displaced millions of people. The majority of these refugees found safety in neighboring countries, especially Lebanon, Jordan, Turkey, and Pakistan, but hundreds of thousands traveled onward to Europe in the hopes of finding a more permanent refuge and brighter prospects. The scale of the influx has triggered varying levels of anxiety among the receiving states. Some apprehensions center on practical concerns, such as the financial burden associated with housing and caring for the largely indigent immigrants. Others center on the ability or willingness of these immigrant groups to integrate into their new host societies, at times feeding blatantly xenophobic attitudes toward non-Christian, 'non-Caucasian' peoples.

The prospect that terrorists aligned with IS or other extremist groups might use these migrant flows to enter Europe and launch attacks further complicates the issue, especially in the wake of the Paris and Brussels massacres. A number of European countries have gone so far as to erect new border fences and implement travel controls in an attempt to stop or at least redirect migrant flows. It is also clear that as many as one third of the migrants originate from countries of comparative stability and therefore have weak claims to refugee status. Even those from war-ravaged countries often have more ambiguous experiences. Alan and his family, for example, were in no immediate danger in Turkey. The family's flight from Syria certainly fit conventional definitions of refugee status, but the family's attempted journey to Greece seemed to be more economically motivated, raising ethical and legal questions about the geographical scope of refugee claims (Barnard 2015). Mass migrations are not unique to the twenty-first century, but they now increasingly unfold within a morally-tangled context regarding freedom of movement, human rights, and trans-border security concerns.

Protection, therefore, emerges prominently in the discourse surrounding the treatment of refugees in Europe. The creation of the EU was rooted in supplanting the jingoisms of the past with enlightened ideals of multiculturalism, tolerance, and a shared future based upon the eradication of barriers to movement, a common economic system, and the notion of common European citizenship. Yet reactions to surging refugee flows have demonstrated the survival of parochialisms rooted in national territoriality as concepts of 'citizenship privilege' acquire new resonance. Put another way, human rights universalism confronts the bordered reality of nationally-defined civil beneficence. Moreover, it seems that fears of terrorism and infiltration of society by ideologies regarded as anathema to Western values have drawn exclusive nationalisms back to the center of the political arena. These reified ideas are reshaping the calculation of what constitutes good and bad mobilities among host societies. Guest workers from Muslim countries were once courted to certain European states, but current discourses of resistance to refugee/migrant flows reflect the contingency of border permeability and the continued value placed on control of national space. In fact, the continued viability of the European Union may rely on the supra-national organization's acceptance of the re-enforcement of member state borders in the short term, while pursuing more stringent border controls along its external borders in the long term.

The networking of borders allows for a multi-scalar security regime that both emphasizes the state, as well as offering new significance to sub-state and supra-state regions (Coleman 2007). The state's mandate to provide services (including protection) to its citizenry, serves as the rational for new multi-layered, multi-locality processes and mechanisms of bordering (Staeheli 2010; Mann 1984). What is clear from the above discussion is that the nation-state need not disappear for new conceptions and practices of globality to emerge or vice versa. Processes of de-territorialization and re-territorialization are occurring simultaneously as borders retain a central role.

7 Conclusion

Even a cursory review of modern history demonstrates that borders are not fixed entities bounding a system of immutable territorial sovereignty. Borders move for various reasons as they become more and less permeable in relation to often-abstract contingencies. Some borderlands remain marred by entrenched divisions (e.g. India/Pakistan, Palestine/Israel), but seemingly intractable conflicts have been ameliorated in Northern Ireland, the Balkans, and Cyprus, even as new arenas of potential partition emerge in Ukraine, Sudan, the Arctic Ocean, and the South China Sea. It is clear that we should not expect any sort of borderless world anytime soon. Yet that does not mean that borders, their functions, and meanings are stagnant. As the above cases suggest, the processes and modalities of bordering continue to evolve in conjunction with changing political, economic, cultural, and technological contexts. Borders are, therefore, likely to evolve in varied and contradictory ways across multiple scales.

It might be more helpful to think of the contemporary world as undergoing a period of re-bordering and re-ordering (Popescu 2012; Diener and Hagen 2012). In some cases, borders are being redrawn, as between Russia and Ukraine, while China is creating new borders by literally creating new territory in the South China Sea. The Islamic State makes a big show of erasing borders in the lands under its control and broadly rejects the entire sovereign state system in favor of its vision for a worldwide caliphate. Yet IS simultaneously employs territorial control much in the same manner as the states it seeks to overthrow. The EU counts the displacement of pejorative nationalism with a cosmopolitan ideology and freedom of movement between its member states as among its greatest accomplishments and a model for a more inclusive world order. Yet the spillover from the disorder in neighboring regions threatens to undermine that achievement and in some cases has already reversed that openness and tolerance, at least temporarily. These four cases illustrate the complex and nuanced nature of contemporary borders and their broad but often overlooked importance to a range of political, cultural, economic, and ethical issues. They also vividly demonstrate that we should expect to live in a very bordered world for the foreseeable future. We conclude this chapter by posing a question—what new form of political territorial organization might emerge capable of replacing, let alone erasing, the continuing allure of the territorial state and the borders that define it? The 'territorial trap' continues to reinforce bounded space as an indispensable political modality and shows little sign of abating.

References

Adamson, F. B. (2016). Spaces of global security: Beyond methodological nationalism. *Journal of Global Security Studies, 1*(1), 19–35.

Agnew, J. (2003). *Geopolitics: Re-visioning world politics* (2nd ed.). Oxford: Routledge.

Agnew, J. (2009). *Globalization and sovereignty*. Lanham, MD: Rowman and Littlefield.

Andreas, P. (2000). Introduction: The wall after the wall. In P. Andreas & T. Snyder (Eds.), *The wall around the West: State borders and immigration controls in North America and Europe* (pp. 1–11). Lanham, MD: Rowman and Littlefield.

Antonsich, M. (2009). On territory, the nation-state, and the crisis of the hyphen. *Progress in Human Geography, 33*(6), 789–806.

Anzaldua, G. (2012). *Borderlands, La Frontera: The New Mestiza*. San Francisco: Aunt Lute Books.

Artman, V. (2013). Documenting territory: Passportisation, territory, and exception in Abkhazia and South Ossetia. *Geopolitics, 18*(3), 682–704.

Ashley, R. (1989). Living on the border lines: Man, poststructuralism, and war. In J. Der Derian & M. Shapiro (Eds.), *International/intertextual relations* (pp. 259–321). Lexington, MA: D.C. Heath.

Barnard, A. (2015, December 28). Family's tragedy goes beyond one boy. *The New York Times*, p. A1. Retrieved from http://www.nytimes.com/2015/12/28/world/middleeast/syria-refugees-alan-aylan-kurdi.html?_r=0

Biersack, J., & O'Lear, S. (2014). The geopolitics of Russia's annexation of Crimea: Narratives, identity, silences, and energy. *Eurasian Geography and Economics, 55*(3), 247–269.

Black, I. (2014, June 18). Isis breach of Iraq-Syria border merges two wars into one 'nightmarish reality', *The Guardian*. Retrieved from http://www.theguardian.com/world/2014/jun/18/isis-iraq-syria-two-wars-one-nightmare

Caney, S. (2005). *Justice beyond borders: A global political theory*. Oxford: Oxford University Press.

Castells, M. (1997). *The power of identity*. Oxford: Blackwell.

Clem, R. (2014). Dynamics of the Ukraine state-territory nexus. *Eurasian Geography and Economics, 55*(3), 219–235.

Coleman, M. (2007). Immigration politics beyond the Mexico-US Border. *Antipode, 39*, 54–76.

Deutsch, K. (1966). *Nationalism and social communication: An inquiry into the foundations of nationality*. Cambridge, MA: MIT Press.

Diener, A. (2014). Russian repositioning: Mobilities and the Eurasian regional concept. In S. Walcott & C. Johnson (Eds.), *Corridor of interconnections: Eurasia from the South China to the Caspian Sea* (pp. 72–109). New York: Routledge.

Diener, A., & Hagen, J. (2009). Theorizing borders in a borderless world: Globalization, mobility and scale. *Geography Compass, 3*(3), 1196–1216.

Diener, A., & Hagen, J. (Eds.). (2010). *Borderlines and borderlands: Political oddities at the edge of the nation state*. Lanham, MA: Rowman and Littlefield.

Diener, A., & Hagen, J. (2012). *Borders: A very short introduction*. New York: Oxford University Press.

Dodds, K. (1994). Geopolitics and foreign policy: Recent developments in Anglo-American political geography and international relations. *Progress in Human Geography, 18*(2), 186–208.

Donnan, H., & Wilson, T. M. (1999). *Borders: Frontiers of identity, nation and state*. London: Bloomsbury.

Friedman, T. (2005). *The world is flat: A brief history of the twenty-first century*. New York: Farrar, Straus and Giroux.

Fukayama, F. (1991). *The end of history and the last man*. New York: Free Press.

Gavrilis, G. (2010). *The dynamics of interstate boundaries*. Cambridge: Cambridge University Press.

Glassner, M., & Fahrer, C. (2004). *Political geography* (3rd ed.). Hoboken, NJ: Wiley.

Hartshorne, R. (1936). Suggestions on the terminology of political boundaries. *Annals of the Association of American Geographers, 26*(1), 56–57.

Hashim, A. S. (2014). The Islamic state: From al-Qaeda affiliate to caliphate. *Middle East Policy, 21*(4), 69–83.

Herz, J. (1957). Rise and demise of the territorial state. *World Politics, 9*, 473–493.

Huang, J., & Billo, A. (Eds.). (2015). *Territorial disputes in the South China Sea: Navigating rough waters*. New York: Palgrave Macmillan.

International Organization for Migration. (2016). *Missing migrants project*. Retrieved from http://missingmigrants.iom.int/Mediterranean

Jones, R. (2012). *Border walls: Security and the war on terror in the United States, India, and Israel*. London: Zed Books.

Khouri, R. (2015). ISIS is about the Arab past, not the future. *Wilson Center Middle East Program, May*, 1–23.

Krause, K., & Williams, M. (Eds.). (1997). *Critical security studies: Concepts and cases*. London: UCL Press.

Kuper, A. (2004). *Democracy beyond borders: Justice and representation in global institutions*. Oxford: Oxford University Press.

Lister, C. R. (2015). *The Syrian Jihad: Al-Qaeda, the Islamic state and the evolution of an insurgency*. Oxford: Oxford University Press.

Mann, M. (1984). The autonomous power of the state. *European Journal of Sociology, 25*, 185–213.

Martinez, O. (1994). The dynamics of border interaction: New approaches to border analysis. In C. Schofield (Ed.), *World boundaries 1: Global boundaries* (World boundaries series, pp. 1–15). London: Routledge.

Megoran, N. (2008). From presidential podiums to pop music: Everyday discourses of geopolitical danger in Uzbekistan. In R. Pain & S. Smith (Eds.), *Fear: Critical geopolitics and everyday life* (pp. 5–36). Aldershot: Ashgate.

Megoran, N. (2010). The Uzbekistan Kyrgyzstan boundary: Stalin's cartography post Soviet geography. In A. Diener & J. Hagen (Eds.), *Borderlines and borderlands: Political oddities at the edge of the nation state* (pp. 33–52). Lanham, MD: Rowman & Littlefield.

Megoran, N. (2012). Rethinking the study of international boundaries: A biography of the Kyrgyzstan–Uzbekistan boundary. *Annals of the Association of American Geographers, 102* (2), 464–481.

Murphy, A. (2012). Territory's continuing allure. *Annals of the Association of American Geographers, 103*, 1212–1226.

Nakamura, D., & Lamothe, D. (2016, March 1). China testing Obama as it expands its influence in Southeast Asia. *Washington Post*. Retrieved from https://www.washingtonpost.com/politics/china-testing-obama-as-it-expands-its-influence-in-southeast-asia/2016/03/01/d60e1248-dbdf-11e5-891a-4ed04f4213e8_story.html

Nevins, J. (2002). *Operation gatekeeper: The rise of the "illegal alien" and the making of the U.S.-Mexico boundary*. London: Routledge.

Newman, D. (2003). On borders and power: A theoretical framework. *Journal of Borderland Studies, 18*(1), 13–25.

Obama, B. (2016, February 16). *Remarks by President Obama at U.S.-ASEAN Press Conference*. Retrieved from https://www.whitehouse.gov/the-press-office/2016/02/16/remarks-president-obama-us-asean-press-conference

O'Brien, R. (1992). *Global financial integration: The end of geography*. New York: Council on Foreign Relations.

Ohmae, K. (1990). *The borderless world: Power and strategy in the interlinked economy*. New York: Harper Business.

Ohmae, K. (1995). *The end of the nation-state*. New York: Free Press.

Ó Tuathail, G. (1996). *Critical geopolitics: The politics of writing global space*. London: Routledge.

Ó Tuathail, G., & Agnew, J. (1992). Geopolitics and discourse: Practical geopolitical reasoning in American Foreign Policy. *Political Geography, 11*(2), 190–204.

Paasi, A. (1998). Boundaries as social processes: Territoriality in the world of flows. *Geopolitics, 3* (1), 69–88.

Pain, R., & Smith, S (Eds.). (2008). *Fear: Critical geopolitics and everyday life*. Aldershot: Ashgate.

Popescu, G. (2012). *Bordering and ordering the twenty-first century: Understanding borders*. Lanham, MD: Rowman & Littlefield.

Ratzel, F. (1969/1896). The laws of the spatial growth of states. In R. Kasperson & J. Minghi (Eds.), *The structure of political geography* (pp. 17–28). London: University of London Press.

Roszko, E. (2015). Maritime territorialisation as performance of sovereignty and nationhood in the South China Sea. *Nations & Nationalism, 21*(2), 230–249.

Sack, R. D. (1997). *Homogeographicus*. Baltimore, MD: Johns Hopkins University Press.

Sahlins, P. (1998). State formation and national identity in the Catalan borderlands during the eighteenth and nineteenth centuries. In T. M. Wilson & H. Donnan (Eds.), *Border identities: Nation and state at international frontiers* (pp. 31–61). Cambridge: Cambridge University Press.

Schechla, J. (1993). Ideological roots of population transfer. *Third World Quarterly, 14*(2), 239–275.

Semple, E. (1907a). Geographical boundaries-I. *Bulletin of the American Geographical Society, 39*(7), 385–397.

Semple, E. (1907b). Geographical boundaries-II. *Bulletin of the American Geographical Society, 39*(8), 449–463.

Shevchenko, V. (2014, March 11). 'Little green men' or 'Russian invaders'? *BBC News*. Retrieved from http://www.bbc.com/news/world-europe-26532154

Sidaway, J. D. (2015). Mapping border studies. *Geopolitics, 20*(1), 214–222.

Staeheli, L. (2010). Political geography: Where's citizenship? *Progress in Human Geography, 35* (3), 393–400.

Walt, S. (2015). Why arming Ukraine is a really, really bad idea. *Foreign Policy*. Retrieved from http://foreignpolicy.com/2015/02/09/how-not-to-save-ukraine-arming-kiev-is-a-bad-idea/

Weldes, J., Laffey, M., Gusterson, H., & Duvall, R. (1999). Introduction: Constructing insecurity. In J. Weldes, M. Laffey, H. Gusterson, & R. Duvall (Eds.), *Cultures of insecurity: States, communities and the production of danger* (Borderlines, Vol. 14, pp. 1–33). London: University of Minnesota Press.

Zelin, A. Y. (2015, January 28). The Islamic state's model. *The Washington Post*. Retrieved from https://www.washingtonpost.com/blogs/monkey-cage/wp/2015/01/28/the-islamic-states-model/

Alexander C. Diener is an Associate Professor of Geography at the University of Kansas. His research engages with geopolitics, borders, identity, mobility, and urban landscape change through an area studies focus in Central Eurasia. He is the author or co-author of three books and has held research fellowships at the Kennan Institute of the Woodrow Wilson Center, George Washington University's Elliott School, Harvard University's Davis Center, and was the Regional Research Fulbright Scholar for Central Asia in 2011–2012.

Joshua Hagen is Dean of the College of Arts and Sciences at Northern State University. He has co-authored works on geopolitics and border studies, most notably the books Borders: A Very Short Introduction (Oxford University Press, 2012) and Borderlines and Borderlands: Political Oddities at the Edge of the Nation-State (Rowman & Littlefield, 2010). He has also published widely on issues related to urban planning, historic preservation, and nationalism. He is currently working on two full-length research monographs related to Nazi Germany: Building Nazi Germany: Space, Place, Architecture, and Ideology (Rowman & Littlefield) and Dictating the Past: Place and Memory in Nazi Germany (Oxford University Press).

Border Disputes Through Ill-Defined Borders: Maritime Territorial Conflicts and Their Impact on Security

Clemens Binder

Abstract Borders as a mean of territorial demarcation have long been a central notion in international relations and have an important impact on states' foreign and security policies. Borders are often disputed, and disputes are often more complex on the sea, as a clear definition of sea borders is missing. The United Nations Convention of the Law of the Seas (UNCLOS) attempts to offer a maritime border regime but lacks the mechanisms that a completely functional border regime would require. UNCLOS fails to regulate conflicting claims and border disputes on the sea. This leads to a lack of clarity concerning territorial demarcation and increases the possibility of conflict, which influences security policies. In this chapter, it is argued that in the absence of clear borders states fear their security is compromised as this absence can create incentives for states to act as a territorial expansionist. This is explored in two case studies, the Arctic Sea and the South China Sea. Both cases represent areas where the lack of defined borders causes conflicting interests, especially economic ones, and where tensions are increasing. The cases will be investigated from a realist perspective as examples of a security dilemma.

Keywords Maritime boundaries • Border Disputes • Security Dilemma • South China Sea • Arctic Sea

1 Introduction

One of the most important principles of national security policy is considered to be the protection of borders, protecting territorial sovereignty and some theorists (such as Mearsheimer 2001) even regard extending power through extending territory as an objective of foreign policy. Territory is often seen as a means and symbol of power, it contains strategic advantages for states and offers access to natural resources. Agnew (1994: 56) sees 'the merging of the state with a clearly bounded territory' as one of the most essential notions of international relations. In the context of borders and territories, the concept of sovereignty assumes an important

C. Binder (✉)
Austrian Institute for International Affairs (oiip), Vienna, Austria
e-mail: Clemens.Binder@oiip.ac.at

C. Günay, N. Witjes (eds.), *Border Politics*, DOI 10.1007/978-3-319-46855-6_3

role as 'with sovereignty, political authority is linked with territory' (Thomson 1995: 227). There is a direct relation between borders and sovereignty, as borders put limits to political, social and cultural sovereignty (Brunet-Jailly 2005, 2011; Paasi 2009). Sovereignty attached to territory has represented an important notion of international relations since the Treaty of Westphalia. In the Westphalian order, the 'political community was created in modern states over an extended period of time. Territory came first; the state building elites first consolidated control over a territory and only in a later phase came the construction of a nation' (Sørensen 1999: 599). The creation of modern statehood through Westphalia defined the linkage of a territorial delimited area and sovereign control. The concept of sovereign statehood was further developed by Max Weber, who in his work 'Economy and Society' assessed that one of the main aspects of sovereignty is the ability of a political organization, in this case the state, to use force within a territorially delimited area. (Weber 1922/1978: 54) Sovereignty according to Weber also includes the limitation of political rule to limited territories. The connection between borders and sovereignty in the Westphalian order and Weber's definition is evident—states only possess control within the territory that is attached to their own political control. Borders therefore assume the role of demarcation lines of sovereignty.

For this chapter, the linkage of economic sovereignty, meaning that a state possesses control over all economic means available on its territory and borders, is particularly important. The notion of sovereignty as the exclusive rule over territory includes the right to extract natural resources. A great amount of scarce resources like natural oil and gas can be found in the high seas. Increasing demand, technological developments with correspondingly better accessibility have accelerated a scramble for natural resources. The high seas have therefore gained new attention. On land, borders are clearly drawn and define and separate sovereign territories, yet still demarcation lines are often disputed and interpreted differently. The integrity and sovereignty of states is, however, guaranteed by International Law. The Charter of the United Nations[1] prohibits territorial shifts through the Use of Force.[2] But in the case of the seas the demarcation of borders for sovereignty is less clear and therefore even more subject to interpretation. Waters beyond the borders of territorial seas are considered to be international waters. The governance of territories in the high seas falls under the guidelines of the United Nations Convention of the Law of the Seas (UNCLOS),[3] which defines various possibilities for states to extend sovereign economic rights, such as establishing an Exclusive Economic Zone (EEZ) in order to secure rights for resource extraction. Besides

[1]Signed by the 51 founding states of the U.N., the U.N. Charter is a constituent treaty whose rules all U.N. member states have to follow.

[2]Charter of the United Nations, Chapter I, http://www.un.org/en/sections/un-charter/chapter-i/. Accessed 05.04.2016.

[3]UN Convention on the Law of the Sea, opened for signature Dec. 10, 1982, 1833 UNTS 396. Available at http://www.un.org/Depts/los/index.htm

ambitions to explore resources, the control of maritime routes constitutes another important incentive for states to claim sovereignty over areas of economic and strategic interest. The lack of sanctioning mechanisms in UNCLOS is problematic in this context, however. Infringement of EEZs is not punishable under international law. Under UNCLOS therefore sovereignty beyond territorial waters is reduced to resource extraction, but full control over an EEZ is not guaranteed. This lack of control is one factor that adds to the feeling of insecurity, as states within EEZs are not protected from infringements, the seizure of territory by another state, or even the use of force.

The consequences of the absence of an all-encompassing border regime on the seas has become highly evident in various disputed areas of the world. Two areas with increasing potential for conflict are the South China Sea and the Arctic Sea, which serve as case studies for this chapter. Both areas are assumed to be resource-rich as well as strategically relevant to their neighboring coastal states. A number of rivaling territorial claims are extant in both regions, but different approaches are visible. The Arctic shows an increasingly cooperative environment where states engage in intergovernmental institutions such as the Arctic Council or conduct bilateral negotiations in order to resolve problems. By contrast, the South China Sea lacks institutions that comprise all adjacent nations, cooperation is at a low level and tensions are rising. This results from the growing demand for resources of neighboring states, which leads to expansive behavior, especially in the case of China. Security concerns are rising as states are not fully assured of their territorial sovereignty because of the unclear nature of border definitions within UNCLOS. This became especially evident when a US destroyer approached Chinese territorial waters in fall 2015, causing a diplomatic row between the two powers. China felt that the US violated its territorial sovereignty while the US argued that it had operated under the freedom of navigation in international waters. This example highlights the problems that different perceptions of borders can cause. Sovereignty issues also threaten stability in the Arctic, where trade routes and the opening up of new extractive resources assume a stronger role in the dispute than increased militarization. The patterns of conflict present in these two areas raise two questions that will be addressed in this chapter.

The first question will assess the effects of the absence of borders on what has been defined by Herz (1950) as the 'security dilemma' and has since been adapted by Jervis (1978, 2011) and Tang (2009). The dilemma derives out of the anarchic structure of the international system, and describes the security concerns of states within an anarchic society due to the lack of a ruling government or sovereign, causing what Hobbes has called 'the war of all against all'. In International Relations theories, especially in Realism, the notion of anarchy is prevalent and central, and the security dilemma is omnipresent. Taliaferro (2000: 129) states that the security dilemma is caused by security being a zero-sum game, if one state increases its security other states could view theirs as threatened. For example, in the case of the South China Sea, China's expansive behavior compromises the security of the other states, who therefore attempt to increase their military capabilities. In addition realism relies on the existence of sovereign territories and borders, therefore, the absence of borders can lead to a deterioration of the security dilemma. ‘Territorial borders and associated rules of sovereignty, territorial integrity and non-intervention have helped states co-exist in an orderly fashion and with less violence and chaos than might otherwise have ensued’ (Williams 2002: 740). Against Williams’ statement, one could argue what Diehl and Goertz (1988: 103) find, that trying to extend territorial control and to force territorial shifts always causes conflicts, which diminish the meaning of borders for security in general. Giordano et al. (2005: 54) view the lack of a settled definition of sovereign territory as being one of the main driving forces for resource conflicts. This adds another dimension to Williams’ argument as resource conflicts imply the expansion of sovereign territories in order to access more resources. Contrary to Herz’ defensive realism, where concerns revolve mainly around defending security and reacting to threats, offensive realism as often described by Mearsheimer (1995, 2001) seeks to expand influence and power. Here, the lack of borders at sea could influence the security dilemma as states may view it as being easier to expand their sovereign territory and therefore gain an economic advantage. The dichotomy between offensive and defensive realism and how the lack of borders influences states’ foreign and security policies in this dichotomy is a central issue in this chapter.

The second question results from the first and projects the problem of an increased security dilemma in the international system onto national security policies. There is a distinction between two possible outcomes—either states engage strengthen cooperation to overcome the Hobbesian ‘State of Nature’ or act autonomously, which leads to the stronger militarization of conflicts. UNCLOS is important in this regard because it represents the only international regime that offers remote governance of border zones on the sea. Hence, from a multilateralist and institutionalist perspective it is important to investigate if states adhere to UNCLOS, seek to strengthen the Convention’s role and attempt to create a sea border regime. Therefore, it is important to evaluate the role that UNCLOS plays safeguarding borders at sea. Jervis (1999: 62) states that defensive realists are inclined to seek cooperation more strongly if the security dilemma is more threatening to them, offensive realists on the other hand are skeptical towards cooperation, as institutions are often regarded as obstacles to the further extension of power (Mearsheimer 1995: 12). Offensive realism, by that logic, would then lead to stronger militarization in the contested areas, while, if defensive realism prevails, states would enter cooperation and use diplomacy rather than force to guarantee sovereignty in contested areas, in the absence of borders. The analysis of specific policies, such as the increase of military capabilities or the adaption of national security strategies will serve as indicators in order to measure if offensive or defensive realism prevails. The assessment will begin by describing the nature of sea borders, as defined by UNCLOS, and examining the resource and sovereignty conflicts in more detail before proceeding to analyze these findings through the case studies.

2 The Characteristics of Borders, Territories and Sovereignty on Sea

2.1 General Definitions of Borders, Territories and Sovereignty

For centuries, Hugo Grotius' concept of the 'Mare liberum', the freedom of the seas was one of the main principles concerning global waters. The principle proposed open access for every nation to maritime resources and the complete freedom of navigation. However, especially since the establishment of UNCLOS in 1982 and its ratification in 1994,[4] the question of sea borders has become increasingly important. An agreement for international waters became necessary when, after World War II, states began to claim sea territories beyond their territorial waters. UNCLOS was preceded by the Convention on the High Seas in 1958, and offered a definition of different maritime territories and their respective legal statuses, providing a framework for border zones on the high seas. However, as will be assessed later, UNCLOS faces various challenges; it has not been ratified by all states, and mechanisms for sanctioning violations are hardly defined. Therefore, it is important to assess if the measures provided by UNCLOS are sufficient to serve as means for territorial demarcation and securing sovereignty. Borders, territoriality and sovereignty need to be defined in order to investigate if the procedures within UNCLOS apply to common definitions of these concepts and therefore offer valid forms of borders on sea.

Academic debate comprises a great variety of border definitions. Brunet-Jailly (2005: 635) traces the existence of borders to the Treaty of Westphalia in 1648 and describes boundaries as the crucial element for establishing the nation state. He also states that borders '[...] result from international agreements that are established by mutual understanding between states' (2005: 636). For Basaran (2008: 342), borders define the inside or outside of a territory and the limits to the territorial rule of the state. However, she distinguishes between the territorial borders and the legal borders of states. Territorial borders are oriented on geographical circumstances such as the Rio Grande, which serves as a territorial base for the legal border between the US and Mexico. Although borders around the globe are predominantly legally drawn and rarely based on geographical circumstances, territorial borders have proven to be less disputable than legally drawn borders. This distinction becomes central in the case of maritime borders, as the regulations for delimiting maritime borders under UNCLOS can be criticized as arbitrary and artificially drawn.

According to these two definitions, in the Westphalian system borders require a legal basis and mutual understanding. However, the perspective of mutual

[4]Until today, 167 states have ratified UNCLOS. States that have not signed the Convention include the United States and Turkey.

understanding excludes the relation between border shifts and the use of force. Although the UN Charter of 1945 restricts the use of force to change borders, cases like Russia's seizure of the Crimea in March 2014 prove that force remains a means to redraw borders. Zacher (2001: 216) describes a 'territorial integrity norm', that states are increasingly respecting existing borders and abstaining from the use of force to change them, as one of the main reasons why forceful border changes have declined. According to Simmons (2002), states often benefit from the peaceful settlement of border disputes. At sea, however, territorial integrity is not as evident as on land and the possibility of states using force under the security dilemma becomes much more likely, while institutionalists would argue that cooperation is fostered by the perceived insecurity. This becomes evident in both case studies in this chapter. As will be assessed later, insecurity over disputed sea areas leads to a stronger inclusion of these areas into security strategies, which includes militarization of conflicts as well as intergovernmental cooperation.

Directly linked to the concept of borders are the concepts of territory and sovereignty, which are highly intertwined. As territory defines a state as an actor and its role in the international system depends largely on various aspects of its territory, such as size or availability of resources, securing territorial integrity becomes a central factor in security policy. Agnew (1994: 60) distinguishes between two approaches in international relations to the concept of territory—a neorealist perspective and an institutionalist perspective. For the neorealist perspective, he states that 'no spatial unit other than territory of the state is involved in international relations' (Agnew 1994: 57). While institutionalists argue that cooperation reduces the effects of the territorial state on international relations, it still 'remains the central actor' (1994: 58). However, while the state is the central actor in institutionalism, it is not the only actor. States, as argued by institutionalists such as Keohane (1984), pursue their interests through cooperation rather than confrontation. Thus, cooperative institutions emerge as actors on an international level. One of the main differences between the two approaches is that institutionalism describes states as being cooperative whereas neorealist theories see states in constant rivalry. Institutionalism therefore relies on the notion that states are willing to give up parts of their sovereignty in order to achieve their goals.

Territory is not the main definition of a state, however. Rather, it encompasses the area within which a state possesses rule and sovereignty. Grimm (2015: 78) defines state rule as being territorially limited. Sovereignty in this context is understood as 'external sovereignty', where a state is defined by the control of its territory, and the control within its territory. This means that a sovereign state has in principal the right to establish any rule on its territory. However, Grimm (2015: 91) holds that through international cooperation, sovereignty has been diminished as international organizations and regimes, such as the EU, shape the politics and governance of states. This is in accordance with Thomson's statement that sovereignty is connected more strongly to state authority rather than to state control, the concept of control is diminishing while states still strive for authority (Thomson 1995: 214). Sovereignty gives the state the possibility to define the political sphere while 'authority concerns rule-making and control, rule-enforcement' (1995: 223).

According to Thomson (1995: 214), authority is a prerequisite for sovereignty and vice versa. Sovereignty hands states authority not only over political, but over economic, social and cultural issues. Therefore, a state can be considered as sovereign if it possesses this kind of authority, but only if a state is considered sovereign it can use its authority. In the context of the high seas, both authority and sovereignty assume a central role, as sovereignty hands economic resources to the adjacent state, while authority gives the state the possibility to formulate specific rules. As UNCLOS extends sovereignty and authority rights in some areas, such as resources, over territorial borders, it is interesting to investigate how states are influenced by the fact that they possess authority and sovereignty in some issues, while in others international law applies.

To sum up, borders can be interpreted as demarcation lines between two sovereign territories separating areas of different jurisdictions, rules and authorities. Basaran (2008: 244) states that the separation of inside from outside that is caused by borders also applies offshore waters. The following section will investigate how UNCLOS defines border zones, their legal foundations and examines their influence on states' foreign policies.

2.2 *Maritime Delimitation According to UNCLOS*

The delimitation of national waters has been widely discussed in the process leading to the establishment of UNCLOS in 1982.[5] Before UNCLOS there were no clear legal guidelines for the demarcation of sea territories, territorial waters were not clearly defined and there were no rules concerning the governance of high seas. UNCLOS has provided guidelines for high sea governance but they have proven to be insufficient in settling disputes over territories and sovereignty. UNCLOS defines three different sorts of maritime border zones, all of these will subsequently be described (Table 1).

Territorial waters: In UNCLOS, territorial waters are defined as follows: 'The sovereignty of a coastal State extends, beyond its land territory and internal waters and, in the case of an archipelagic State, its archipelagic waters, to an adjacent belt of sea, described as the territorial sea' (UNCLOS, Article 2.1). Territorial waters, simply put, extend the territory and the sovereignty of a state beyond its natural land. The width of territorial waters is defined as a 12-mile zone from the coastal baseline. In general, territorial waters contain the lowest potential for conflict—their demarcations are clear, as well as the consequences of a violation of the

[5]For example by Boggs (1930, 1937) or Minghi (1963: 422), who stated: 'A maritime boundary, unlike a land boundary which directly affects only the two states it separates, marks the limits of the spatial encroachment of a state's sovereignty into the area of the high seas, and thus affects many states'. However, as these discussions took place before the introduction of UNCLOS, their contemporary impact is highly questionable. It is important, however, to highlight the extensive duration of this debate.

Table 1 Summary of UNCLOS territories (Table designed by author)

	Extension from baseline	Jurisdiction of coastal states	Demarcation of adjacent states
Territorial Water	12 nautical miles	National jurisdiction in all areas	Border equally distant from both
Contiguous Zone	24 nautical miles	National jurisdiction in certain areas e.g. customs	None
Exclusive Economic Zone	200 nautical miles	Right to resource extraction	Bilateral agreements
Continental Shelf	Max. 350 nautical miles	Right to resource extraction	Bilateral agreements

12-mile border. Archipelagic states represent an exception to this notion, these are states that have islands off the shore of another country, and therefore conflict over territorial waters becomes more probable. UNCLOS hands states the right to defend their territory, states can take any measure necessary to defend their territorial integrity in territorial waters in case of a threat. Ships of other nations, however, have the right to navigate through territorial waters under the freedom of navigation. It is stated that ships are entitled to 'innocent passage', which means they are allowed to pass territorial waters as long as 'it is not prejudicial to the peace, good order or security of the coastal State' (UNCLOS, Article 19.1). Warships are under particular scrutiny in this context, compliance with the national law of the coastal state is absolutely necessary in order to guarantee a warship innocent passage. There is, however, potential for controversy in the demarcation of the territorial sea of two adjacent states. Under UNCLOS, states are compelled to agree bilaterally on a line of demarcation at points that are equally distant from both states' baselines. Within the bilateral agreements however, there is potential for disputes in cases where states fail to strike an agreement. In conclusion, territorial waters are in fact maritime extensions of a state's territory with all the sovereignty rights that are also valid on land. In addition to territorial waters, UNCLOS defines the so-called Contiguous Zone. In this zone, which extends 24 miles from the baseline, states may '(a) prevent infringement of its customs, fiscal, immigration or sanitary laws and regulations within its territory or territorial sea; (b) punish infringement of the above laws and regulations committed within its territory or territorial sea' (Article 33.1). That means, the contiguous zone is not equivalent to territorial waters, but remains under the legal control of the coastal state in specified areas, which to a certain degree entails the expansion of national sovereignty.

Exclusive Economic Zone: The definition of the Exclusive Economic Zone (EEZ) is the most important notion for maritime sovereignty conflicts as it defines the right to exploit a certain area of the sea economically. The advantages of claiming an EEZ of 200 miles beyond the territorial waters signifies a massive expansion of exclusive economic exploitation and of control over maritime routes. Claiming an EEZ gives a state the 'sovereign rights for the purpose of exploring and exploiting, conserving and managing the natural resources [. . .]' (UNCLOS, Article 58.1). In an EEZ, the rules and laws of the coastal state do not apply, rather the coastal state, as well as any other state, has to abide by the rules defined in the Convention. EEZs are treated in the same way high seas—freedom of navigation and exploration applies for all states. Most importantly, the fact that the EEZ extends a state's right to explore, exploit and manage natural resources largely from an area much beyond its territorial sea, possesses a large potential for conflict with the interests of other littoral states as well as the international community. As the establishment of an exclusive 200-mile zone can easily interfere with other claims for EEZs, delimitation is often contested and controversial. UNCLOS offers a settlement process for EEZ demarcation disputes. However, the International Court of Justice (ICJ) has the right to rule in such cases, which again undermines the authority of UNCLOS to guarantee maritime border security. UNCLOS, in addition, defines certain rights and duties of coastal states regarding resource exploitation. For example, the right to build artificial islands is given to states, which is especially evident in the South China Sea conflict, as China is constructing artificial structures causing considerable controversy.

Another problem arises from the fact that although EEZs are partly considered as sovereign, their sovereignty has not been legally tested and secured, as has been the case with territorial waters. The mere legal, highly arbitrary definition of a border at a 200-mile distance and the complicated mechanisms of settling disputes add to the unclear status of EEZs. However, the separation of 'inside' and 'outside' also occurs in EEZs, as only the state 'inside' is given the right to extract natural resources. This, however, raises the question of how states handle control of the 'inside' as their rights are limited to economic extraction. '[T]here is considerable legal confusion and controversy over the right to exercise innocent passage through territorial seas, especially by warships and the right to conduct military surveillance activities in the EEZ of a coastal state' (Rosenberg 2011: 10). The unclear legal situation causes an uncertainty about the security of EEZs which might force states into military action in order to strengthen security. This is one factor to take into account when discussing the influence of the territories defined by UNCLOS on the security dilemma. As uncertainty is one of the main issues causing a security dilemma, the legal controversies contribute to the deterioration of the dilemma.

Continental shelf: The continental shelf of a state marks an extension of the EEZ, however, a claim for the extension of the continental shelf requires the acceptance by agreement of the Commission on the Limits of the Continental Shelf (CLCS). Claims need to contain significant scientific proofs in order to be accepted by the commission. The continental shelf comprises all areas that 'extend beyond its territorial sea throughout the natural prolongation of its land territory to the outer edge of the continental margin' (Article 76.1). As the 200-mile boundary of the EEZ is valid regardless of the limit of the continental shelf, this chapter will only consider the extension of the shelf beyond the 200-mile mark. Continental shelves are limited to areas within 350 nautical miles measured from the baseline.

Concerning sovereignty over the continental shelf, the same rules apply that exist for the EEZ. States have the unique right to extract resources in their respective continental shelves, navigation and discovery are, however, open to anyone. The delimitation of adjacent continental shelves follows the same principles as the delimitation of EEZs, conflicting states should attempt to achieve a bilateral agreement under the guidance of international law. Dutton (2011: 49) describes this as a jurisdiction, where states only have authority over specific matters in the respective areas, in this case resource extraction, whereas in contrast to that sovereignty would entail the full authority of the state over all policy areas.

The definitions prove that 'UNCLOS fundamentally changes the exclusive nature of territorial sovereignty, because it defines multiple spheres of overlapping rights, responsibilities and political authority' (Carlson et al. 2013: 23), which can be interpreted as different intensities of sovereignty. However, the controversies mentioned before highlight the problems UNCLOS fails to prevent, as there is no binding legal mechanism to resolve border disputes. In the case of the EEZ and the extension of the continental shelf, authority is given only to the respective state over a limited number of policy areas, opening up dangers of conflict in areas where authority is not given. Therefore, it is not clear to what extent EEZs can be considered as territorially invulnerable, as states can practice their right of economic extraction of these areas but do not enjoy full legal protection of the territory the EEZ comprises.

3 Maritime Conflict, the Impact of UNCLOS and the Roles of Institutions

The question that arises out of the definition of the different border zones on sea is how these impact potential conflicts. Before assessing the impact, it is important to outline which areas contain a considerable potential for conflict and therefore can be regarded as security threats. The two main areas where economic and security interests conflict are access to resources and to sea lanes that are considered important trade routes. The two case studies of this chapter have been selected as these two patterns of conflict apply strongly in both regions.

Giordano et al. (2005: 51) relate resource availability and resource demand with the emergence of conflict. They hold that conflicts are usually fostered by the scarcity of resources. However, if resources are abundantly available, scarcity disappears and the marginal value of using force in order to secure the resources declines. Therefore, they conclude; great amounts of resources reduce the danger of conflict (ibid.).

The steady increase in demand for oil and gas, as well as the evolution of offshore-drilling technologies, have caused a new scramble for resources. Great amounts of natural resources are assumed to be under the sea floor. This has fostered claims for EEZs and the extension of the continental shelves. A case in point is the Arctic where all states but the US have applied for an extension of their respective continental shelves, the US as a non-member state of UNCLOS does not have this option. Giordano et al. (2005: 55) highlight that oceans are a prime example of how the lack of a definition of territorial sovereignty might cause resource conflicts. However, Nyman (2013: 9) holds that, as private companies tend to abstain from resource extraction in disputed areas, this might serve as a motivation for states to resolve border issues quickly and peacefully.

Giordano et al. (2005: 54) also regard the lack of regulatory institutions as being a problem in resource conflicts. In the Arctic as well as in the South China Sea, regional institutions (Arctic Council and ASEAN) exist but they suffer from shortcomings that limit their utility for conflict resolution. For example, the Arctic Council has a ban on debating security issues, and ASEAN does not include China, making it difficult to include the region's main actor in security processes. However, there is dialogue between ASEAN and China. Both institutions therefore play an important role as a forum for debate but do not possess sufficient competences to resolve conflict.

A problem is posed by the insufficient capability of mechanisms to resolve disputes. There are a variety of dispute settlement mechanisms in the Convention but these lack effectiveness. The settlement process in UNCLOS obliges all states in disputes to reach a settlement. However, if there is no settlement to be agreed upon bilaterally, there are different procedures (Boyle 1997: 38) in existence in order to reach a settlement, for example the inclusion of independent courts, such as the International Court of Justice (ICJ).

The next section will explain these conflicts by referring to the South China Sea and the Arctic Sea respectively as case studies and assess how states act in the light of these conflicts in order to investigate the impact of the territories defined by UNCLOS on states' foreign and security policies. The definition of the territories in UNCLOS shall be investigated through the theoretical lens of offensive and defensive realism. This should prove that the lack of a clear border regime at sea and ill-defined territoriality and sovereignty increases the danger for territorial disputes. Therefore, in the light of this danger, states might pursue protection as well as resolution.

4 Case Studies

4.1 The South China Sea

The South China Sea, surrounded by China and Southeast-Asian states such as Vietnam, Thailand and Indonesia is a resource-rich region and possesses important trade routes such as the Strait of Malacca. As previously stated, rising world energy demand has increased prospective profits from the extraction and exploitation natural resources. Emerging powers in the region, such as China, Indonesia and Malaysia not only need to meet their own increasing domestic energy demand but also want to establish themselves as global energy powers. However, more than the existence of natural resources it is the importance of the South China Sea for maritime trade routes that renders this region situated between China, Vietnam,

Malaysia, Taiwan, and the Philippines strategically and economically extremely important. More than 50 % of the world's merchant fleet and oil tanker traffic passes through the South China Sea every year (Rosenberg 2011: 7). One of the most active routes is the aforementioned Strait of Malacca in Malaysia, which is one of the central connections between the Indian and Pacific Ocean. Therefore, not only littoral states, but also the United States and Japan have a vital interest in this area. They are especially interested in securing freedom of navigation through South China Sea Waters and maintaining maritime security in the area.

In terms of sovereignty and territorial conflict, disputes have arisen over possession of the Spratly Islands, a group of uninhabited islands that are situated in the seas between Vietnam, Malaysia and the Philippines. The area around the Spratly Islands is considered to be resource-rich, and control over the islands would secure considerable advantages to the coastal state that possesses them. However, the areas claimed by the neighboring states that include China, Vietnam, the Philippines and Indonesia conflict and are not demarcated properly, as the claims of EEZs overlap. Dutton (2011) describes three areas of dispute that apply for the region, sovereignty, jurisdiction, and control. The sovereignty issue has become especially prevalent, as territorial claims do not only comprise EEZs, but, particularly in China's case, the extension of territorial waters. China's claims are oriented on the so-called 'Nine-Dash-Line', which 'has become synonymous with a claim of sovereignty over the island groups that have always belonged to China' (Gao and Jia 2013: 108) The Nine-Dash-Line defines China's claims within the South China Sea, exceeding any Chinese EEZ or Extension of the Continental Shelf. China rests these claims on historical reasons and claims historical rights over South China Sea waters and the Spratly Islands, including resource extraction. However, the claims made within the Nine-Dash-Line interferes with the EEZs of other adjacent states, such as Vietnam and the Philippines. The problem of the sovereignty claims relates to the problem of the ambiguous jurisdiction in the area. 'All states with coastlines that border the South China Sea claim continental shelves and EEZs; however, very little actual delimitation of the boundaries between coastal-state zones has occurred' (Dutton 2011: 50).

The verdict by an international tribunal, within the Permanent Court of Arbitration in The Hague on July 2016, might intensify the conflict in the South China Sea. The verdict found China's claims within the Nine-Dash-Line untenable and rebukes them in accordance with UNCLOS. By judging that parts of the region are either considered as Philippine EEZs or as international waters, the tribunal's decision has strongly supported the Philippine's claims (Phillips et al. 2016). China immediately refused to recognize the court's decision (Perlez 2016). The issue highlights that while international courts would have the competence to conciliate conflicts and define maritime borderlines, the character of UNCLOS as a legally non-binding agreement, and the courts' inability to establish legally binding rules, render the enforcement of decisions on maritime boundaries nearly impossible. Verdicts of this nature can cause negative effects, by triggering increasingly assertive measures on the side of the defeated party. They can even escalate conflicts and delegitimize international institutions.

Two conclusions can be drawn from these observations. First, before the verdict in July 2016 the Nine-Dash-Line symbolized a specific kind of expansionism. Even though China claimed the South China Sea as being its historic territory, this territorial claim would likely have required support by military force and therefore would have caused counter-reactions if there were strict and clear borders on sea, as territories would be demarcated clearly and could only be shifted through force. China's expansionism, as well as the defense by the other adjacent states is driven by the motive of securing economic rights in this region. Second, the fact that disputes around interfering neighboring claims of EEZs require bilateral agreements to be resolved, which contain additional obstacles, proves the weakness of UNCLOS in resolving border issues. Therefore, the border regime established by the Convention cannot be seen as a security guarantee. However, as the verdict of the tribunal proves, international law can at least provide partial protection from expansionist behavior, albeit the effect is subject to debate as China did not accept the verdict.

This raises the question of how the lack of a comprehensive border regime on seas influences states' security policy. The Nine-Dash-Line can of course be interpreted as an offensive action, as China, albeit peacefully, attempts to extend its sovereign territory and draw the borders in the South China Sea according to its interests. Taylor Fravel (2011) defines two components of Chinese strategy in the South China Sea, a diplomatic and a military one. Blazevic (2012: 92) assesses that especially China and Vietnam have made efforts to cooperate on an institutional level, however, these attempts have not proven to be useful, ASEAN states have increasingly worried about China's expansive role. China has addressed the issue of maritime security in its 2015[6] military strategy, in which it states that '[i]t is necessary for China to develop a modern maritime military force structure commensurate with its national security and development goals, safeguard its national sovereignty and maritime rights and interests' (People's Republic of China 2015). Taylor Fravel (2011: 307) regards two aspects of the military dimension as important, first, a considerable modernization of China's South Sea Fleet, and second, the increase of naval exercises in the area. Rahman and Tsamenyi (2010: 324) also find that states in the South China Sea have claimed security zones to restrict foreign military activities in their EEZs. That underlines that EEZs do not necessarily guarantee safety from military infringement, and there may lie the danger that coastal states might militarize the EEZ. However, as freedom of navigation has to be granted in EEZs, these areas are unlikely to obtain the same status as territorial waters.

[6]China's Military Strategy. Retrieved from http://news.usni.org/2015/05/26/document-chinas-military-strategy

4.2 The Case of the Arctic Sea

At first glance, the disputes Arctic and the South China Sea are of similar nature. Both are contested, resource-rich and strategically important regions, with important connections between oceans and bordered by great powers as well as small states. There is however one central difference between the two regions, this difference is the impact of climate change. Whereas in the South China Sea, resources are comparably easily available and trade routes such as the Strait of Malacca are open the entire year to navigation, resources and trade routes in the Arctic are dependent on the decrease of ice in the Arctic Sea. Therefore, sovereignty claims in the Arctic result from strategic endeavors to secure economically important areas of the Arctic Ocean that might become significant in the future through climate change.

A symbolic event that highlighted the rising conflict over sovereignty in the Arctic occurred in 2007, when a Russian submarine planted a Russian flag into the Arctic seabed, in order to claim it as Russian territory. This, albeit only symbolic action, caused anger among the other Arctic coastal states. Even though this act did not cause big consequences, it can be estimated as being significant—Russia, driven by the fear of losing territory that is not clearly defined, attempted to at least symbolically claim it. Although EEZs or Continental Shelves give states economic rights, this case shows that the lack of sovereignty leads to insecurity and in consequence, to expansive behavior. In the Arctic, interfering territorial claims are plentiful—Canada and the United States are in dispute over the Beaufort Sea and the Northwest Passage, Russia and Norway were in dispute until recently over the Barents Sea, Russia is contested by the other Arctic nations concerning the Northern Sea Route and the dispute over Hans Island between Denmark and Canada remains unsolved (see Byers 2009).

The Northwest Passage is one example where even territorial waters can be a subject of dispute. Mainly used as an important sea lane, Canada attempts to claim the Northwest Passage as an internal water (Emmerson 2011: 111) The United States, by contrast, claims that the Passage is an international strait as it connects two bigger sea areas. Byers (2009: 75) defines the main difference as being in the opportunity of passage—in internal waters, the coastal state has to permit every passage, whereas in international straits, freedom of navigation applies. While the Northwest Passage is unlikely to cause major military conflict, as both are members of NATO, it shows that even allied states like the US and Canada can be drawn into conflict by the lack of clarity in UNCLOS's definitions of sovereignty.

The other example is the dispute between Norway and Russia in the Barents Sea. An assumed resource-rich region, both adjacent states have claimed large parts as EEZs, however, these claims overlapped in various areas. The long-ongoing dispute, however, was solved through a bilateral treaty[7] that came into force in 2011

[7]Treaty between the Kingdom of Norway and the Russian Federation concerning Maritime Delimitation and Cooperation in the Barents Sea and the Arctic Ocean. Retrieved from https://www.regjeringen.no/globalassets/upload/ud/vedlegg/folkerett/avtale_engelsk.pdf

that clearly defines the Russian-Norwegian border in the Barents Sea. While this can be regarded as success in establishing recognized sea borders other aspects, such as the general cooperative environment in the Arctic, should be taken into account as well and the bilateral agreement has not lead to a completely calm situation. Since the Ukraine crisis, Norway held military exercises in the Barents Sea together with Sweden and Finland, which is a prime example of further militarization.

Having debated border and sovereignty disputes, the question arises how these shape security in the High North. As Heininen (2012: 28) assesses, sovereignty is the prime priority in every Arctic state's Arctic strategy. The settlement of border issues does also assume an important role in the respective strategies. However, as the non-coastal states approach security more comprehensively, the coastal states focus on defense and security. This is in line with the question posed by Järvenpää and Ries (2013: 136) for whom 'the extent to which littoral powers feel the need to back up their Arctic claims and activity with a military presence' is of importance. Only two Arctic powers have strengthened their Arctic fleet so far, but Wezeman (2012) concludes that, with the exception of the US, all Arctic nations have adopted Arctic defense strategies and significantly build up their Arctic forces. Huebert (2010: 23) interprets for example Norway's build-up as a direct reaction from skepticism towards Russia but as Huebert's assessment was made before the enforcement of the treaty between Norway and Russia, the military build-up can be interpreted as a reaction to the unsolved border issue. While in the Arctic expansive endeavors remain at a low level while and cooperation high, the short-comings of the border regime provided by UNCLOS has definitely increased the demand for security measures in the Arctic.

In conclusion, both case studies represent an example of a deterioration of the security dilemma caused by the unclear drawing of borders and the lack of protection of sovereignty within UNCLOS. The visible militarization in both regions proves that states perceive an increased threat to their already reduced sovereignty in EEZs. Furthermore, different interpretations of territorial demarcation can also lead to offensive behavior, as proven by China's Nine-Dash-Line. Institutions might be able to mitigate the deteriorated security dilemma, in both cases, the lack of territorial demarcation and ill-defined sovereignty alter the security environments.

5 Conclusion

It was attempted to explain how a border regime that allows interfering claims and territorial disputes influences what has been defined as the 'security dilemma'. Also, this chapter tries to explain whether this border regime fosters offensive or defensive behavior. Mearsheimer (2001: 29) claims that 'Great Powers [. . .] are always searching for opportunities to gain power over their rivals.' As power can be described by territorial possession, and especially by economic capabilities, unsettled borders offer an opportunity for greater powers to extend their influence in certain areas of the globe. This, at least partially, applies to China's strategy in the South China Sea, where it could also be seen as the only Great Power. The Nine-Dash-Line symbolizes an expansive approach, the military build-up has not only taken place to guarantee security, but also to underline China's territorial claims. This threatens other adjacent nations as well as international actors like the US who themselves have responded with a military build-up in order to guarantee their respective securities. This offers a great example of how disputed borders on the high seas can foster expansive behavior, and how the lack of sanctioning mechanisms in the case of possible violations leads to greater insecurity among other actors, therefore deteriorating the security dilemma.

On the contrary, defensive realism, as defined by Taliaferro (2000: 129), assumes that states only seek expansion under certain conditions and try to reach security by more comprehensive and cooperative means. This definition applies more readily to the Arctic than offensive realism, which may be due to the fact that more great powers are involved in the Arctic. Sovereignty issues do not mainly deal with the endeavor of a state to extend its influence, but more with securing the own territorial integrity, often following cooperative and diplomatic approaches. Some aspects of defensive realism can also be seen in the South China Sea, especially in the actions of countries like Vietnam and the Philippines, the Arctic however can be interpreted as acting nearly entirely under the notions of defensive realism.

Unsettled borders contribute to perceived insecurity and therefore lead to increasing security measures, such as military build-ups. Especially in the context of resources it is important to resolve border issues, as resource extraction depends highly on economic sovereignty. However, it is difficult to assess to what extent borders affect the security dilemma and which role other factors, for example cooperative structures, assume. It is clear though that if territorial demarcation is disputed, states are motivated to seek other measures to increase their security. In certain configurations, like the South China Sea, disputes can even add to expansive endeavors, especially if economic or power motives are underlying. So I will conclude this chapter by answering the two questions asked at the beginning. For the first question, it is quite obvious that the security dilemma as formulated before is negatively affected by ill-defined borders—the lack of territorial integrity and guaranteed sovereignty increases the perception of insecurity and therefore leads to intensifying conflicts. For the second question, national security policy is influenced by ill-defined borders as the legal protection of territory is lacking, therefore, military protection assumes a greater role. This also adds to the deterioration of the security dilemma. In order to avoid a break-out of possible maritime conflicts, UNCLOS would need to be strengthened and especially stronger sanctioning mechanisms for the coastal states need to be installed.

References

Agnew, J. (1994). The territorial trap: The geographical assumptions of international relations theory. *Review of International Political Economy, 1*(1), 53–80.

Basaran, T. (2008). Security, law, borders: Spaces of exclusion. *International Political Sociology, 2*(4), 339–354.

Blazevic, J. J. (2012). Navigating the security dilemma: China, Vietnam and the South China Sea. *Journal of Current Southeast Asian Affairs, 31*(4), 79–108.

Boggs, S. W. (1930). Delimitation of the territorial sea: The method of delimitation proposed by the delegation of the United States at the Hague conference for the codification of international law. *American Journal of International Law, 24*, 541–555.

Boggs, S. W. (1937). Problems of water-boundary definition, median lines and international boundaries through territorial waters. *The Geographical Review, XXVII*, 445–456.

Boyle, A. (1997). Dispute settlement and the law of the sea convention: Problems of fragmentation and jurisdiction. *International and Comparative Law Quarterly, 46*(1), 37–54.

Brunet-Jailly, E. (2005). Theorizing borders: An interdisciplinary perspective. *Geopolitics, 10*(4), 633–649.

Brunet-Jailly, E. (2011). Special section: Borders, borderlands and theory: An introduction. *Geopolitics, 16*(1), 1–6.

Byers, M. (2009). *Who owns the arctic? Understanding sovereignty disputes in the high north.* Vancouver: Douglas & McIntyre.

Carlson, J. D., Hubach, C., Long, J., Minteer, K., & Young, S. (2013). Scramble for the arctic: Layered sovereignty, UNCLOS and competing maritime territorial claims. *SAIS Review of International Affairs, 33*(2), 21–43.

Diehl, P. F., & Goertz, G. (1988). Territorial change and militarized conflict. *Journal of Conflict Resolution, 32*(1), 103–122.

Dutton, P. (2011). Three disputes and three objectives. China and the South China Sea. *Naval War College Review, 64*(4), 42–65.

Emmerson, C. (2011). *The future history of the Arctic. How climate, resources and geopolitics are reshaping the north, and why it matters to the world.* London: Vintage Books.

Gao, Z., & Jia, B. B. (2013). The nine-dash line in the South China Sea: History, status and implications. *The American Journal of International Law, 107*(1), 98–124.

Giordano, M. F., Giordano, M. A., & Wolf, A. T. (2005). International resource conflict and mitigation. *Journal of Peace Research, 42*(1), 47–65.

Grimm, D. (2015). *Sovereignty. The origin and future of a political and legal concept.* New York: Columbia University Press.

Heininen, L. (2012). State of the Arctic strategies and policies—A summary. *Arctic Yearbook, 2012*, 2–47.

Herz, J. H. (1950). Idealist internationalism and the security dilemma. *World Politics, 2*(2), 157–180.

Huebert, R. (2010). *The newly emerging Arctic security environment.* Canadian Defence & Foreign Affairs Institute.

Järvenpää, P., & Ries, T. (2013). The rise of the Arctic on the global stage. In J. Kraska (Ed.), *Arctic security in an age of climate change.* Cambridge: Cambridge University Press.

Jervis, R. (1978). Cooperation under the security dilemma. *World Politics, 30*(2), 167–214.

Jervis, R. (1999). Realism, neoliberalism, and cooperation: Understanding the debate. *International Security, 24*(1), 42–63.

Jervis, R. (2011). Dilemmas about security dilemmas. *Security Studies, 20*(3), 416–423.

Keohane, R. (1984). *After hegemony: Cooperation and discord in the world political economy.* Princeton, NJ: Princeton University Press.

Mearsheimer, J. J. (1995). The false promise of international institutions. *International Security, 19*(3), 5–49.

Mearsheimer, J. J. (2001). *The tragedy of great power politics.* New York: W.W. Norton.

Minghi, J. (1963). Review article: Boundary studies in political geography. *Annals of the Association of American Geographers, 53*(3), 407–428.
Nyman, E. (2013). Oceans of conflict: Determining potential areas of maritime disputes. *SAIS Review of International Affairs, 33*(2), 5–14.
Paasi, A. (2009). Bounded spaces in a 'borderless world': Border studies, power and the anatomy of territory. *Journal of Power, 2*(2), 213–234.
People's Republic of China. (2015). China's military strategy. Retrieved from http://news.usni.org/2015/05/26/document-chinas-military-strategy. Accessed 15 Jan 2016.
Perlez, J. (2016). Beijing's South China Sea claims rejected by Hague Tribunal. *New York Times*. Retrieved from http://www.nytimes.com/2016/07/13/world/asia/south-china-sea-hague-ruling-philippines.html. Accessed 13 July 2016.
Phillips, T., Holmes, O., & Bowcott, O. (2016). Philippines wins South China Sea case against China. *The Guardian*. Retrieved from https://www.theguardian.com/world/2016/jul/12/philippines-wins-south-china-sea-case-against-china. Accessed 12 July 2016.
Rahman, C., & Tsamenyi, M. (2010). A strategic perspective on security and naval issues in the South China Sea. *Ocean Development & International Law, 41*(4), 315–333.
Rosenberg, D. (2011). Governing the South China Sea. From freedom of the seas to ocean enclosure movements. *Harvard Asia Quarterly, 12*(3&4), 4–12.
Simmons, B. A. (2002). Capacity, commitment and compliance. International institutions and territorial disputes. *Journal of Conflict Resolution, 46*(6), 829–856.
Sørensen, G. (1999). Sovereignty: Change and continuity in a fundamental institution. *Political Studies, 47*(3), 590–604.
Taliaferro, J. W. (2000). Security seeking under anarchy: Defensive realism revisited. *International Security, 25*(3), 128–161.
Tang, S. (2009). The security dilemma: A conceptual analysis. *Security Studies, 18*(3), 587–623.
Taylor Fravel, M. (2011). China's strategy in the South China Sea. *Contemporary South East Asia, 33*(3), 292–315.
Thomson, J. E. (1995). State sovereignty in international relations: Bridging the gap between theory and empirical research. *International Studies Quarterly, 39*(2), 213–233.
Weber, M. (1922/1978). *Economy and society*. Los Angeles: University of California Press.
Wezeman, S. T. (2012). *Military capabilities in the Arctic*. SIPRI Background Paper.
Williams, J. (2002). Territorial borders, toleration and the English school. *Review of International Studies, 28*(4), 737–758.
Zacher, M. W. (2001). The territorial integrity norm: International boundaries and the use of force. *International Organization, 55*(2), 215–250.

Clemens Binder is a Researcher at the Austrian Institute for International Affairs (oiip) where he focuses on Science, Technology and International Relations. In addition, he conducts research on maritime conflicts, resource conflicts and Arctic affairs. He obtained his Master's degree from the University of Vienna, with experience abroad in Norway and the United States.

Border (Power) Politics Reborn in the Refugee Crisis: Contested Lines of Demarcation and the Re-emergence of Identity Conflicts: The Case of Serbia and Croatia

Vedran Dzihic

Abstract The refugee crisis in 2015 and 2016 has brought the region of the Western Balkans back into the international news headlines. For months the so-called 'Western Balkans-Route' was a major arterial road for refugees with the ultimate goal of reaching Germany and other Western European countries. This chapter starts by establishing a conceptual model, based on Rogers Brubaker's relational argument, to explain the continued importance of nationalism and consequently of border (power) politics in the region. By illustrating the conflict between Croatia and Serbia over refugees in fall 2015, the chapter reveals the structure of newly emerging political battles and identity discourses surrounding the concept of borders and demarcations in the Balkans. The chapter argues that developments on and around the 'Western Balkans-Route' contributed to the re-emergence of concepts of borders and demarcations in the political realm. The refugee crisis re-opened and re-fueled old identity conflict lines thus contributing to an increase in nationalist rhetoric and behavior. More substantially, the refugee crisis and subsequent events have contributed to the reaffirmation of borders, and thus strengthening of exclusive nation-state concepts in the Balkans.

Keywords Border politics • Refugees • Nationalism • Western Balkans • Serbia • Croatia

1 Introduction

The refugee crisis of 2015 and 2016 has brought the region of the Western Balkans back into the international news headlines. For months the so-called 'Western Balkans-Route' was a major arterial road for refugees from Syria, Iraq and Afghanistan with the ultimate goal of reaching Germany and other Western European

V. Dzihic (✉)
Austrian Institute for International Affairs (oiip), Vienna, Austria
e-mail: Vedran.Dzihic@oiip.ac.at

C. Günay, N. Witjes (eds.), *Border Politics*, DOI 10.1007/978-3-319-46855-6_4

countries. The already fragile and rather unstable Western Balkans states have struggled to cope with the mass influx of refugees, which has resulted both in the appearance of new demarcation and identity conflict lines as well as the emergence of new nationalisms throughout the region. The closure of the Croatian and Serbian border in fall 2015, during the peak of the refugee crisis, reinforced old animosities and enhanced conflicting rhetoric. From the beginning of the crisis Southeastern Europe has witnessed the erection of new fences on the border between Slovenia and Croatia, between Macedonia and Greece, etc. This has sparked debates about the consequences of new border regimes, both on regional stability and cooperation, as well as on broader issues such as EU-integration, national identities and the further development of democracy in the region.

Against the background of the recent refugee crisis, in this chapter I argue that since fall 2015, developments in the Western Balkans have contributed to the re-emergence of concepts of borders and demarcations in the political realm. I use consciously the terms 're-emergence' as the events and debates relate directly to the discourses and narratives of the early 1990s. Or to put it more precisely, the 1990s are the birth-place of border (power) politics in the Balkans, while recent events can be described as a prolongation and a re-birth under new circumstances. In any case, following a period of enhanced and intensified regional cooperation and normalization since 2000 (at least between Croatia and Serbia, but also more broadly), the recent refugee crisis has re-opened and re-fueled old identity conflict lines thus contributing to an increase in nationalist rhetoric and behavior. More substantially, the refugee crisis and subsequent events have contributed to the reaffirmation of borders and thus the strengthening of exclusive nation-state concepts in the Balkans. Here I argue that the process of political instrumentalization of (ethnic/national) differences and borders (real and discursive ones) between the states in the Balkans based on nationalism and old identity conflict lines from the 1990s can be described as a border (power) politics. I describe this kind of border politics as power politics, alluding to the ultimate goal that is pursued by political (nationalist) elites in the region, which is basically equal to remaining in power. Based on theoretical thoughts on nationalism, the following chapter aims at (a) establishing a conceptual model to explain the continued importance of nationalism, and consequently of border (power) politics in the region based on Rogers Brubaker's relational argument, (b) sketching out the newly emerged border (power) politics in the regional context of Southeastern Europe based on the conflict over refugees between Croatia and Serbia in fall 2015, and (c) uncovering the structure of newly emerging political battles and identity discourses surrounding the concept of borders and demarcations between countries in the Western Balkans.

This chapter draws on an extensive analysis both of the general literature on nationalism as well as the regional literature on the effects and consequences of nationalism in the Western Balkans. The case study on Serbia and Croatia during the course of the refugee crisis is based on an analysis of statements of policy-makers, as well as content analysis of media reporting in major regional news outlets.

2 Background: Roots and Persistence of Ethno-nationalism and Border (Power) Politics in the Balkans

Politics in the last years of the Former Yugoslavia were shaped by nationalism and nation-state building processes, based on strict borders between nations and newly established exclusive identity boundaries. The annual celebrations on the Field of Blackbirds (Kosovosko polje) on 28 June marked the beginning of the end of Former Yugoslavia. The celebrations eventually became a symbol of new demarcation lines forming within the broader Yugoslav society. Nearly one million Serbs gathered to celebrate the 600th anniversary of the Battle of Kosovo Polje in 1989.[1] Slobodan Milošević, who took power in Serbia in 1987, gave the key address during the celebrations and launched the final phase of his nationalist-populist campaign against the alleged discrimination of Serbia within the Yugoslav state. By reminding the crowd of possible violent conflicts in the near future and deploying all his rhetorical power to draw thick lines of distinction between Serbs and 'unfriendly' nations within the Yugoslav federation Milosevic marked the beginning of border (power) politics based on the resource of nationalism (Magaš 1992; Jović 2003; Allcock 2000).

From this point onwards, the crisis of the Yugoslav state became acute and its dissolution unfolded. Milosevic's Serbian nationalism triggered new forms of nationalist political formations in other Yugoslav republics. Franjo Tudjman emerged as Milosevic's counterpart in Croatia. Tudjman promoted an ethnically homogenous Croatian nation-state and emphasized the differences between Croatia and the other republics. At the beginning of the 1990s, the already deep gap between the Western republics of Slovenia and Croatia on the one side, and an alliance formed around Serbia on the other, was rapidly widening. It culminated in the demolition of the League of Communists of Yugoslavia in January 1990 and would subsequently lead to violent ethnic conflicts and wars. Socialist Yugoslavia went up in flames (Ramet 1992; Woodward 1995; Jović 2003). The 'rebirth' of nations, and consequently new national borders in Southern Europe, led to a nationalistic frenzy with numerous victims and erection of new national borders in the Balkans marked not only by new states, but also new strong and exclusive ethnic and national identities (Mappes-Niediek 2005). The fight for the demarcation from the ethnic 'other', fought by all means, became the main feature of politics in the region in the 1990s, only to be perpetuated in the subsequent period of so-called 'transition to democracy'. The interpretation of the recent past, based on exclusive narratives about the events of the 1900s (Ingrao and Thomas 2009), became a power resource fully in place until today, able to nurture new potential conflicts and re-affirm strict border and demarcation lines between ethnic groups, nations and newly established states in the Balkans. Deep and still persistent demarcation lines and cleavages between the Croatian and Serbian narrative, the Bosniak, Croatian

[1]The Battle of Kosovo Polje took place on 28th June 1389, when a Christian army faced the invading Ottomans. The Battle figures prominently in the Serbian national mythology.

and Serbian narrative in Bosnia and Herzegowina, or the narrative between Kosovo Albanians and Serbs (and further to the South between Greek and Macedonians), function until today as a repository for any kind of border (power) politics that emerge. This is precisely the background against which I try to frame and explore the newest emergence of border (power) politics in the course of the refugee crisis in 2015 and 2016.

3 Conceptualizing Nationalism and Border (Power) Politics in South Eastern Europe: Relational Framing and Creation of 'Groupness' Around Borders

Already the ancient term 'ethnic' marked boundaries between groups, based on their self-attributed 'ethnic' distinctiveness and exclusivity (Volkan 1999). Ethnic boundaries are, therefore, usually 'the result of a reflexive selection process; they occur only in opposition to other, similarly structured groups' (Orywal and Hackstein 1993: 600). Such a process ultimately results in bringing borders and demarcation lines (both in terms of discourse as well as territorial/material borders) to the forefront. Opposition to the other, and selection according to the distinction between 'we' and 'you', is a permanent process with conjunctures and fluctuations, and where the opposite is not necessarily always present. Quite often the 'imagined other' (Anderson 1988), even within one ethnic group or nation, is sufficient to draw boundaries between 'us' and 'them'.

The construction of this 'uniqueness and exclusivity' is made possible through massive and deliberate manipulation and mythologizing of history as well as through processes of exclusion (of the real or imagined other). At the core of this narrative stands an identifiable ethnic group living within borders of 'our nation-state' which is considered to be better, stronger, more resistant and superior, exclusive 'we' group different than the 'other' groups, which are generally perceived and constructed as being a threat. This is what is described as the construction of 'otherness' (see Ćurak 2004; and Džihić et al. 2006). It is important to note that different ethnicities or national belongings *a priori* do not provide a reason and an explanation for conflicts. Their conflictive potential develops only, and where, one's own uniqueness and exclusivity is perceived as being endangered, and where—speaking in terms of political power games—the interests of power groups and networks (including political parties, oligarchs, etc.) are endangered (Barth 1969). Thus, ethnicity is a tool that can be interpreted and instrumentalized differently in different political circumstances.

> Ethnicity is a relationship between two or several groups, not a property of a group; it exists between and not within groups. . . . Ethnicity is the enduring and systematic communication of cultural differences between groups considering themselves to be distinct. It appears whenever cultural differences are made relevant in social interaction, and it should thus be studied at the level of social life, not at the level of symbolic culture. Ethnicity is thus relational, and also situational; the ethnic character of a social encounter is contingent on the situation. It is not, in other words, absolute. (Eriksen 2002: 58)

An important insight into the relational character of ethnic groups and nations that is relevant for my conceptualization of border (power) politics is provided by Rogers Brubaker's theoretical and analytical frameworks. Brubaker's point of departure is a critical re-consideration of the concept of the 'group', which is a concept that is usually taken-for-granted in the context of theories of nationalism and often not further scrutinized. Brubaker describes the tendency to take groups for granted as 'groupism' (see Brubaker 2002). He postulated the need to stop uncritically adopting categories of ethnopolitical and nationalist practice as categories of social analysis.

> By invoking groups (actors) evoke them, summon them, call them into being. Their categories are for doing—designed to stir, summon, justify, mobilize, kindle, and energize. By reifying groups, by treating them as substantial things-in-the-world, ethnopolitical entrepreneurs may, as Bourdie notes, 'contribute to producing what they apparently describe or designate' (Brubaker 2002: 7)

Taking Brubaker's thinking and re-conceptualisation of groups and nations a step further I suggest that borders, and consequently border (power) politics, can be thought of and conceptualized along the lines of Brubaker's thinking about 'groupness'. Usually, territorial borders are, once negotiated and agreed upon, taken for granted, and there is good reason for them lying at the heart of international law and their being connected with the conceptualization of the modern state and its sovereignty. However, in cases like in Former Yugoslavia, where we have had several layers of conflicts over borders and demarcation lines in the past, borders taken as 'things-in-the-world' (Brubaker 2002) become categories of doing. In this process the borders are capable of 'stirring, summoning, justifying, mobilizing, kindling and energizing' differences, and thus able to reinforce the power of nationalism, and in the very end, to fortify power positions. It is precisely the process of (a) mobilizing, energizing and utilizing differences (more precisely ethnic differences in the Former Yugoslavian context) for power purposes (gaining and retaining power), and (b) creating borders as lines of distinction between 'our' group and the 'other' that I define as 'border (power) politics'.

Returning to the events in Former Yugoslavia at the beginning of the 1990s Brubaker's analytical model can provide an explanation for the emergence of nationalism and border (power) politics in the 1990s. Based on Pierre Bourdieu's theory of fields, and relations between fields, Brubaker developed a new analytical framework that brought in an analysis of the dynamics of nationalism (Brubaker 2006). According to Brubaker's argument, nationalism is generated within political fields, which he describes as a 'triadic relational nexus' or 'triangular relationships' (Brubaker 2006). Brubaker's nexus involves a 'dynamic interdependence' among the following three 'fields': a newly emergent 'nationalizing state', an ethnocultural or 'national minority' residing within it, and an external 'national homeland' state of the expatriate 'national minority'. In applying his framework to the '*locus classicus*' of national self-determination in post-Cold War Central and Eastern Europe and the former Soviet Union, Brubaker predicted a downward spiral of conflict, and potentially the emergence of explosive violence resulting from interactions among the three fields of his triad (Ibid.). This downward spiral is precisely the one that occurred in the 1990s in the territory of Former Yugoslavia. Brubaker's idea is that specific interests and demands, which are formulated and pursued within individual fields, create a framework of diverging relations (based on distinct national and exclusive narratives of the past and nationalist instrumentalisation of these narratives) in which the population can be mobilized, and which bestow upon actual conflicts between ethno-national groups the appearance of 'naturalness' and 'eternity'. Once the conflicts appear 'natural' and 'eternal', the dynamics between the three fields can be orchestrated by political forces, thus becoming a power tool par excellence. Our case study, with the seemingly 'natural' and 'eternal' conflict line between Serbs and Croats, fits perfectly into the analytical model provided by Brubaker.

Stephen Del Rosso highlights a certain lack of explanatory power in Brubaker's thesis. Del Rosso proposed an essential fourth field: external influences, and refers to the implications of these on the dynamics between the three fields defined by Brubaker. Del Rosso speaks about globalization, and more precisely in the context of Eastern and Southeastern Europe, of the processes of 'Europeanization', involving political/economic, normative, and technological/cultural elements (Del Rosso 2004). Indeed, in the context of the Post-Yugoslav region the international community, and in particular the EU, need to be included as important external agents into analysis.

Selectively appropriating key elements of Brubaker's model and adding this external variable provided by Del Rosso helps us to transfer Brubaker's concept into the realm of border (power) politics of today, in the context of the refugee crisis in the Western Balkans. Borders in the context of the former Yugoslavia are here understood as being 'subject to constant reinterpretation, reincarnation and redrawing' (Iveković 2008).

My general argument would be the following: The triadic nexus of the 'nationalizing state', an ethnocultural or 'national minority' residing within it, and an external 'national homeland', sparked the ethno-nationalist forces in the period of the dissolution of Former Yugoslavia, creating a fertile ground for the persistent instrumentalisation of this triadic nexus since the 1990s until today. As a result, new border regimes emerged on the territory of Former Yugoslavia, materialized as the borders of new national states (leaving huge minorities outside) and as mutually exclusive narratives. Since 2000, the EU-integration process became a dominant external variable (Džihić and Wieser 2011; BIEPAG 2015) and emerged as a fourth field, which has influenced the triadic nexus. Although the EU has been able to exercise power politics by its own, it has, so far not been able to substantially alter the dynamics of ethno-nationalism. Finally, I argue that in times of fundamental turbulence within the EU and of weakened power politics in the framework of Europeanization, the actors in the region tend to retreat to the original dynamics of nationalism and border (power) politics from the 1990s.

4 The Refugee Crisis and Conflict Between Croatia and Serbia[2]

The latest border-crisis in the Balkans was triggered by a fence. In July 2015, Hungary began building a fence along its 110-mile border with Serbia. When Hungary closed its doors to the tens of thousands of refugees heading north partly violent clashes including water cannons and tear gas occurred, leading to high tensions in both countries. There were chaotic scenes near the border crossing at Horgos, with burning fires, police vehicles and ambulances arriving on the Serbian side of the border across from massed ranks of riot police on the Hungarian side (Radio Free Europe 2016). The Prime Minister of Serbia, Aleksandar Vučić, reiterated that the current Hungarian policy towards refugees is harmful and dangerous. In the following days he stepped up the rhetoric with statements where he draw comparison to the World War II (Ibid.).

Nevertheless, Hungary's fence-building caused a domino effect that played out across the Balkan region (Ernst 2015). As the war of words intensified, masses of weary refugees continued their way up the 'Western Balkans route', this time choosing the way from Macedonia to Serbia and further north to Croatia, Slovenia and finally into Austria and Germany. As Serbia started diverting refugees to Croatia the Serbian-Croatian relationship started to deteriorate rapidly.

Zoran Milanović, the prime minister of Croatia, demanded that Serbia send some of the refugees to Hungary or Romania and pledged that he would not allow Serbia to 'make fools of us'. The refugee dispute between Serbia and Croatia escalated leading to a trade war. Belgrade closed the main border crossing Bajakovo-Batrovci to all trucks with Croatian plates and to all those transporting goods produced in Croatia. In retaliation, Croatia closed the crossing to cars with Serbian plates. At that time, Bajakovo-Batrovci was the last of eight crossing points that had remained open to both trucks and cars after the dispute of the previous week. Croatia than went on to block trucks coming from Serbia at Bajakovo-Batrovici, in a further attempt to pressure Belgrade to redirect the migrant flow towards Hungary and Romania (Balkan Insight 2015).

Both Serbia and Croatia ramped up the rather nationalist rhetoric. They started trading blame and accusations of lying, while at the same time openly and aggressively disparaging each other's actions as 'pathetic' or a 'disgrace'. What was striking is the fact that the highest officials were engaged in reviving the old inflammatory rhetoric, reminiscent of that of the 1990s. The infamous exchange between Serbian Prime Minister Vučić and Croatian Prime Minister Zoran Milanović is one of the most illustrative examples. The debate was sparked by Serbian Social Affairs Minister Aleksandar Vulin who, following the closure of all but one border crossing between Croatia and Serbia by Croatia authorities, said 'I

[2] If not differently stated the events and developments here are based on the continuous following of media reporting around the refugee crisis provided by Radio Free Europa, T-Portal, B92.net and Al Jazeera Balkans.

am sorry to see that Croatian humanity and solidarity lasted just two days,' immediately warning the neighbors that Serbia intended to take the issue to the international courts. From its new strong position in the region as a member state of the EU, the Croatian Prime Minister Milanović responded sharply, and compared Serbia state power with a fly, which symbolizes something small and unimportant. He added that '(An) eagle does not hunt flies. Croatia is an eagle' (B92.net 2015a, September 18). The Foreign Minister of Serbia, Ivica Dačić, answered with a quote from a very famous Former Yugoslav movie 'The spy from the Balkans' (Balkanski špijun), 'The eagle was downed'. And finally, Prime Minister Vučić said that he wouldn't take the bait sending a message to Zagreb that Serbia will do everything it can to protect its interests (Ibid.).

The past also figured dominantly in the conflict, which was seen in a further statement issued in September 2015. For example, the protest letter by the Serbian Ministry of Foreign Affairs sent to the Croatian Embassy in Belgrade called for a travel ban for the Serbian passport holders, a measure that was not appropriate for the 'civilized world'. The Statement of the Ministry continued: '[The] discriminatory character of such measures can be compared only with the measures undertaken in the past, at the time of the fascist Independent Croatian State' (B92.net 2015b, September 24). While Serbia cried Nazism and recalled Storm (the operation of the Croatian forces against territory in Croatia ruled in 1999 by the Serbs), the Croatian side mentioned Vukovar,[3] which is paradoxically a city near where the refugees were crossing the border between the two countries.

This fierce exchange happened against the background of an already shaky relationship between Serbia and Croatia, full of historical resentments (Gagnon 2004). The major dispute between these two former adversaries is fueled by different interpretations of the war. While Croatian narratives see Croats as a victor in a rightful war to protect their sovereignty, Serbian narratives depict Serbs as victims of ethnic cleansing and a 'fascist' Croatia (Jović 2012). Nationalist forces on both sides have been keeping these mutually exclusive narratives high on the agenda and use every opportunity to define the other side as the absolute 'Other'. This border between the two national narratives was re-installed and strengthened as a real border during the events of 2015 related to the refugee crisis.

The current hostility between Croatia and Serbia has been shaped by domestic political considerations and power dynamics both in Zagreb and Belgrade. In Croatia, elections were due to be held in February 2016. The Croatian economy had been in recession for 6 years and only recently begun to show small signs of growth. This was a welcome moment for Croatian political representatives to revive old nationalist rhetoric as a distraction from domestic problems. On the other side, the Serbian Prime Minister Vučić found himself facing rising pressure from right-wing parties, and partly from some parts of his own Serbia Progressive Party (SNS),

[3]Vukovar was the major site of fighting between Croatian armed forces and Yugoslav Peoples' Army (JNA) and Serb paramilitaries in the second half of 1991. During the siege of the city and the final surrender to the JNA major war crimes were committed.

to react to what was widely perceived as aggressive behavior and humiliation by Croatia. In the following months Serbia and Croatia continued with harsh rhetoric, which even included a debate about buying new offensive weapons (Nikolić 2016). This debate can be seen as a continuation of the conflict sparked by the refugee crisis and events of fall 2015. During this armament debate, media outlets in both countries stepped up their sensationalist coverage, with politicians on both sides sending controversial messages to each other. For example, Prime Minister Vučić stated that 'Serbia will never attack anyone, but must be able to protect its territory and citizens at any moment. We are keeping quiet, doing nothing faced with the threats of those others who are not giving up on acquiring very powerful offensive weapons' (Nikolić 2016). Croatian politicians responded with harsh accusations against Vučić and Serbian Foreign Minister Ivica Dačić, blaming them for being senior officials of the Serbian government during the 1990s which initiated conflicts in Slovenia, Croatia, Bosnia and Kosovo (Ibid.).

To sum it up, the above described events once again emphasised how an externally induced crisis (the refugee crisis) can immediately reinforce old conflict lines and fuel animosities. The political reasoning in Croatia and Serbia, and the fact that both sides have been using the refugee crisis to fortify their power positions, serves internally as a paradigmatic case of border (power) politics. For both the Croatian government, which at that time was already entering an intensive election campaign, as well as for the Serbian government, which shortly after the events announced the date for new elections, the refugee crisis and the newly sparked conflict lines served the purpose of strengthening the position and the image of 'strong leaders' (Milanović and Vučić).

Vessela Tcherneva and Fredrik Wesslau argued: 'This humanitarian crisis is leading to rapidly deteriorating relations between the countries in the region, with politicians eagerly channelling long-veiled animosities and gaining electoral wins though rough exchanges with neighbours' (Tcherneva and Wesslau 2015). The speed at which Serbia and Croatia resorted to vicious mutual insults was rapid and can be explained by the already available framework for the emergence of nationalism from the 1990s, within Brubaker's triadic nexus, and by the instrumentalisation of nationalism and border (power) politics since the 1990s.

Moving from the events of 2015 to more recent developments, we've witnessed a decrease in the relevance of the Western Balkans route during the course of 2016. At the beginning of 2016, the debate on dealing with the refugee crisis on the European level quickly moved towards the introduction of more rigid measures on the borders by Western European states like Austria and the closure of the Western Balkans Route to refugees. This development came after February 2016 when Austria decided to introduce a new general limit for refugees arriving in 2016 (Selo Šabić and Borić 2016), and a daily limit of refugees allowed to enter and to be registered in the country. This triggered EU fears of a domino effect along the so-called Balkan 'migrant' route, a fear that was only fueled by the events following the so called Western Balkans conference organized by Austria on February 24, that was harshly criticized by Greece, Italy, Germany and the EU Commission. Western Balkan states decided to follow Austria's example and either drastically limit the number of refugees allowed to cross their borders on a daily basis or close their borders to them altogether. After March 2016, the border between Macedonia and Greece, and particularly the refugee camp in Idomeni, became the new and rather violent hot spot, adding a new dimension to the refugee crisis.

As the focus of the refugee crisis in the first few months of 2016 shifted away from the Western Balkans towards Greece, Turkey and the Mediterranean Sea, the status of the relationship between Croatia and Serbia remains open. Formally, and in terms of border and migration management, the relations between Western Balkan countries have improved, particularly as they have begun to share information, open communication lines and better coordinate plans and policies to deal with refugees and migrants. However, the tensions and rather nationalist rhetorics that emerged in the fall of 2015 continued and even escalated against the background of the final verdict against (and acquittal of) Vojislav Šešelj at The Hague Tribunal at the end of March 2016. Croatian authorities and public opinion reacted angrily. The newly appointed Croatian Prime Minister, Tihomir Orešković, described the verdict as a setback for justice. 'This verdict is an embarrassment for the Hague Tribunal and represents a defeat for the Hague prosecution.. . .This is a man who has never shown remorse for the things he has done, not even now. He's the man who is burning the flags of Croatia and the EU' (Balkan Insight 2016). Just a few days following the Seselj verdict, Croatia took formal action against Serbia demanding better treatment of Croats in Serbia and more action on war crimes, forcing the European Council to postpone negotiations with Belgrade on two chapters of EU legislation. The reaction of Serbian officials and the public came immediately. Prime Minister Vučić, finding himself in the middle of the election campaign, was 'stunned' by Croatia's decision and sent a strong message to Zagreb that 'Croatia did not have a single good reason for that decision. Serbia . . . will not allow anyone in Europe and the world, including Croatia, to blackmail, humiliate and demean it in any way' (Euractiv). This latest episode in the newly re-emerged conflict between Croatia and Serbia in the aftermath of the refugee crisis is again proof of the re-emergence of nationalist border (power) politics in the region.

5 Conclusion: The Refugee Crisis as a Crystallization Point for a New Kind of Nationalist Border (Power) Politics in the Western Balkans

The recent and ongoing developments in the refugee crisis provide a picture of insecurity in terms of further development of border (power) politics in the Balkans. As the Croatian-Serbian dispute since the fall 2015 shows, the nationalist border (power) politics remains a dominant feature of the Balkans entailing potential for further escalation of the situation and continued mobilization in their societies around nationalism. This chapter departed from theoretical considerations on nationalism against the background of the ethno-nationalism and mutually exclusive narratives from the 1990s. It went on to establish a conceptual model for the explanation of the continued importance of nationalism, and consequently of border (power) politics in the region, based on Rogers Brubaker's relational argumentation. By illustrating the conflict over refugees between Croatia and Serbia in fall 2015, the paper uncovered the structure of newly emerging political battles and identity discourses surrounding the concept of borders and demarcations in the Balkans.

We can conclude that the recent refugee crisis re-opened and re-fueled old identity conflict lines, thus contributing to an increase in nationalist rhetoric and behavior. More substantially, the refugee crisis has contributed once again to the reaffirmation of borders, and thus the strengthening of nation-state concepts in the Balkans, described as a border (power) politics based on ethnic differences and nationalism. The final argument presented was that in times of fundamental turbulence within the EU, and of weakened power politics in the framework of Europeanization, actors in the region retreated to the original dynamics of nationalism and border (power) politics from the 1990s. Obviously, looking at the region today and applying Rogers Brubaker's triadic nexus, the original 'triadic nexus' between a 'nationalizing state', an ethnocultural or 'national minority' and an external 'national homeland' has been altered in the meantime, resulting in more or less stable nation states (Croatia and Serbia) and 'national minorities' (of Serbs in Croatia, and Croats in Serbia) in a less prominent position than in the 1990s. Even though the 'triadic nexus' has changed, the construction of the 'other' based on 1990s divisions and the nexus has continued to exist, both in discursive as well as in 'Realpolitik'-terms (see events around Cirilica in Vukovar, annual celebrations of the Oluja/Storm-Operation or recent commemorations of the Jasenovac concentration camp).[4] The additional fourth field of the European refugee crisis, that played out on the border between an EU-member state (Croatia) and a candidate country for the EU-membership (Serbia) acted as a variable that shaped this conflict. The Croatian blockade of further EU-negotiations in the spring 2016 provides evidence for the intensity of this conflictual relationship between two neighbors.

A final and highly relevant additional argument in terms of nationalism and border (power) politics, as seen in the refugee crisis in the Western Balkans, can be found in the work of the Bosnian sociologist Dzemal Sokolovic. His argument is related to the fluctuating nature of ethnic nationalism and thus of border (power)

[4]'Ćirilica in Vukovar' refers to the conflict in the city of Vukovar over the decision of the Croatian government to implement the constitutionally guaranteed usage of the Cyrillic alphabet in public/state institutions. The official name plates of institutions written in Cyrillic were repeatedly destroyed by the local population and accompanied by sharp protests of Croatian conservative and nationalistic forces.

Oluja/Storm, was a major military operation of Croatian army in the summer of 1995 that resulted in the re-capture of Serb controlled territories in the Croatian Krajina. Croatia celebrated the date of the operation as a national holiday while the Serbian side accuses Croatia of committing major war crimes during its course.

Jasenovac concentration camp is an extermination camp established in Slavonia by the authorities of the Independent State of Croatia (NDH). The annually held commemorations are widely contested in the Croatian public, as some parts of conservative-nationalist forces in Croatia tend to deny the genocide committed in Jasenovac. The commemoration in 2016 following the victory of the conservative HDZ in the elections and was particularly disputed.

politics (Sokolović 1997). Sokolović argues that ethnic identities are prone to fluctuations, which means that phases of euphoric and hypertrophic eruptions of national identity and nationalism alternate with periods of national lethargy and indifference. The transitions from one state to the other very often take place quickly and surprisingly. Following this argument, the state of euphoric and hypertrophic eruption of national identity and nationalism can be triggered particularly rapidly and surprisingly in situations where (like in the Former Yugoslavia) a sufficient repository of nationalism and identity politics continues to shape the political arena. What we have been witnessing since the beginning of the refugee crisis is precisely this kind of trigger revealing the underlying conflicts in the region. And it is precisely in such a situation that borders are capable of 'stirring, summoning, justifying, mobilizing, kindling and energizing' differences (Brubaker), reinforcing the power of nationalism, and in the very end, fortifying not only existing borders but more fundamentally power positions.

References

Allcock, J. (2000). *Explaining Yugoslavia*. London: Pluto.

Anderson, B. (1988). *Die Erfindung der Nation*. Frankfurt am Main: Suhrkamp.

B92.net. (2015a, September 18). Refugee crisis: Croatia "moves to Plan B". *B92.net*. Retrieved from http://www.b92.net/eng/news/politics.php?yyyy=2015&mm=09&dd=18&nav_id=95483

B92.net. (2015b, September 24). Serbia's protest note references fascist Croat WW2 entity. *B92.net*. Retrieved from http://www.b92.net/eng/news/politics.php?yyyy=2015&mm=09&dd=24&nav_id=95545

Barth, F. (1969). *Ethnic groups and boundaries. The social organization of culture difference*. Michigan, IL: Little & Brown.

BiEPAG. (2015). Western Balkans and the EU: Beyond the Autopilot Mode. Policy Brief. Retrieved from http://www.suedosteuropa.uni-graz.at/sites/default/files/article_attach/BIEPAG-Western-Balkans-and-the-EU-Beyond-the-Autopilot-Mode.pdf

Brubaker, R. (2002). Ethnicity without groups. *Archives Europénnes de Sociologie, 2*, 163–189.

Brubaker, R. (2006). *Ethnicity without groups*. Los Angeles: University of California.

Ćurak, N. (2004). *Dejtonski nacionalizam: Ogledi o političkom*. Sarajevo: Buybook.

Del Rosso, S. J. (2004). Bringing the globe back. In *An analysis of the effects of globalization on national self-determination through application of Rogers Brubaker's "triadic nexus" of nationalism to the case of Estonia* [Dissertation]. Retrieved from ProQuest Paper AAI3125807.

Džihić, V., Nadjivan, S., Paic, J., & Stachowitsch, S. (2006). *Europa—Verflucht Begehrt. Europavorstellungen im Kontext sich wandelnder Staatlichkeit in Bosnien-Herzegowina, Kroatien und Serbien*. Wien: Braumüller.

Džihić, V., & Wieser, A. (2011). Incentives for democratisation? Effects of EU conditionality on democracy in Bosnia and Herzegovina. *Europe-Asia Studies, 63*(10), 1803–1825.

Eriksen, T. H. (2002). *Ethnicity and Nationalism* (2nd ed.). London: Pluto Press.

Ernst, A. (2015, September 9). Scheingefechte auf dem Balkan. *Neue Zürcher Zeitung*. Retrieved from http://www.nzz.ch/international/europa/scheingefechte-auf-dem-balkan-1.18621765

Gagnon, V. P. (2004). *The myth of ethnic war: Serbia and Croatia in the 1990s*. Ithaca, NY: Cornell University Press.

Ingrao, C., & Thomas, E. (Eds.). (2009). *Confronting the Yugoslav controversies: Scholars' initiative*. Washington, DC: United States Institute for Peace.

Iveković, R. (2008). Translation borders. Limits of nationalism, transnationalism, translationalism. *Transversal 03*. Retrieved from eipcp.net/transversal/0608/ivekovic/en/print

Jovanović, I. (2015, September 24). Serbia-Croatia refugee dispute escalates into trade war. *Balkan Insight*. Retrieved from http://www.balkaninsight.com/en/article/serbia-croatia-start-trade-war-09-24-2015

Jović, D. (2003). *Država koja je odumrla. Uspon, kriza i pad Kardeljeve Jugoslavije (1974-1990)*. Zagreb: Prometej.

Jović, D. (2012). The war that is not allowed to be forgotten: Nationalist discourse on the "Homeland War" (1991–1995) in contemporary Croatia. *Südosteuropa Mitteilungen, 3*, 52–69.

Magaš, B. (1992). *The destruction of Yugoslavia. Tracking Yugoslavia's break-up 1980-1992*. London: Verso.

Mappes-Niediek, N. (2005). *Die Ethno-Fälle. Der Balkan-Konflikt und was Europa daraus lernen kann*. Berlin: Ch. Links.

Milekic, S., & Dzidic, D. (2016, March 31). Croatia reacts angrily to Vojislav Seselj acquittal. *Balkan Insight*. Retrieved from http://www.balkaninsight.com/en/article/croatia-reacts-angrily-to-vojislav-seselj-acquittal-03-31-2016

Nikolić, I. (2016, January 11). Belgrade-Zagreb weapons row sparks media offensive. *Balkan Insight*. Retrieved from http://www.balkaninsight.com/en/article/belgrade-zagreb-weapons-war-hits-media-01-11-2016

Orywal, E., & Hackstein, K. (1993). Ethnizität: Die Konstruktion ethnischer Wirklichkeiten. In T. Schweizer, M. Schweizer, & W. Kokot (Eds.), *Handbuch der Ethnologie* (pp. 593–609). Berlin: Dietrich Reimer.

Radio Free Europe/Radio Slobodna Evropa. (2016, September 16). Retrieved from www.slobodnaevropa.org

Ramet, S. P. (1992). *Nationalism and federalism in Yugoslavia 1962-1991* (2nd ed.). Bloomington, IN: Indiana University Press.

Selo Sabic, S., & Boric, S. (2016). *At the gate of Europe. A report on refugees on the Western Balkan Route*. Friedrich Ebert Stiftung, SOE Dialog Südosteuropa.

Sokolović, D. 1. (1997). *Nacija protiv naroda. Bosna je samo jedan slučaj*. Oslo.

Tcherneva, V., & Wesslau, F. (2015, October 30). Refugee road to nowhere: The Western Balkans. *European Council on Foreign Affairs*. Retrieved from http://www.ecfr.eu/article/commentary_refugee_road_to_nowhere_the_western_balkans4089

Volkan, V. (1999). *Blutsgrenzen. Die historischen Wurzeln und die psychologischen Mechanismen ethnischer Konflikte und ihre Bedeutung bei Friedensverhandlungen*. Bern: Scherz.

Woodward, S. L. (1995). *Balkan tragedy. Chaos and dissolution after the Cold War*. Washington, DC: Brookings Institution Press.

Vedran Dzihic is a Senior Researcher at the Austrian Institute for International Affairs (oiip) and lecturer at the Institute for Political Sciences, University of Vienna. He has been an Austrian Marshall Plan Fellow and is currently a non-resident Senior Fellow at the Center for Transatlantic Relations, SAIS, John Hopkins University, Washington. Dzihic is author of 4 monographs, editor/co-editor of further 14 edited volumes/books and of numerous book chapters, scholarly articles and policy papers (in journals like Nationalities Papers, East European Politics and Society, Southeastern Europa, JEMIE, Europe-Asia Studies and others).

Part II
Practices of Border Crossing and Border Making

Reframing Migrant Smuggling as a Form of Knowledge: A View from the US-Mexico Border

Gabriella Sanchez and Nicholas Natividad

Abstract While empirical research on human smuggling worldwide is scant, there is a vast, well defined narrative pertaining to irregular migration: its facilitation as controlled by heinous transnational networks of exploitative traffickers who operating in the dark corners of the migrant universe take advantage of infantile migrants and asylum seekers, traffic virginal women, allow for the smuggling of drugs and weapons, and do not think twice about leaving their human cargo stranded in desolate deserts or deadly oceans. Over the last decade this rhetoric has been challenged by the scholarship of brokerage and precarity, and by attempts by social scientists to articulate new theoretical approaches to labor that incorporate illegitimized forms of work among marginalized populations in late modernity within its definition. Despite these critical efforts, scholarship on the facilitation of irregular migration has reached an impasse. Emphasis on providing data over migration routes, costs, distances, and an over-emphasis on narrating the most tragic journeys as a way to generate awareness on the experiences of migrants and asylum seekers, provide a narrow counter-narrative to the visually powerful rhetoric of smuggling as criminal, in fact often reinscribing perceptions of migrants as prone to violence and crime. How can the field of irregular migration facilitation articulate new visions that foreground critical analysis of its own concepts, while identifying new research and analysis paths? In this essay I return to the field to revisit and reconsider with the help of migrants who were successful in crossing the border extra-legally the very notion of smuggling. Through their testimonies, border crossings emerge as grounded on notions not of profit or risk alone, but instead, as connected to people's survival strategies under new forms of globalization, where human security, solidarity, friendship, love and humor emerge as the organizing principles of migratory journeys.

Keywords Migrant smuggling • *Coyotes* • US Mexico Border • Knowledge

---

G. Sanchez (✉)
National Security Studies Institute, University of Texas at El Paso, El Paso, TX, USA
e-mail: gesanchez4@utep.edu

N. Natividad
Criminal Justice Department, New Mexico State University, Las Cruces, NM, USA

C. Günay, N. Witjes (eds.), *Border Politics*, DOI 10.1007/978-3-319-46855-6_5

1 Introduction: The Border

At almost 3200 km long the US Mexico Border is embedded in the collective, global imagination as a lawless stretch of crime and death separating two very different countries. While, due to its proximity to Mexico, the border is often depicted as a dangerous place ridden by the heinous violence of Mexican drug *cartels*, its reputation is also derived from its paradigmatic role in the imaginarium of global irregular migration. As one of the most often crossed borders in the world, the US Mexico border is portrayed as being under a permanent state of siege by herds of people seeking to penetrate it illegally. Images of thousands of desperate dark-skinned migrants attempting to overcome the US fence at any cost, of frightened women and children turning themselves over to the immigration authorities, and of abandoned, lifeless bodies lying in the Arizona desert have further enhanced the perception of the US Mexico border as a land of decay, despair and death.

Also central to the narrative of the US Mexico border and irregular migration flows is the practice of migrant smuggling and its most notorious actors: the human smugglers or *coyotes*, as they are referred to colloquially in this part of the world. *Coyotes* are most commonly depicted as violent, exploitative and greedy men organized in transnational networks of vast reach. Within the official narrative, smugglers have complete disregard for the lives of migrants: they strip them of their hard earned money, abandon them to their fate along desert trails, kidnap their infant children and force women into the inferno of the sex trade.

While we do not deny the precariousness inherent to clandestine migration journeys, the vulnerability of migrants nor the specific forms of violence they face in the course of their journeys across the US Mexico border, the official and media narratives constructed in association with migrant smuggling have hardly been the subject of critical analyses. Rarely are migrant deaths explained as being a result of the environmental exposure faced by migrants in their search for remote crossing places to avoid the detection of law enforcement (Slack et al. 2013), or their reliance on *coyotes* explained as being a result of the virtual impossibility to fulfill visa or passport requirements (Sanchez 2015) imposed by governments throughout the Americas. Even less present, amid the criminalization of irregular migrants and their journeys are discussions on the social dimensions of migrant smuggling—on how mechanisms like friendship, solidarity and emotional support amid the uncertainty and instability of the route ultimately allow for said journeys to take place.

Scholars have long argued that borders are essential elements in the creation and the perpetuation of geographies of power. In this sense borders have been theorized as being emblematic examples of the everyday performance of state violence. Yet borders have simultaneously been challenged and transgressed by people in their daily practices. Borders are often depicted as the gates to the state—the spaces where surveillance, discipline, punishment and their consequences coalesce. However, everyday liminal practices on the margins carry, as Anzaldúa once wrote, the power to threaten the sovereignty of rulership (1987: 16).

As part of our contribution to this edited volume on defining spaces of governance and forms of transgressions on the border, we propose a critical revision to mainstream engagements with the practice of migrant smuggling. Relying on ethnographic data on coyote-led journeys taking place on the US Mexico Border, and deploying notions and methods articulated by indigenous and postcolonial thought and methodologies, we reframe migrant smuggling as being, rather than a criminal practice alone, but as a component of the community-originated forms of protection that are crafted in an attempt to reduce the vulnerability inherent to clandestine journeys—a form of human security from below that carries deep epistemological roots. Rather than reinscribing monolithic notions of smuggling and smugglers as deviants, we propose a critical re-definition of the practice that acknowledges not just the migrants' individual efforts but the collective dimensions of their communities to secure mobility amid the risks created by border controls and the criminalization of migration.

We argue that the series of practices that constitutes the facilitation of irregular migration—of which smuggling is an element—are rooted in historical, generation-long efforts dependent upon notions of community, solidarity, friendship, tradition and affect. Under neoliberalism, and in response to states' concerns over sovereignty and national security, these efforts have increasingly become criminalized, labeled as dangerous, exploitative and criminal, smuggling becoming in turn an increasingly dangerous premise for those who historically have relied on it as a mechanism for mobility. Our contribution is therefore an attempt to critically analyze the frameworks present in the academic engagements with migrant smuggling and potentially articulate solutions to move the field beyond oversimplified accounts of victimized migrants and inhumane smugglers.

2 Human Smuggling: A Definition

The practice of entering a country different than one's own, with the assistance of a broker or facilitator for a fee or in kind payment, while avoiding state controls is defined by international law conventions as human smuggling. Smuggling is often depicted as an exploitative and violent practice controlled by groups of *men* organized in vast and complex networks that operate transnationally and regularly in collusion with other criminal groups like drug trafficking organizations, even terrorists. Smugglers are also portrayed as being solely driven by the allegedly immense profits they obtain from banking on the desperation of migrants and asylum seekers, whom they often scam or even abandon while in route. There are also multiple reports of smugglers forcing women and children into the sex trade, or of migrants being sold or delivered into forced labor, becoming unwitting victims of human trafficking. Globally, and in response to the mobilization of these narratives, smuggling has become increasingly typified as a criminal, punishable offense.

While graphic representations and reports on exploitative forms of migrant smuggling are abundant, empirical work on the practice is surprisingly scant. Most data pertaining to smuggling activity is originated by law enforcement or other government officials, who in turn rely on examples from the most tragic and graphic of failed clandestine journeys. In this context, an important source of official smuggling narrative data are the testimonies of migrants who were the targets of violence in the context of their journeys, often at the hands of other criminals and state actors, rather than smugglers, and/or who were unsuccessful in their attempts to reach their final destination.

Critical, empirical engagements on migration facilitation practices have questioned the monolithic characterizations of smuggling as violent, establishing that irregular or clandestine journeys occur in far less dark, tragic or sensationalist conditions than what politicized and mediated narratives indicate.

In the case of smuggling facilitators, ethnographic evidence indicates they do not fit a specific demographic profile. Rather they are ordinary citizens (Zhang and Chin 2002), men as well as women of all ages—including minors (Sanchez 2015). The majority of those arrested for smuggling and smuggling-related offenses tend to be adult men of working age (Achilli 2015). While they are also important actors in the smuggling market, women are less likely to be detained (Zhang et al. 2007; Sanchez 2016). The majority of *coyotes* are working class individuals who hold regular jobs in the mainstream economy or support themselves by performing side jobs, income from smuggling activities is limited, seasonal and only occasional in nature (Zhang 2007). Most often they are migrants and/or refugees in transit themselves who share the same nationality or place of origin as their clients (Achilli 2015, 2016). Furthermore, interactions between this market and other transnational crime or even terrorist organizations, while existing, are most often of limited nature and reach (Sanchez and Zhang 2016).

The official narrative of clandestine migration as being under the control of smuggling facilitators on the one hand, and of constituting an individual, tragic and irrational journey on the part of naïve migrants in search of a better life on the other, has obscured the social dynamics that support migration flows. The web of protection provided to migrants by friends and family members, despite being a fundamental component of clandestine journeys, has remained largely absent in academic engagements on migration. Friends and family members extend financial, emotional and logistical support for those who migrate, and most importantly, constitute the source of social capital that provides recommendations and access to reliable smuggling facilitators (Koser 2008). This access is highly valued amid the desire and/or the need to migrate and the abundance of reports involving the risks associated with clandestine migration. Yet this information is more than a simple referral or tip. We argue that information on contacts, recommendations, specific details regarding routes, hotels and places for respite, advice on self-care to name but few, constitute a body of accumulated knowledge that is purposely shared in order to provide a protection mechanism for those who travel amid the inherent vulnerabilities of the clandestine journey. These protective and epistemological dimensions pertaining to the facilitation of border crossings are most often ignored amid larger narratives of crime, border control—even by those seeking to raise awareness over the precariousness faced by migrants in transit. As academics we have systematically failed to identify, theorize and incorporate notions of solidarity and support as constituting legitimate forms of knowledge in scholarly engagements of irregular migration.

3 Towards Theorizing Irregular Migration Facilitation from the Margins

Caribbean philosopher Eduard Glissant introduced the notion of *chaos monde*—the ways in which individuals and communities 'go beyond vainglory and suffering, power and impatience, together, however imperceptibly' to argue that memory within a marginalized community is capable of transcending a state of non-history (1997). Along these lines, the collective memory of past migratory experiences allows migrants to transcend the vulnerabilities inherent to their journeys when deployed as a form of knowledge amid the contradictory, multi-layered dynamics of clandestine migration. By framing migrant smuggling as a collective response seeking to address the precarity of late modernity, we refer, identify and acknowledge the information shared with migrants by their friends, families and community in support of their journeys as epistemological mechanisms to challenge historical conditions of marginalization and colonization. In so doing this challenges the dominant narrative of clandestine migration that frames contemporary migration flows as unprecedented crises and which has wittingly erased the long-standing history of migration from the global south. Recognizing the value of clandestine migrations as constituting forms of knowing, we can reverse the process that has rendered migrants to a condition of non-history and which has asserted legitimate practices from the margins as criminal or deviant.

The decision not to recognize the collection of actions and interactions of a community on behalf of its migrating members as history, nor as carrying epistemological meaning, has been central to the maintenance of state-centric discourses of irregular migration. These discourses have instead opted for privileging narratives of migrants embarking in irrational, even suicidal journeys motivated solely by their individual economic or security goals, rather than framing migration processes as mediated, structured, organized and sustained from and within migrant communities' own geo-historical and epistemic locations. The bootstrap, protestant and self-centered rhetoric of self-determination and self-sufficiency favored in colonial or imperial iterations of past migratory flows is not only not extended to the journeys of the colonized. Narrated as rational, orderly, justified and civilized efforts in search of freedom, past migrations within the global north have instead been systematically used to advance narratives of current clandestine migration flows from the global south as constituting illogical, disorderly, savage processes. Central to the advancement of this narrative is the persona characterized as the quintessential predator of late modernity: the criminal, immoral and primitive man from the margins—the smuggler.

The narrative of the facilitation of irregular migration as being in the hands of transnationally organized smuggling networks—and its continued treatment as such by many scholars—is also connected to much larger discourses of the nation-state as single-handedly holding the right as a sovereign nation to exclude those that are perceived as unfit or undesirable (Spener 2008: 116). As Spener has previously articulated, the very term smuggling 'privileges the state authorities regarding the phenomenon of [clandestine] cross-border migratory movements' (2008: 115), often reducing or in fact eliminating the ability to articulate the facilitation of clandestine migration in terms other than those used by the state or which emphasize the practice's ascribed criminality.

The state-centered conceptualization and discourses surrounding smuggling have prevailed, remaining central to most scholarly iterations of clandestine migration facilitation and limiting critical, empirical engagements with the community dynamics that support the efforts of individuals or groups of people to migrate clandestinely. Most often, and in an attempt to raise awareness over the vulnerability faced by those in transit, academic engagements with smuggling have rather opted to document the incidence of its most graphic aspects—to wit, the reliance on victimization—and used them as a cornerstone of the clandestine migration experience analysis. This has been accomplished with varying levels of success, as most engagements have continued to reinscribe imperialistic notions of the migrant body as docile and complying and smugglers as exploitative and vile, rather than conceptualizing views of migration and borders that can be mobilized into actual change (Weber 2015).

There have been effective attempts to reframe the facilitation of clandestine migration from a non-state centered perspective. Rodriguez's notion of autonomous international migration acknowledges that the movement of people across nation-state borders often occurs outside of state regulations, as 'people in peripheral countries ... develop their own policies of international employment independent of state planning' (Rodriguez 1996: 22, quoted in Spener 2008: 117). Framing the practice of irregular migration among Mexican migrants to the United States as tied to global apartheid, Spener argues that clandestine, facilitated migration to the United States constitutes a survival strategy by Mexican migrants to resist 'the territorial confinement to a low-wage region by crossing the border ... in spite of the considerable efforts by [the United States] police forces to prevent their entry' (Spener 2008: 117–118). While aware that this kind of resistance has no structural consequences for the overall system of inequality, Spener uses the notion of *resistencia hormiga* (literally, 'ant resistance') as his way to designate the collection of strategies Mexican migrants rely upon to migrate and allows them and their families to survive, and which draw from social and cultural resources present in their communities.

Spener's framework, and call, to re-conceptualize clandestine crossings as a form of resistance, is fundamental in any attempt to critically engage with the dominant narratives present in migration facilitation discourse. In fact, his attempt to employ an alternate angle from where to map the practice and strategies of irregular migration facilitation[1] and to recognize these as embedded within larger processes of community formation and support remains the most complete effort to date at articulating the need for critically reframing the facilitation of irregular migration from a sociological and anthropological perspective. However, it continues to frame migration along the parameters of economics and production, where migrants appear represented solely as workers.

Despite the fact that clandestine migration and the journeys it involves are embedded in the complex and rich fabric of human relations, the causes shaping migration beyond the productive sphere (the economic survival that is central to aspects of Spener's argument) have hardly been the subject of migration research (Ahmad 2015).[2] Those who migrate clandestinely are still mainly perceived as being guided by economic need, the complexity of their journeys remaining largely unexplored. Migrants' life choices are described as limited by the pressures of a transnational, global economy, that they are described as being forced to join in order to survive and support their families. Spener's framework, while cognizant of the community dimensions of border crossings, still focuses on treating migration as an economically-oriented form of resistance, perhaps unwittingly undervaluing the epistemological dimensions of clandestine journeys in the configuration of the knowledge that allows for journeys to occur.

Recent anthropological work on clandestine migration makes a strong argument for the need to frame the practice within a historical, community and tradition-embedded context, that recognizes migrants' experiences in the provision of care and protection as constituting legitimate forms of knowledge. Vogt, describing the intimate care strategies built among migrants and their smugglers (2016) and Bridgen, documenting the efforts of Central Americans to 'pass' for Mexican in the context of their US-bound journeys (2016) provide examples of how migration journeys produce an epistemological corpus that is collectively devised and mobilized by migrants, their friends and families that seeks to reduce the risk of clandestine journeys and allow for successful, if still acknowledgedly precarious, transits. Ayalew refers to this accumulation as constituting 'a diasporic system of

---

[1]Scholars in the US and Latin America have often favored the terms *coyotaje* and *coyoterismo* responding to Spener's critique of the migratory discourse as being state-centered to designate the provision of migration services. There is also a body of scholarship that has further explored the use of the term *coyote* as being tied to indigenous narratives and story-telling traditions, where the coyote (*Canis latrans*, a wild wolf species) is depicted as the trickster, able to circumvent challenges and to outsmart its captors. In contemporary Latin American folklore and life, *coyotes* are not only the individuals who facilitate irregular migration, but are also the brokers of burdensome, bureaucratic processes, primarily those concerning state services (Spener 2008; Spener 2009).

[2]Feminist scholarship on transnational parenting is one of the few exceptions, however it often situates the migrant's identity primarily in the context of labor, or of her condition as a source of financial support for family members in her country of origin. Hagan has also raised concerns over how faith, hope and the meaning of the migration journey have often been absent in migration research and analysis (2008: 19).

knowledge that challenges immobility regimes and impediments to transits,' (2016) allowing migrants not just to arrive to their destinations but to do so safely. Consequently, these scholars' work suggests that analyses of clandestine migration should not focus merely on the outcomes of the journey, but rather should also identify how, despite structural limitations, communities can effectively deploy systems of knowledge across borders that provide protective mechanisms that seek to reduce the levels of vulnerability of their members. While successful migrations allow for the eventual production of additional material resources, which allow for the diaspora's further mobility, their importance also resides on how journeys increase and strengthen the collective knowledge that allows for its members' survival. In this context, the smuggling process, rather than being a criminal activity, becomes a fundamental, collectively constructed body of knowledge deployed in the provision of safe transits, built upon a system of reciprocating social obligations existing in migrants' communities of origin, aspects largely absent in mainstream engagements on irregular migration. In summary, while in the context of their journeys those on the move face intense experiences that can include significant forms of violence and trauma, journeys are ultimately experiences that forge collective, intimate social bonds whose dimensions ought to be explored and recognized not merely as experiences on migration, but as constituting legitimate forms of knowledge that then become part of the history of a people.

4 Researching Smuggling on the US Mexico Border

How can scholars mobilize critical engagements with heavily criminalized, stigmatized migratory practices? Influenced by indigenous methodologies, we argue that the re-framing of migrant smuggling (the western obsession deeply embedded in state-centric notions of sovereignty and order) depends on the deployment of methods that acknowledge individual and collective exercises into migration as being inherently epistemological. While researching smuggling processes on the US Mexico border, we seek to accomplish this goal methodologically by:

1. Acknowledging practices pertaining to the facilitation of clandestine journeys as constituting legitimate forms of knowledge informed upon collective interactions particular to a location/space and which serve to create a spirit of reciprocity and respect among a people (Battiste and Henderson 2000; Brown and Strega 2015).
2. Recognizing the relationships migrants, their families and friends have forged with the land and the people they have relied upon for their journeys as carrying epistemological meaning and constituting elements of their collective history (Battiste 2000; Little Bear 2000). While scholarly and law enforcement interventions against smuggling often focus on identifying routes, business models or ways in which financial frameworks that can be dismantled, indigenous

methodologies reposition those in transit into the center of the migratory process, and as possessing a body of pluralistic, epistemological and empirical knowledge informed with collective experience that is deployed in the exercise of their migrations, rather than as merely naïve, submissive or scared bodies on the run.

3. Validating the major role orality and storytelling play in communicating migration-related community practices, and as epistemological elements (Archibald 2008; Thomas 2015). Mainstream narratives of migration privilege accounts that frame the migrant journey as individual or solitary, and therefore as requiring the researcher to become its interpreter or teller. Even some attempts by supportive social scientists to 'give a voice to the voiceless' have been dependent on testimonies portraying migration as centered on individual experiences, failing to identify the communal, collective and social dimensions of migration. There is also a dangerous tendency to emphasize the experiences of injured, traumatized and even deceased migrants in ways that further frame the migrant body as inherently fallen, dead, and therefore as voiceless.

5 Smuggling as Community

This section summarizes data collected from 2007 to 2014 through research projects conducted among migrants who successfully crossed the US Mexico Border with *coyotes*, informed by the methodological strategies outlined above. It involves data from face-to-face interviews conducted among smuggling facilitators, their friends and family members as well as their clients, who ultimately settled in the US states of Arizona and Utah. Informants were identified in the community through one of the researcher's social contacts. Court records were identified via online court records searches.

Research has identified smuggling as one of multiple strategies mobilized by migrants and their communities to facilitate transborder, transnational clandestine journeys with the least amount of risk possible, while aware of the vulnerabilities inherent to irregular migration. Smuggling itself is also identified by its actors as constituting a legitimate form of labor that, when collectively and successfully performed, leads to the arrival of a migrant to his or her final destination. In the paragraphs that follow we highlight the social organization of smuggling, the perceptions connected to the facilitation of smuggling tasks, the economy of smuggling, and the function of violence in the market.

Social Organization The men and women who participate in the provision of smuggling services most often enter the market by two routes: through friends and family members already active in the provision of smuggling services, or when approached to participate in the smuggling process in the context of their own journeys as migrants, most often in exchange for a reduction of their fees, as the remarks of a migrant who was eventually charged with committing a smuggling offense attests:

> One of the *coyotes* asked us if anyone knew how to drive, and I raised my hand said I did. The *coyotes* offered to reduce my fee to US$2000 if I drove one of the vehicles. They gave me a radio and I was taken to a location where I picked up ten people. I am not a *coyote* though, I was only offered to drive a van. (*Ramiro*)

Most smuggling facilitators operate independently, relying on their personal resources and social networks, and performing a single, specific task (driving; cooking; guiding groups). There is no specialized or technical training required to participate in smuggling, which further eases the incorporation of those who participate into it, and who must often rely on skills or knowledge they already possess. Tasks may include recruitment of migrants, driving, guiding groups, serving as lookouts, even work as *borra-huellas* or 'step-erasers' whose role is to eliminate the footsteps left on the sand by migrants in transit in order to avoid being tracked by immigration law enforcement, as explained by a female migrant:

> The ones who crossed us were a group of three: the *coyote*, the guide and *el huellas*. That is how they referred to him, because he was walking behind the group erasing the tracks we left behind with a tree branch. (*Annette*)

Smuggling groups lack a centralized leadership or hierarchy mechanism. Tasks are performed in coordination with other facilitators, but most often participation is dependent upon each facilitator's individual availability, time and skills, which often means that a successful crossing requires multiple attempts. On occasion, smuggling facilitators rely on the services of individuals who coordinate contacts between facilitators, clients, and community members; yet this role is one of a logistical nature only. Occasionally individual smuggling facilitators may assume control over the organization of a particular journey or the border crossings of individual groups. Yet this control is temporary and always dependent on logistical contexts. In other words, there is no indication that successful smuggling journeys require the existence of a single head or lead to be successful; rather it is the ability of smuggling facilitators to improvise and take decisions when needed that most often allows for the successful facilitation of irregular border crossings (Brigden 2016). This does not suggest individual facilitators with leadership abilities or inclinations do not exist in the market, but rather that the performance of smuggling groups is not dependent upon the existence of leadership.

Self/Perception of Smuggling Tasks Despite the reputation of smuggling facilitators, migrant smuggling is as a general rule not a frowned upon activity among migrant and refugee communities. Information on how to access reliable, trusted facilitators is highly valued, amid the desire or the need to migrate and the abundance of reports on the inherent risks pertaining to clandestine journeys across borders. Those seeking to travel, and their families, solicit references from friends and relatives who have completed the journey in the past and 'shop around' until they identify the facilitator that suits their needs in terms of reliability, cost and risk factors.

Researchers have argued that the continued success of a smuggling group or facilitator (defined as his or her ability to secure work opportunities) relies on referrals from past clients and from other facilitators. Reports of clients of the reliability, punctuality, cost, risk levels, transportation quality, distance of smuggling services are important in their decision to travel with a specific coyote. Yet the affective realm of the transaction—factors like respect, treatment received during transit, quality of the food, and levels of care—play a role in the ability of facilitators to generate business for themselves and others.[3] Here, the mother of a young adult explains her decision to entrust him to a specific group of young *coyotes*:

> I told the smuggler: 'I know you. I know who you are. We are from the same town. So let me tell you. I put my son in your hands. If anything, and I do mean anything happens to him, I will find you!'[laughs]. But the truth is that those kids—they were very young—took very good care of my son. I went with them for my son's [crossing] because they were the ones who crossed me the last time I crossed, and they were always very kind, very well mannered. They had even taken us to church to pray for a successful crossing. (*Sacramento*)

Smuggling facilitators and their clients do not perceive the tasks they provide as criminal, although they recognize its illicit nature and the potential for prosecution. Many facilitators and their clients instead perceive the work of *coyotes* as being beneficial and as needed amid the challenges posed by immigration and border enforcement (Achilli 2015). To some *coyotes* their work, in addition to constituting an income generating strategy, is an attempt to pay forward the favors done onto them by the *coyotes* behind their journeys; to assist others like themselves in achieving their migration goals, and as a mechanism to increase their social status and reputation—a tool that may come in handy when in need to access goods and services within their community, often once having left the smuggling industry. A woman who often worked coordinating transportation for migrants explained:

> [Looking at her hands which were already showing the signs of rheumatoid arthritis:] "I have been getting sick too often lately and I am starting to worry that soon I will no longer be able to work. But I am not too worried, you know ... I know enough people in Phoenix. If the time comes when I am too sick to work, I am going to know who to call. People owe me favors. When people needed to cross, we were here to help them." (*Cynthia*)

The Economy of Smuggling The cost involved in the facilitation of a smuggling journey varies considerably, yet it is often dependent on the distance between place of origin and destination, means of transportation, routes, and the age, gender or health status of the person who seeks to travel, among other factors. Some facilitators provide specialized, even guaranteed crossings for children, the elderly or pregnant women at a cost many times higher than those of a 'regular' trek which may involve several days of walking, and extreme, often lethal levels of environmental exposure. A phone conversation between a coyote and a potential client explains the advantages of traveling with a specialist:

> [Crossing a pregnant woman] is more expensive, yes. But [crossing with us] she will only have to walk from the house on this side of the border to the other. The two houses are

[3]For an expanded discussion on how the work of *coyotes* can constitute a form of intimate labor and care in mobility, refer to Vogt's analysis of smuggling along Mexico's migrant route (2016).

connected by a tunnel. She comes in through one side, comes out the other, gets in the van and that's all! No walks, no danger, no *migra*,[4] nothing. (*Virginia*)

There appears to be a relationship between the cost of a journey and its level of risk, which in turns creates a hierarchy of protection among those who travel. Those with the largest amount of resources will most likely face the lowest level of risk, as capital ensures the use of private routes (Hagan 2008), the existence of pre-arranged crossings in collusion with law enforcement (Izcara-Palacios 2013), use of specially adapted or non-conspicuous vehicles (Trujillo 2011), etc. Those unable to secure financial or social capital to cover the cost of these more expensive services often travel on their own, or depend on less-reliable, more dangerous routes and mechanisms and on less experienced, poor or ill-reputed *coyotes* under whose care risks are exponentially higher.

Despite the often exorbitant prices quoted in association with smuggling costs, research indicates that individual facilitators' earnings are quite limited. After all the costs associated with the journey have been recovered, the reminder of the fee is most often split among the many individuals who perform different tasks along the route. Tasks performed by men had a tendency to be compensated at a much higher rate than those of women (Sanchez 2016). Most facilitators do in fact maintain full time jobs, smuggling providing only a supplemental, occasional form of income. Most earnings are immediately circulated into the local economy, as the majority of those involved in the smuggling industry are members of working-class, migrant families (Sanchez 2015).

Violence The smuggling market is often described as being plagued by high levels of risk, danger and violence, or as being under the control of transnational criminal organizations. Research on criminology shows that the forms of violence in criminal markets are specific to the market and not random in nature (Reuter 2009). Tensions between facilitators and clients, and among facilitators themselves, often over the payment or non-payment of fees are quite common. Many facilitators add additional charges and fees to initially agreed-upon smuggling prices, and refuse to allow clients to leave security or drop houses until these additional costs are covered.

[There was] one incident where the boss of the house got into an argument with a husband and a wife over the increased smuggling fee. Originally, the couple was to be [sic] US$2500 a piece. When they arrived at the drop house, the fee was increased to US$3500. The girl told the boss that he was robbing them. The two started yelling at each other and the boss told her husband to have his bitch shut up or that he would fuck her up. (*Unidentified Migrant 1*)

Loud arguments and threats as exemplified by the one above are common, yet hardly ever escalate as both parties most often negotiate to avoid damaging their reputation, the loss of capital, or being detected by or reported to law enforcement (Sanchez 2015). Facilitators also reconcile their differences among each other in order to ensure continued business opportunities.

[4]Immigration agents.

Cases of migrants being forcefully removed during their transits or from safety houses are common. On the US Mexico border these acts are often conducted by groups of *bajadores* who as their name in Spanish suggests 'unload' migrants from *coyotes* (Slack et al. 2013; Sanchez 2015) with the attempt to profit through the placement of extortion or ransom calls. Prosecuted by the criminal justice system as kidnappings, these cases often involve migrants being subjected to psychological, physical and sexual forms of abuse, many times at the hands of other migrants (themselves unable to cover their own ransom fees). While women are often the target of sexual violence, threats and actual incidents of sexual assault are also committed regularly against men (Sanchez 2015).

6 Discussion and Conclusion: Smuggling Strategies as a Form of Knowledge

Mainstream articulations of borders situate them as inherent sites of poverty, violence, conflict and decay. We argue that this continued conceptualization is part of a larger colonizing narrative, where borders as geopolitical margins appear as unconquered, wild and remote spaces deemed unsafe, residual and lethal, that must be disciplined back into order.

In our contribution we have wittingly referred to a practice of the margins, of the border—the facilitation of migrant smuggling—as an example of how attempts to bring order to the border are challenged and contested by the people. Smuggling constitutes for some scholars a form of economic resistance, one where migrants as workers contest the geographic limitations imposed on their ability to support themselves and their families. But we envision those on the move as more than individual workers motivated by the economic demands of globalization. Informed by the testimonies on migrant smuggling along the US Mexico border that our respondents have shared, we call for the recognition of narratives of migration as constituting a system of knowledge, that when transmitted allows for the survival and protection of those traveling clandestinely—a form of human security from below. Yet we find in these narratives elements that reveal deeper understandings of daily social life—reciprocity; conflict; fear; trust. These elements collectively are more than a series of strategies to overcome border surveillance and enforcement. Together they constitute and reflect the efforts of people to know and relate with the world and with one another, and therefore carry deep epistemological meanings. In this sense they also constitute a fundamental element of the history of people. While much of the scholarship on clandestine migration and border crossings has focused on documenting the victimization and violence faced by those in transit, we instead opt to frame smuggling as a mobility strategy, that attempting to overcome state controls on mobility depends on the construction and the maintenance of social interactions, many of which involve varying degrees of conflict and the potential for violence—as the ethnographic evidence shows. Reframing the facilitation of migrant smuggling involves the re-articulation of notions of borders and the periphery as places of violence to places of knowledge, while not ignoring borders role as part of a much larger hegemonic project carried out by the state.

Establishing a research narrative and agenda of migration that privileges and conceptualizes notions of people's efforts for self-determination, survival and the struggle to take control over a collective or individual destiny, demands 'more than rhetoric' or than identifying 'acts of defiance' (Tuhiwai Smith 2005: 142). Indigenous methodologies can situate irregular migration facilitation processes taking place along borders in a way they can be reclaimed, reformatted and reconstituted in a manner 'strategic in its purpose and activities and relentless in its pursuit of social justice' (Tuhiwai Smith 2005: 142). Here we argue that recognizing that the facilitation of irregular migrations as taking place in a communal context rather than solely in a criminal or even immoral context, implies revaluing migrant and refugee experiences as constituting not merely data but rather forms of knowledge: as 'a collection of individual stories, ever unfolding through the lives of the people who share the life of that community' (Bishop 1996: 24, in Tuhiwai Smith 2005: 145) and which carry deep epistemological meaning, in this way borders become key spatial elements in the constitution of people's collective history and knowledge.

Extralegal journeys build upon collective, accumulated, and also improvised forms of knowledge acquired, developed and shared by those in transit and their communities. As efforts to control or contain irregular migration continue to emerge globally (the closing of the Balkans route in Europe, or the decision on the part of the Australian government to redirect asylum seekers to Nauru), and new routes and mechanisms to travel clandestinely emerge (the consolidation of Libya as the top smuggling hub in North Africa), knowledge seeking to create forms that provide a level of physical safety for those who travel—a form of security from below—will simultaneously appear, its efficacy however varying.[5] It is true that stepped-up border and immigration enforcement is almost immediately followed by migrants devising routes more remote and more dangerous in order to avoid detection, and that as Slack and Whiteford argue in reference to the victimization and violence migrants may face at the hands of *coyotes* on the US Mexico border 'the goals of people trying to cross and those assisting them are not the same' (2011: 16). Yet our contribution seeks to craft a scholarship of migration that does not simply frame migrant smuggling as being monolithically violent, but as a one of the many practices that in the context of global attempts to control mobility of, and from, the margins generates ways of knowing that are employed by those on the move in the course of their journeys.

Our contribution is a call to jumpstart academic engagements with smuggling facilitation, framing the US Mexico border—and by borders we refer to the spaces, geographies and those who live on and from the fringes—as localities of

[5]Between 2009 and 2015 the US Border Patrol reported a total of 2624 deaths registered along the US Southwestern Border (Williams 2016).

knowledge. We do not seek to provide a romanticized perspective of smuggling, but rather to empirically re-energize the academic dialogues on a body of knowledge whose scholarship has become stagnant amid often moralistic discussions over the role of facilitators and the development of measures to stop their actions. Finally, we also call for closer analysis of the way in which the deployment of narratives of violence and victimization, as cornerstones of the academic treatment of the migratory experience along the US Mexico Border, narrows potential spaces to articulate change, and the risks that this approach has of further perpetuating the mobilization of problematic characterizations of people on the move, and their experiences, in an imperialistic and colonial fashion, where their physical suffering and death have become mere objects of the Western gaze.

Interviewees

Ramiro	Male; irregular Mexican migrant detained in Arizona, 2009.
Anette	Female, irregular Mexican migrant, interviewed in Utah, 2014.
Sacramento	Female, irregular Mexican migrant, interviewed in Utah, 2014.
Cynthia	Female, Mexican born US citizen. Interviewed in Arizona, 2011.
Virginia	Female, unknown nationality. Phone conversation registered in Arizona, 2010.
Unidentified migrant 1	Testimony reported in Maricopa County Superior Court vs. Chacón-Perez, CR2009-153051 and included in Phoenix Police Department Report DR200991074559. Interview conducted by law enforcement in Arizona, 2009.

References

Achilli, L. (2015). *The smuggler: Hero or felon?* Policy Brief. Robert Schuman Centre for Advanced Studies. Florence: European University Institute.

Achilli, L. (2016, April 5–6). This is Jihad: Piety and morality among Syrian smugglers [conference paper]. In *Critical approaches to irregular migration facilitation: Dismantling the smuggler narrative*. Florence, Italy: European University Institute.

Ahmad, A. N. (2015). *Masculinity, sexuality and illegal migration: Human smuggling from Pakistan to Europe*. London: Oxford University Press.

Anzaldua, G. (1987). *Borderlands/La Frontera: The new Mestiza*. San Francisco: Aunt Lute Books.

Archibald, J. A. (2008). *Indigenous storywork: Educating the heart, mind, body, and spirit*. Vancouver, BC: UBC Press.

Ayalew, T. M. (2016, April 8). The struggle of mobility: Organising high risk migration from the Horn of Africa. *Open Democracy Roundtable on Smugglers*. Retrieved from https://www.opendemocracy.net/beyondslavery/hsr/tekalign-ayalew-mengiste/struggle-of-mobility-organising-high-risk-migration-from-horn

Battiste, M. (Ed.). (2000). *Reclaiming indigenous voice and vision*. Vancouver, BC: UBC Press.

Battiste, M., & Henderson, J. Y. (2000). *Protecting indigenous knowledge and heritage: A global challenge*. Saskatoon, SK: Purich.

Bishop, R. (1996). *Collaborative research stories*. Parmerston North: Dunmore Press.

Brigden, N. (2016). Improvised transnationalism: Clandestine migration at the border of anthropology and international relations. *International Studies Quarterly, 0*, 1–12.
Brown, L. A., & Strega, S. (Eds.). (2015). *Research as resistance: Revisiting critical, indigenous, and anti-oppressive approaches* (2nd ed.). Toronto, ON: Canadian Scholars' Press.
Glissant, É. (1997). *Poetics of relation*. Ann Arbor, MI: University of Michigan Press.
Hagan, J. (2008). *Migration miracle: Faith, hope and meaning on the undocumented journey*. Cambridge, MA: Harvard University Press.
Izcara-Palacios, S. (2013). Corrupción y Contrabando de Migrantes en Estados Unidos. *Política y Gobierno, 20*(1), 79–106.
Koser, K. (2008). Why migrant smuggling pays. *International Migration, 46*(2), 3–26.
Little Bear, L. (2000). Jagged worldviews colliding. In M. Battiste (Ed.), *Reclaiming indigenous voice and vision*. Vancouver, BC: UBC Press.
Reuter, P. (2009). Systemic violence in drug markets. *Crime, Law and Social Change, 52*, 275–284.
Rodriguez, N. (1996). The battle for the border: Notes on autonomous migration, transnational communities, and the state. *Social Justice, 23*(3), 21–38.
Sanchez, G. (2015). *Border crossings and human smuggling*. London: Routledge.
Sanchez, G. (2016). Women's participation in human smuggling: The case of the US Southwest. *Geopolitics, 21*(2), 387–406.
Sanchez, G., & Zhang, S. (2016, April 5–6). Casual encounters? Changing market conditions and organizational responses among smugglers of migrants and drugs [conference paper]. In *Critical approaches to irregular migration facilitation: Dismantling the smuggler narrative*. Florence: European University Institute.
Slack, J., Martinez, D., Whiteford, S., & Peiffer, E. (2013). *In the shadow of the wall: Family separation, immigration enforcement and security*. Tucson, AZ: The Center for Latin American Studies, University of Arizona.
Slack, J., & Whiteford, S. (2011). Violence and migration on the Arizona-Sonora border. *Human Organization, 70*(1), 11–21.
Spener, D. (2008). Global Apartheid, Coyotaje and the discourse of clandestine migration: distinctions between personal, structural and cultural violence. *Migración y Desarrollo*, 115–140.
Spener, D. (2009). *Clandestine crossings: Migrants and coyotes on the Texas-Mexico border*. Ithaca, NY: Cornell University Press.
Thomas, R. (2015). Honoring the oral traditions of my ancestors through story telling. In L. A. Brown & S. Strega (Eds.), *Research as resistance: Revisiting critical, indigenous, and anti-oppressive approaches* (2nd ed., pp. 237–254). Toronto, ON: Canadian Scholars' Press.
Trujillo, A. (2011). *Felix: Self-fictions of a human smuggler* [Video]. Creativetime Reports.
Tuhiwai Smith, L. (2005). *Decolonizing methodologies: Research and indigenous people*. Dunedin/London: University of Otago Press/Zed Books.
Vogt, W. (2016). Stuck in the middle with you: The intimate labours of mobility and smuggling along Mexico's migrant route. *Geopolitics, 21*(2), 366–386.
Weber, L. (Ed.). (2015). *Rethinking border control for a globalizing world: A preferred world*. London: Routledge.
Williams, J. (2016, June 7). Deaths in the desert. Kino Border Initiative. Retrieved from https://www.kinoborderinitiative.org/deaths-desert-2/
Zhang, S. X. (2007). *Chinese human smuggling organizations: Families, social networks and cultural imperatives*. San Francisco: Stanford University Press.
Zhang, S., & Chin, K. (2002). *The social organization of Chinese human smuggling—A cross-national study*. San Diego, CA: San Diego State University.
Zhang, S., Chin, K., & Miller, J. (2007). Women's participation in transnational human smuggling. *Criminology, 45*(3), 699–733.

Gabriella Sanchez is a professor in human security at the National Security Studies Institute at the University of Texas at El Paso. Her work explores the social dynamics to the inside of smuggling facilitator groups. She is the author of "Human Smuggling and Border Crossings" (Routledge 2015). She lives on the US-Mexico Border.

Nicholas Natividad is an assistant professor in the Department of Criminal Justice at New Mexico State University. His current research focuses on transnational and local community practices of human rights informed by indigenous and post-colonial methodologies that address inequality, crime and violence.

Humanitarian Borderwork

Polly Pallister-Wilkins

Abstract Over the last 10 years border practices by European member states and supranational EU actors such as Frontex have changed. Increasingly border practices, including border policing have taken account of humanitarian concerns and actively pursued humanitarian practices concerned with saving lives. These changes are in large part a result of the reduction in safe and legal routes for those fleeing conflict, human rights abuses and poverty. These restrictions produce increasingly violent border spaces that result in the need for humanitarian, lifesaving interventions to relieve the effects of such violence. I call this humanitarian borderwork. Here the enactment of humanitarian principles changes older forms of borderwork concerned with stopping, defending and securing territory to work concerned with securing lives. Humanitarian borderwork considers two main areas: one concerns the ways demands to save lives in border contexts impacts on the practices and performances of those engaged in border policing; and two concerns the ways humanitarian actors who have entered the field of border performances in order to save lives and alleviate suffering impact the production of borders.

Keywords Humanitarianism • Borderwork • Biopolitics • Mobility • Intervention

1 Introduction

On 28 October, 2015 a wooden boat carrying more than 250 people capsized two kilometres off the northern shore of Lesbos, Greece with the loss of at least 42 lives. It was crossing the narrow straight that separates the island from Turkey. The boat's passengers, mostly Syrian refugees, were rescued by a combination of the Greek Coastguard, a Norwegian Search and Rescue (SAR) boat seconded to the European Union's External Border's Agency, Frontex, Spanish volunteer life guards from an NGO called Proactiva Open Arms and Turkish and Greek fishermen. Those rescued were taken to the nearby town of Molyvos, a well-known tourist resort during the

P. Pallister-Wilkins (✉)
Department of Political Science, University of Amsterdam, Amsterdam, The Netherlands
e-mail: p.e.pallister-wilkins@uva.nl

C. Günay, N. Witjes (eds.), *Border Politics*, DOI 10.1007/978-3-319-46855-6_6

summer months. Here they were met on the harbour side by a host of volunteers, from NGOs and individual citizens both local and from across Europe and the Mediterranean neighbourhood. This event was not unique. Humanitarian action at the borders of Europe saves lives, but more than that, it changes border practices in two principal ways: through re-orienting existing border control and policing towards humanitarian concerns and through the emergence of new humanitarian actors involved in borderwork.

As safe and legal routes are closed to those fleeing conflict, persecution, and poverty through the imposition of a strict visa regime, carriers liability and the increasing use of border fencing (see Pallister-Wilkins 2016a, b) Europe's borders have become places of suffering and death. Within this context people on the move are acutely vulnerable in border spaces (Weber and Pickering 2014). For example, between 1990 and 2013, 3188 people are known to have died at Europe's Mediterranean borders (Last 2015). As a result border control is changing and humanitarian principles increasingly shape border control practices. In response to the danger and suffering of Europe's border regime that prohibits safe and legal routes for those fleeing conflict and poverty a range of actors from state agencies, humanitarian organisations, volunteer NGOs and individual citizens undertake a range of practices to relieve suffering and prevent deaths. I call these practices 'humanitarian borderwork'.

In humanitarian borderwork, humanitarian principles concerned with saving lives, alleviating suffering and bearing witness are enacted in border spaces. These borders in turn are the products of a range of practices by people, organizations and states and they are produced and reproduced through constant work known in the border studies literature as borderwork (Rumford 2008). The enactment of humanitarian principles changes borderwork from work concerned with stopping, defending and securing territory to work concerned with securing lives. This chapter aims to introduce the concept of humanitarian borderwork and show how it re-orients border politics and practices.

The chapter proceeds as follows. Firstly, humanitarian borderwork will be situated within the relevant literatures on humanitarianism and border control. Secondly, the conceptual innovation of humanitarian borderwork in studies of humanitarianism and border studies, that moves beyond biopolitics and reiterates the importance of territory will be briefly laid out. Thirdly, the chapter moves on to discuss in empirical detail how humanitarian borderwork changes border practices and produces new territorial configurations through a focus on the introduction of humanitarian practices into border policing, the emergence of new humanitarian actors in border spaces and the creation of new spaces of borderwork through humanitarian action. These empirics are based on sustained fieldwork in European borderlands, in the southern central Mediterranean and Greece as well as in Amsterdam, Brussels and Warsaw. This fieldwork has focused on the practices of Frontex, member state border police, humanitarian actors such as Médecins Sans Frontières (MSF) and local volunteers. It has involved participant observation of rescue missions, transit spaces, border patrols and operational meetings as well as semi-structured interviews and informal conversations with border police, policy officers, risk analysts and a host of humanitarian actors (see Pallister-Wilkins 2015a–d).

2 Humanitarianism and Borderwork

Border control has traditionally been concerned with maintaining state sovereignty over exclusive territorial spaces through the control of who and what can move across state borders and into and out of exclusive state spaces. This has been done through: the defence of territories by state militaries (Andreas 2003); the control of goods by state customs agents (Hollifield 2004); and the control of population movements through bureaucratic inventions such as the passport (Torpey 2000). Moreover the production of exclusive spaces and the everyday practices that go into maintaining and governing them involves a variety of practices that can be characterized as violent (Hindess 2006). These practices range from the structural violence of the restriction and denial of movement; to the ever-present immanent possibility of physical force embodied in the work of the border police; to the actualized use of physical force unleashed on irregular border crossers such as that witnessed in April 2016 at Idomeni on the Greek-FYROM border. During this encounter FYROM border officers used tanks, rubber bullets and tear gas to prevent the movement of irregular people on the move (Independent 2016).

As a result of events such as these it is important to understand that any discussion of humanitarian borderwork must be grounded in the particular structural politics of borders themselves as violent constructs that territorially prescribe processes of inclusion and exclusion. It is within this context that the changes to Europe's external borders in the last two decades must be understood. These changes saw the introduction of the Schengen *acquis* in 1997 and the removal of internal borders between EU member states along with a concomitant strengthening of the external borders. These changes to Europe's border practices can be characterised as both a hardening of territorial control at the edges (Rosière and Jones 2012; van Houtum 2010) and a coterminous shift to focusing on the population as the subject of border control through biopolitical forms of government (Amoore 2006; Bigo 2002). Within border studies, a biopolitical approach to borders that focuses on the bodies of people on the move as a site of border policing, as opposed to more traditional forms of territorial control at the border line, 'opens up an entirely different spatial configuration of security' based on the *circulation* of people rather than their interdiction (Dillon 2007: 11).

This circulation of bodies and the recognition of people on the move as a category or terrain of government intertwine with other forms of production and control. In order for this circulation to be governed alongside territory in border policing, populations and spaces come to be calculated and categorised (Elden 2007a). Meanwhile recent work on border practices has stressed the diverse ways actors beyond the state are involved in these processes that 'envision, construct, maintain and erase borders' (Rumford 2008: 2). However, up until now, studies of borderwork by non-state actors have primarily focused on various forms of policing to keep people out such as the Minutemen border militia, the self-appointed guards of the United States-Mexico border (Doty 2007) or individuals informing on suspected 'illegal immigrants' in the UK (Vaughan-Williams 2008).

This structural and physical violence enacted on the bodies and life-chances of people on the move is mitigated through practices of humanitarianism predicated on universal principles of humanity. Humanitarianism enacts these supposedly universal principles through a commitment to saving lives and reducing suffering (Calhoun 2008). As such 'humanitarianism describes a worldview, aspirations, professional vocabularies and actions affirming the common dignity of humankind regardless of difference in race, gender, religion, national belonging, political creed, or any other accident of birth of contextual circumstance' (Belloni 2007: 451). Building on this worldview and the practices that follow, humanitarianism is often presented as a humanist alternative to the international system made up of sovereign and exclusive territorial spaces. Such an idea is present in the name Médecins Sans Frontières for example. However, a genealogy of humanitarian thought and practice roots such an universalist approach in a particular European enlightenment history that challenges the universal claim of humanitarianism that suggests a transcendence of the sovereign and importantly, territorialised state (Fassin 2012; Hopgood 2013; Pupavac 2010; Weizman 2011). In addition, humanitarian practice while making claims to a universal ideal of humanity that seeks to de-territorialize and challenge sovereign claims to life and death, in many instances works to re-territorialise and reaffirm sovereignty in practice (Debrix 1998). Such transversal practices are brought to the fore in humanitarian borderwork.

Humanitarianism's relationship to sovereignty is linked to its politics even while it is claimed by humanitarian practitioners that humanitarian intervention becomes necessary when sovereign—read state—politics has failed (Redfield 2013). These politics can be summarised as concerning one that speaks and acts for a universal humanity; the powerful subject positions produced by practices such as those between giver and receiver, rescuer and victim (Feldman and Ticktin 2010); and the reproduction of the very same categories of life between race, gender, religion and nationality that humanitarian universalism tries to overcome (Belloni 2007). These categories of life are central to humanitarian borderwork. The category of 'refugee' as opposed to 'migrant' is one of the clearest ways these categories of life are central to humanitarian practice (Agier 2011; Fassin 2005). The category 'refugee' carries with it a whole set of rights, responsibilities, politics, values and meanings. In contrast, 'migrant', denotes the act of mobility but is exempt from the same rights or responsibilities and represents different politics, values and meanings. In practice at the border this has played itself out in, for example, the imposition of different places and systems for registration with the border police and differential access to humanitarian relief and temporary shelter. Therefore, 'it is important to see humanitarianism not as a value-neutral field but as a practice based on the relations and hierarchies of power utilised for the governance of populations' (Pallister-Wilkins 2015a: 59).

In recognition of the way a humanitarian rationality changes border practices, there has been an increased focus across the social sciences on the 'humanitarian border'. The humanitarian border emerges as a concept in recognition of how 'border-crossing is a matter of life and death' (Walters 2011) caused by the violence of borders and territory (Elden 2007b; Hindess 2006). But moreover, the humanitarian border is also a set of practices whereby 'humanitarian concerns increasingly shape and strengthen border policing practices' (Aas and Gundhus 2015; Pallister-Wilkins 2015a; Williams 2015). This humanitarianism frames and legitimises interventions at sea, such as Italy's Mare Nostrum. It promotes certain technologies such as drones, and shapes the operational responses of the border police. Furthermore, humanitarianism is articulated and practiced at multiple sites and scales and by multiple actors: border police, state ministries, experts, facilitators and practitioners. In addition humanitarianism also forms the basis for many civil society responses (Pallister-Wilkins 2015a: 54).

The focus on border*work* here stresses the productive nature of the humanitarianism being done in border settings. Like much humanitarian practice and borderwork based on categorisation, humanitarian borderwork enacts differentiated categories of life between those deemed worthy of help and those not, and between those who help and those who need help (Fassin 2012; Pallister-Wilkins 2016c; Redfield 2013). Humanitarian borderwork is therefore focused on the enactment of humanitarian principles premised on a humanist belief in the universality of humanity and concerned with preserving human life and relieving suffering in border settings (Fassin 2012; Redfield 2013; Weizman 2011) while at the same time working to reproduce exclusive categories of life and exclusive territorial spaces.

3 Categories of Life and the Production of Borders

Humanitarian borderwork shows how at the border humanitarian practice, as a rationality of government with specific meanings and values about life and specific practices of intervention and assistance, is a form of borderwork producing particular borders in particular ways. As we have seen, thinking about humanitarian borderwork conceptually requires bringing the literatures on humanitarianism and categorisation together with literatures on borderwork and territorial production. A focus on the intersection of humanitarianism and borderwork unsettles the large body of literature on the securitisation of migration and borders (Hyndman 2012). Humanitarian borderwork considers 'other' forms of security in border practices, such as the security of life and wellbeing for people on the move. It moves discussions of humanitarianism beyond being a functional technique of border management and examines how, as a rationality of life (Fassin 2012), humanitarianism is not just 'something that happens at the border' or 'something that happens in response to the violence of the border' (Aas and Gundhus 2015; Pallister-Wilkins 2015a; Williams 2015) but is part of the production of the border itself.

As such it moves discussions on borderwork beyond an understanding of the multiple actors involved in producing and reproducing borders and adds an exploration of the categories of life and types of spaces and territories that are produced through this borderwork. It therefore adds to the nascent literature on the 'humanitarian border' and advances this beyond the biopolitical idea of the 'borders as a place of life and death' (Walters 2011). This moves the discussion on border practices and policing beyond a biopolitical one focused on the bare life of migrants, even as risk to life invokes humanitarian action, and begins to introduce ideas of wellbeing as being more than life or death. In turn this brings the politics of what it means to live well into discussions of security.

Humanitarian borderwork also challenges the biopolitical focus of much work in recent border studies by drawing our attention to its relationship to territory, both as a determinant of practice and as something that comes to be configured or re-configured in particular ways by humanitarian intervention. There has been considerable work in border studies over the past decade or so on the 'vacillating' nature of borders today, in that they are not only found at the borderline but are increasingly understood more in terms of borderlands and borderscapes (Balibar 2009; Mezzadra and Neilson 2013). This focus on the spatially disaggregated nature of borders is the result of two interrelated processes: a focus on populations and their circulation/mobility and the resulting technologies and techniques designed to police these mobile populations. This biopolitical focus on border policing captures some of the notable changes in border control of recent years, however, where these controls take place and their relationship to space is important to consider.

Here humanitarian borderwork focuses our attention on this relationship. As a biopolitical practice concerned with the security of mobile populations, even as in practice it moves beyond biopolitics and practices a politics of life, humanitarian borderwork also has an intimate and productive relationship with space. Traditionally humanitarian practice has created 'new' semi-sovereign spaces most notably encapsulated by the 'refugee camp' (Agier 2011; Debrix 1998). However, humanitarian borderwork in practice moves the study of humanitarian spaces out of the territorially fixed setting of the refugee camp. Through having to respond to people on the move humanitarianism's relationship to space is better understood in terms of borderscapes.

Borderscapes here enable a recognition of the 'spatial and conceptual complexity of borders today as fluid and shifting, established while at the same time continuously traversed by a range of bodies, discourses, practices and relationships that highlight the continual production and reproduction of inside and outside, self and other.' A focus on borderscapes allows for a concomitant focus on border practices and *where* these take place while recognising that this 'where' is constantly dis-placed, negotiated and the product of multiple actors (Brambilla 2015: 19).

4 Search and Rescue Operations: Border Policing, Saving Lives and the Expansion of European Space

In the political declaration that accompanied the Joint Africa-EU Valletta Summit on Migration in November 2015, the participants stressed their 'deep concerns for the suffering, abuse, exploitation and loss of life' of refugees and migrants stressing that such suffering and death had 'serious humanitarian consequences and security challenges' with the first priority being 'to save lives' (European Council 2015). This was followed in December by the announcement that the EU would launch a new 'European Border and Coast Guard' that would lead to greater levels of integrated border management and re-enforce the mandate of Frontex (European Commission 2015). The need for this 'new' European Border and Coast Guard—the actual newness of such a body is debatable as what is proposed is more a consolidation of existing practices using existing personnel rather than an altogether new institutional body—was justified thus:

> The crisis has shown that the limitations of Frontex—limited resources in terms of staff and equipment, an inability to initiate and carry out return or border management operations and the *absence of an explicit role to conduct search and rescue operations*—have hindered its ability to effectively address significant increases in migratory pressure. (European Commission 2015)

The inclusion of the need for a SAR mandate is of specific interest here and builds on the slow realisation within Frontex and other European border control practitioners that search and rescue, with or without a mandate, has come to play an increasingly integral part of their day-to-day borderwork.

The increase in SAR operations sees a growth in both who is considered a humanitarian actor but also a growth in who comes to be engaged in borderwork (Pallister-Wilkins 2015b). SAR operations are the most prominent form of humanitarian borderwork. Saving lives at sea and reducing the risk of the sea crossings in the southern Mediterranean and Aegean have come to determine a large proportion of the operational duties of those border police and coastguard charged with policing the Mediterranean and Aegean against irregular migration. This practice has grown steadily in public consciousness in conjunction with the ever hardening of Europe's external borders and the increasing reduction of safe and legal routes. Such SAR operations are undertaken by a range of actors from state coastguard agencies and others tasked with border policing such as Italy's Guardia di Finanzia, as well as member state naval forces as with Italy's Mare Nostrum SAR operation.

Alongside state-actors such as the Guardia di Finanzia, search and rescue, coordinated by the coastguard has been increasingly undertaken by private philanthropic organisations, activist groups and humanitarian organisations have increasingly undertaken specific SAR operations again in co-ordination with the coastguard. Building on the earlier SAR work of Cap Anamur (Basaran 2015) two of the most prominent non-state actors involved in SAR at sea are Migrant Offshore Aid Station (MOAS) and MSF.

MOAS, that first began SAR operations in 2014, was initially a private philanthropic effort financed by the Catrambone family. Residents of Malta, the Catrambones were compelled to use their own personal wealth to engage in rescue operations following the Lampedusa shipwreck of October 2013 in which 360 people drowned. This was understandably a development for SAR in the Mediterranean, and heralded something of a return to a Victorian era private philanthropy concerned for the physical suffering of others and the possible social unrest such suffering could cause. This philanthropy highlighted both the normative and instrumental rationalities of caregiving and was something of a precursor to modern humanitarian action (Haskell 1985a, b; Pupavac 2010). Importantly MOAS differed from earlier efforts at private, activist inspired SAR efforts such as Cap Anamur through both its disavowal of the political and its subsequent sovereign mandate. Cap Anamur articulated a clear political position with regards to the rights of people to cross borders and it operated beyond the sovereign control of European maritime control. MOAS in contrast has come to actively co-operate with and take orders from the relevant sovereign authorities such as the Italian Maritime Rescue Coordination Centre (MRCC) in Rome.

In April 2015, MOAS was joined in maritime SAR in the southern Mediterranean by MSF. In the first instance MSF worked in conjunction with MOAS through providing funding and medical staff for the MOAS rescue boat the MY Phoenix. A month later MSF launched their own SAR boat, the Dignity I that was later joined by a second boat, the Bourbon Argos. Again like their MOAS counterparts MSF's SAR operations are undertaken in full co-operation with the Italian MRCC in Rome (Pallister-Wilkins 2015c). In late 2015 both MOAS and MSF also turned their attention to the risks to life in the Aegean and have started undertaking SAR operations there also. These are currently operational predominantly off the northern shore of Lesbos and differ in operational practice to those in the southern Mediterranean due to differences in the operational environment. These differences are predominantly geopolitical. SAR operations in the southern Mediterranean often take place hundreds of kilometres out at sea in international waters. Like those in the Mediterranean, rescues in the Aegean are fully coordinated with the Greek coastguard but take place in Greek territorial water and much closer to shore as the straight between Turkey and northern Lesbos averages 10 km in width.

These operational differences are important for the types of humanitarian borderwork that are undertaken. They are also important for the ways such work impacts on traditional border policing practices that could traditionally only take place in territorial waters. They appeal to a humanitarian SAR logic that enables border policing to operate in both territorial *and* international waters thereby extending the zone of European intervention. In the southern Mediterranean the humanitarian SAR operations undertaken by both state actors, like those seen during Mare Nostrum and those of MOAS and MSF can and do take place in international waters. Here the humanitarian imperative to rescue and the Safety of Life at Sea (SOLAS) directive expands the space of operations into international waters. Legally vessels can only be intercepted in policing operations in international waters if they are at risk. Under the SOLAS directive many migrant boats are now pre-emptively categorised as at risk and in need of rescue (Andersson 2012). In practice this means that boats can be intercepted in international waters when previously the coastguard would have been restricted to more traditional border policing practices in territorial waters.

Rescue might be the primary motive for SAR operations but in practice they are also border policing operations. Increasingly border police authorities in the USA and Europe have realised that humanitarian concerns and the alleviation of risk for people on the move does not necessarily stand in contrast to policing the border (Pallister-Wilkins 2015a; Williams 2014). In fact Frontex and EU member state border police have realised that rescue works to justify and in many instances increase temporally and spatially the field of intervention allowing more people to be intercepted overall while reducing the numbers of deaths. This is especially clear when you consider the SAR operations of MOAS and MSF. Operating in conjunction with the sovereign authority of the Italian MRCC the presence of these non-state humanitarian SAR vessels increases the capacity for SAR operations alongside the existing capacity of state actors. They facilitate a greater number of rescues, or in border policing terms, interceptions of vessels. In addition rescue boats such as the Dignity I and the Bourbon Argos are instructed by state authorities where to disembark those they have rescued, where they are met and registered by the Italian authorities as part of traditional border policing practices.

Therefore, SAR operations do not stand in contradiction to more traditional border policing operations that seek to control movement of people on the move by intercepting bodies and making them legible (Torpey 2000). In fact in some instances they expand these border policing practices. They expand border policing in terms of when interventions can take place; they expand border policing in terms of capacity for rescue/intervention and they expand the spatial zone of operation into international waters. But more than this, as SAR takes place in both territorial and importantly international waters SAR also expands a European space of possible intervention. Here SAR shifts the European border into 'new' supposedly 'international zones' creating a new distinctly European border space in the southern Mediterranean (see Fig. 1) in processes that are reminiscent of the earlier externalisation of 'Europe's' borders in North Africa (Bialasiewicz 2012; van Reekum 2016).

5 Spaces of Transit: Policing People on the Move and Humanitarian Borderscapes

Through a long-running sustained investigation of humanitarianism in European border policing, and in response to the violence of Europe's border regime, it has become clear that humanitarian borderwork does not just take place at sea or only performed through SAR practices. The humanitarian borderwork I have encountered in my fieldwork is concerned with alleviating the suffering of mobile

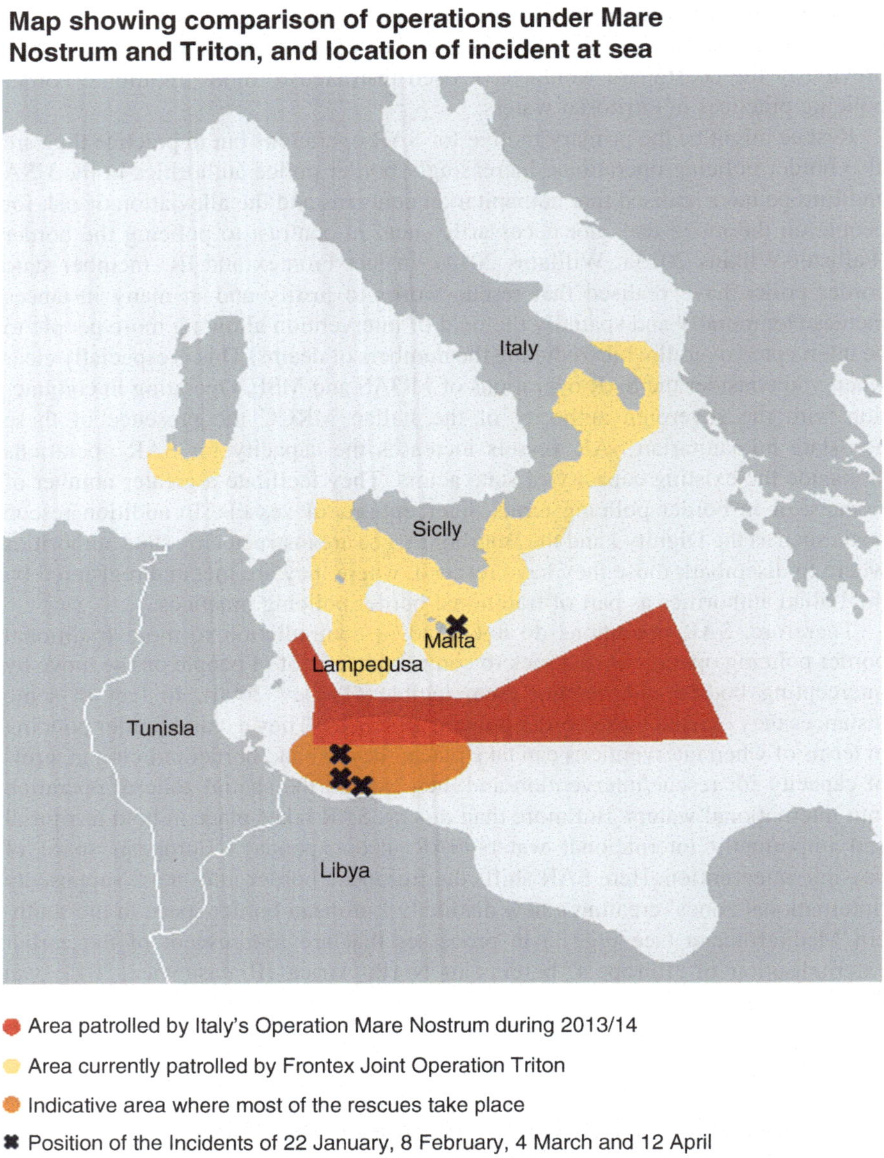

Fig. 1 The expansion of Europe's borders. © Amnesty International

populations in border spaces and occurs in multiple sites wherever these mobile populations are present. This often means humanitarian action is territorialised in the corridors, hubs and nodes of the transport network traversed by people on the move on their life-seeking journeys. As such humanitarian borderwork comes to be

Fig. 2 Borderscapes. © MSF

concerned with policing people on the move in a variety of spaces. In many instances this borderwork produces a politics of categorisation between different groups of people based on nationality, or differential categories of vulnerability and victimhood and, as it traces the journeys people make, it occurs in what we can understand as humanitarian borderscapes (see Fig. 2).

When refugees and migrants started arriving in large numbers on the islands of the eastern Aegean in the summer of 2015 as the Syrian war continued to rage, violence intensified in Iraq and the Taliban became resurgent in large parts of Afghanistan, various forms of humanitarian responses were mobilised, somewhat slowly, to attend to their needs. One of the major European places of arrival for these people on the move was Lesbos where a host of humanitarian (transit) spaces emerged to provide basic humanitarian relief. These spaces of critical humanitarian infrastructure, varying in facilities and quality, started on the beaches where the small and overloaded rubber dinghies arrived and extended almost piecemeal across Lesbos to spaces around the island's capital, Mytiline, and the port from where people could continue their journeys to Athens (Pallister-Wilkins 2015d).

Close to Mytiline, on an old military site near the village of Moria the Greek authorities, belatedly supported by the EU and Frontex, have created a 'hotspot' as they are commonly known, where refugees and migrants in transit have to undergo

Fig. 3 Moria 'hotspot', Lesbos, November 2015. © Polly Pallister-Wilkins, 2015

systems of traditional border policing such as identification verification and biometric registration on the EURODAC (European Dactyloscopy) database (see Fig. 3). At the time of writing Moria has been turned into a site of detention as opposed to transit under the EU-Turkey deal and humanitarian organisations have pulled out refusing to be party to systems of detention and removal that they claim are illegal under International Humanitarian Law. Prior to the enactment of the EU-Turkey Deal that aims to see all those arriving in Greece returned to Turkey unless successful in their asylum applications, Moria was a site of humanitarian interventions intended to lessen the poor conditions people on the move found there.

Before being turned into a detention and removal site Moria was more akin to a large checkpoint than a transit space and far removed from the organised humanitarian governance of established refugee camps (Agier 2011). Here people had to wait for anything up to a week to register with little access to adequate shelter or food. At Moria it was clear that the violence of the European border regime that forces people into using irregular and unsafe routes and to subsequently register in spaces such as Moria was alleviated by the presence of humanitarian workers who provided temporary relief.

In Moria, like other sites in the humanitarian borderscape, processes of triage dictated both border policing and the provision of temporary relief with people assessed according to how much they are believed to be suffering. This triage often plays itself out according to basic practices of categorisation between women and children on the one hand, and single men on the other, or between different nationalities pre-emptively determined according to risk. At Moria this pre-emptive categorisation of those *at* risk dictated how people registered with different lines for different nationalities and differential access to temporary shelter. In other instances, like that at Idomeni on the Greek-FYROM border this differentiation between nationality dictated mobility. People on the move created the border crossing point at Idomeni as the railway line was used to circumvent the official border crossing on the highway a kilometre to the east. This space, while a non-official border crossing, has become a de facto one in recognition of the impossibility of preventing all crossing and amid scenes of repeated physical violence against migrants and refugees by border police since the summer of 2015. As a result Idomeni has become the site of a large-scale humanitarian effort organised principally by MSF (see Fig. 4).

Idomeni is a textbook example of the risks faced by mobile populations when they come into contact with borders. At Idomeni people on the move are made acutely vulnerable by a border regime that at times denies them passage and at others selectively determines who can and cannot move. Here it is clear that the presence of the border is what generates vulnerability and suffering and the subsequent need for humanitarian assistance. In late 2015, Idomeni became a site of differentiation after Slovenia pre-emptively determined that only Syrians, Iraqis and Afghans could be considered 'genuine refugees and asylum seekers' resulting in only these nationalities being able to move across its borders. Responding to Slovenia's decision, Croatia, Serbia and then FYROM decided to allow admission to only Syrians, Iraqis and Afghans to try and prevent other populations becoming 'stuck' in their territory. This resulted in Idomeni becoming a site for the performance of a spatialised and situated politics of life. Now not only was humanitarian assistance determined by differential categorisation but also movement and access to certain spaces became determined by such politics.

In this instance the Greek-FYROM border came to be re-made as one where humanitarian considerations determining who was a 'genuine refugee' were made and governed the border space, while the accompanying practices of differentiation were undertaken by the Greek police with the assistance of the UNHCR. Here an ostensibly humanitarian organisation founded to protect the rights of refugees, and

Fig. 4 MSF built transit point, Idomeni border crossing point, Greek-FYROM border, January 2016. © Polly Pallister-Wilkins, 2016

provide them with relief, engaged in border policing practices and pre-emptive acts of determining who was and was not a 'genuine refugee and/or asylum seeker' based on nothing more than nationality. While the humanitarian consideration of refugees is one that ultimately rests on biopolitical concerns over life, the border in this instance was more than a biopolitical border as movement across it was not denied to all 'refugees' but was governed by differentiated categories of refugee-status pre-emptively determined by nationality. It was in this sense governed by a politics of life that produced hierarchies between those people in transit at Idomeni (Fassin 2012).

In early 2016 the humanitarian borderwork that occurred at Idomeni moved 20 km south to a service station on the E75 highway next to the village of Polykastro. Idomeni was not in use as MSF, who built and managed large parts of the site, refused to allow the Greek police to carry out border policing in what MSF considered a humanitarian space. The Greek police for their part wanted to carry out such policing efforts to prevent similar scenes of protest by those nationalities blocked at the border to those seen in late 2015. In practice what this meant was that people on the move were no longer allowed to wait, in transit at Idomeni for the irregular border crossing to open. The Greek police instead required people travelling north by bus from Athens to first stop and wait at the service station at Poykastro until the FYROM police opened the crossing at Idomeni. As a result the border shifted, re-appeared, or multiplied at the service station in Polykastro and became a site of humanitarian borderwork. Polykastro was thus produced as another zone of humanitarian triage for people on the move (see

Fig. 5 Humanitarian borderwork at Polykastro, January 2016. © Polly Pallister-Wilkins, 2016

Fig. 5). Therefore, the spaces of transit where borderwork occurs are continually shifting, being consolidated and contested as both state authority in the form of border policing and humanitarian practitioners attempt to govern mobile lives according to rationalities of security and wellbeing.

At the time of writing Idomeni is now open again but FYROM has now closed its borders to all irregular people. This has meant that Idomeni is now less of a transit space and rapidly becoming more of a traditional refugee camp. There are, however, those refugees and migrants who, wanting to evade the intervention of the border police and to continue their journeys across the border elsewhere, remain outside of Idomeni and other, similar organised spaces. In response to these scattered communities MSF now runs a mobile medical clinic. Such an initiative recognises and responds to the specific spatial configuration and highly mobile nature of both people on the move and subsequently renders assistance mobile changing the possible space and time of humanitarian intervention.

6 Conclusion

Practices concerned with saving lives and relieving suffering have re-oriented border control in Europe, as SAR operations have become a central everyday practice of European border policing. Such operations in turn work to expand both the potential for intervention and the spaces in which such intervention can take place. This has the overall effect of working to reproduce Europe's borders both in terms of their exclusive nature but also in terms of 'where' they are as SAR operations can and do take place in international waters. In addition, humanitarian borderwork has introduced new actors into borderwork. These actors at times compliment traditional border policing practices and, in fact, work to expand its capacity as with SAR missions. At other times these practices work to disrupt and resist such policing through the provision of humanitarian care and accompanying calls for safe and legal forms of travel for refugees and migrants (Pallister-Wilkins 2015c).

Through the times and spaces of care-provision new border spaces come to be produced and new categories of life performed and consolidated. In short, new forms of borderwork emerge that complicate Europe's borders further. Humanitarian borderwork simultaneously highlights the violence of borders with serious, biopolitical consequences for life, while moving beyond biopolitics through the types of borderwork that attached values and meaning to a range of differentiated categories of people on the move. These in turn work to produce new borders and reproduce existing ones as humanitarian borderwork, even if accompanied by political calls for reforms to Europe's restrictive border regime only ever go as far as assuaging the effects while the underlying structural violence—of territory itself—remains (Pallister-Wilkins 2016c).

Providing humanitarian assistance, as well as policing people on the move as opposed to static populations, is complex and creates new challenges for practitioners. The varied practices that have arisen to manage these transit populations, from providing short-term shelter, food and clothing, to designated buses, and mobile medical clinics can be understood through the vacillating forms of sovereignty and continual contestation and consolidation of borders suggested in the concept of borderscapes. Here the border and thus spaces of humanitarian borderwork follow the trajectories of people on the move in an intimate relationship with mobility. Traditional thinking about borders is insufficient to think about the relationship between the violence of borders, its alleviation through humanitarianism and subsequent forms of borderwork.

The concept of borderscapes better captures the shifting spaces and terrains of practice, the places that emerge as spaces of intervention and the complexities of response. The multiplicity of humanitarian borderwork becomes easier to analyse when we think in terms of borderscapes that are continually traversed by a number of bodies and the practices and relationships that render visible endless categorisations and shifts in categorisation between self and other, saviour and victim, legal and illegal, worthy and unworthy, refugee and migrant. The concurrent performance of state sovereignty and its contestation by mobile bodies and humanitarian actors can more easily be understood as an everyday border practice in itself, as opposed to something that threatens to disrupt the foundations of both how we think about borders but also borders themselves. As such, thinking in terms of borderscapes better helps us to see humanitarian intervention in border spaces as border*work* by enabling a consideration of the complex humanitarian dispositions and practices that go into producing the border.

References

Aas, K. F., & Gundhus, H. O. I. (2015). Policing humanitarian borderlands: Frontex, human rights and precarious life. *British Journal of Criminology, 55*(1), 1–18.

Agier, M. (2011). *Managing the undesirables: Refugee camps and humanitarian government*. Cambridge: Polity.

Amoore, L. (2006). Biometric borders: Governing mobilities in the war on terror. *Political Geography, 25*(3), 336–351.

Andersson, R. (2012). A game of risk: Boat migration and the business of bordering Europe. *Anthropology Today, 28*(6), 7–11.

Andreas, P. (2003). Redrawing the line: Borders and security in the twenty-first century. *International Security, 28*(2), 78–111.

Balibar, É. (2009). Europe as borderland. *Environment and Planning D: Society and Space, 27*(2), 190–215.

Basaran, T. (2015). The saved and the drowned: Governing indifference in the name of security. *Security Dialogue, 46*(3), 205–220.

Belloni, R. (2007). The trouble with humanitarianism. *Review of International Studies, 33*(3), 451–474.

Bialasiewicz, L. (2012). Off-shoring and outsourcing the borders of Europe: Libya and EU border work in the Mediterranean. *Geopolitics, 17*(4), 843–866.

Bigo, D. (2002). Security and immigration: Toward a critique of the governmentality of unease. *Alternatives: Global, Local, Political, 27*(1), 63–92.

Brambilla, C. (2015). Exploring the critical potential of the borderscapes concept. *Geopolitics, 20* (1), 14–34.

Calhoun, C. (2008). The imperative to reduce suffering: Charity, progress, and emergencies in the field of *humanitarian* action. In M. Barnett & T. C. Weiss (Eds.), *Humanitarianism in question: Politics, power, ethics* (pp. 73–97). Ithaca, NY: Cornell University Press.

Debrix, F. (1998). Deterritorialised territories, borderless borders: The new geography of international medical assistance. *Third World Quarterly, 19*(5), 827–846.

Dillon, M. (2007). Governing terror: The state of emergency of biopolitical emergence. *International Political Sociology, 1*(1), 7–28.

Doty, R. L. (2007). States of exception on the Mexico-U.S. border: Security, "decisions", and civilian border patrols. *International Political Sociology, 1*(2), 113–137.

Elden, S. (2007a). Governmentality, calculation, territory. *Environment and Planning D: Society and Space, 25*(3), 562–580.

Elden, S. (2007b). Terror and territory. *Antipode, 39*(5), 821–845.

European Commission. (2015). *European agenda on migration: Securing Europe's external borders* (MEMO/15/6332). Strasbourg.

European Council. (2015). *Political declaration Valletta migration summit 11–12 November* (EUCO 809/15). Brussels.

Fassin, D. (2005). Compassion and Repression. *Cultural Anthropology, 20*(3), 362–387.

Fassin, D. (2012). *Humanitarian reason: A moral history of the present*. Berkeley, CA: University of California Press.

Feldman, I., & Ticktin, M. (Eds.). (2010). *In the name of humanity: The government of threat and care*. Durham, NC: Duke University Press.

Haskell, T. L. (1985a). Capitalism and the origins of Humanitarian sensibility, part 1. *The American Historical Review, 90*(2), 339–361.

Haskell, T. L. (1985b). Capitalism and the origins of Humanitarian sensibility, part 2. *The American Historical Review, 90*(3), 547–566.

Hindess, B. (2006). Terrortory. *Alternatives: Global, Local, Political, 31*(3), 243–257.

Hollifield, J. (2004). The emerging migration state. *International Migration Review, 38*(3), 885–912.

Hopgood, S. (2013). *The endtimes of human rights*. Ithaca, NY: Cornell University Press.

Hyndman, J. (2012). Introduction: The geopolitics of migration and mobility. *Geopolitics, 12*(2), 243–255.

Last, T. (2015). *Deaths at the borders database for the Southern EU*. Retrieved from www.borderdeaths.org/?page_id=11

Mezzadra, S., & Neilson, B. (2013). *Border as Method, or, the Multiplication of Labor*. Durham, NC: Duke University Press.

Pallister-Wilkins, P. (2015a). The humanitarian politics of European border policing: Frontex and border police in Evros. *International Political Sociology, 9*(1), 53–69.

Pallister-Wilkins, P. (2015b). The humanitarian policing of 'our sea'. *Border Criminologies*. Retrieved from https://www.law.ox.ac.uk/research-subject-groups/centre-criminology/centreborder-criminologies/blog/2015/04/humanitarian

Pallister-Wilkins, P. (2015c). The politics of 'illegality' in the humanitarian borderwork of Médecins Sans Frontières. *Border Criminologies*. Retrieved from https://www.law.ox.ac.uk/research-subject-groups/centre-criminology/centreborder-criminologies/blog/2015/10/politics

Pallister-Wilkins, P. (2015d). There is a focus on the boats because the sea is sexier than the land: A reflection on the centrality of boats in the recent 'migration crisis'. *The Disorder of Things*. Retrieved from http://thedisorderofthings.com/2015/12/09/theres-a-focus-on-the-boats-because-the-sea-is-sexier-than-the-land-a-reflection-on-the-centrality-of-the-boats-in-the-recent-migration-crisis/

Pallister-Wilkins, P. (2016a). How walls do work: Security barriers as devices of interruption and data capture. *Security Dialogue, 47*(2), 151–164.

Pallister-Wilkins, P. (2016b). The tensions of the ceuta and melilla borderfences. In A. Bellagamba, S. Dünnwald, & P. Gaibazzi (Eds.), *EurAfrican borders and migration management: political cultures, contested spaces and ordinary lives* (pp. 44–63). Basingstoke: Palgrave Macmillian.

Pallister-Wilkins, P. (2016c). Personal protective equipment and the humanitarian governance of Ebola: Between individual patient care and global biosecurity. *Third World Quarterly, 37*(3), 507–523.

Pallister-Wilkins, P. (2016d). Interrogating the Mediterranean 'migration crisis'. *Mediterranean Politics, 21*(2), 311–315.

Pupavac, V. (2010). Between compassion and conservatism: A genealogy of humanitarian sensibilities. In D. Fassin & M. Pandolfi (Eds.), *Contemporary states of emergency: The politics of military and humanitarian interventions* (pp. 129–152). New York: Zone Books.

Redfield, P. (2013). *Life in crisis: The ethical journey of doctors without borders*. Berkeley, CA: University of California Press.

Rosière, S., & Jones, R. (2012). Teichopolitics: Re-considering globalisation through the role of walls and fences. *Geopolitics, 17*(1), 217–234.

Rumford, C. (2008). Introduction: Citizens and borderwork in Europe. *Space and Polity, 12*(1), 1–12.

Torpey, J. (2000). *The invention of the passport: Surveillance, citizenship and the state*. Cambridge: Cambridge University Press.

Van Houtum, H. (2010). Human blacklisting: The global apartheid of the EU's external border regime. *Environment and Planning D: Society & Space, 28*(6), 957–976.

Van Reekum, R. (2016). The Mediterranean: Migration corridor, border spectacle, ethical landscape. *Mediterranean Politics, 21*(2), 336–341.

Vaughan-Williams, N. (2008). Borderwork beyond inside/outside?: Frontex, the citizen-detective and the war on terror. *Space and Polity, 12*(1), 63–79.

Walters, W. (2011). Foucault and frontiers: Notes on the birth of the humanitarian border. In U. Bröckling, S. Krasmann, & T. Lemke (Eds.), *Governmentality: Current issues and future challenges* (pp. 138–164). New York: Routledge.

Weber, L., & Pickering, S. (2014). *Globalization and borders: Death and the global frontier*. Basingstoke: Palgrave Macmillan.

Weizman, E. (2011). *The least of all possible evils: Humanitarian violence from Arendt to Gaza*. London: Verso.
Williams, J. M. (2014). The safety/security nexus and the humanitarianisation of border enforcement. *The Geographic Journal, 182*(1), 27–37. doi:10.1111/geoj.12119
Williams, J. M. (2015). From humanitarian exceptionalism to contingent care: Care and enforcement at the humanitarian border. *Political Geography, 47*(1), 11–20.
Yeung, P. (2016, April 10). Idomeni: Macedonian police fire tear gas and rubber bullets at refugees trying to break through Greek border [Video]. *Independent*. Retrieved from http://www.independent.co.uk/news/world/europe/idomeni-macedonia-police-tear-gas-refugee-border-greece-a6977141.html

Polly Pallister-Wilkins is an assistant professor of International Relations in the Department of Politics, University of Amsterdam. She specialises in the intersection of humanitarian intervention and border control. Her current research is concerned with what she calls 'humanitarian borderwork' in Europe and it builds on previous research into humanitarianism, border policing and the political sociologies of walls, fences and security barriers. Her regional areas of expertise are the Mediterranean, specifically Greece, and the Middle East.

Part III
European Border Politics

The Politics of Digital Borders

Paul Trauttmansdorff

Abstract Information and communication technologies (ICTs) and large-scale digital databases play a crucial role in the European management of borders and mobility governance. Since the 1990 Schengen Agreement three large-scale IT systems and a number of information sharing mechanisms have emerged. This chapter scrutinizes the relationship between digital technology and border politics by following the idiom of co-production, which focuses on the interconnectedness between techno-political developments and the (re-)construction of social orders. It examines how digital systems are deployed and enacted in the processes of identification, data collection and categorization. The analysis is based on various documents issued by the main official authorities and actors, from official communications and regulation by the European Commission and Council to the information brochures and technical reports of the eu-Lisa agency. The chapter will first present the main developments of ICTs and digital systems in European border management, and then point to the ways in which digital technologies are deployed for the governance of cross-border mobility. In particular, it highlights the de-territorialization effects of digital border governance and the important role of the human body in identification and categorization processes. Finally, it argues that digital borders are co-produced by the interaction and interplay of human actors and technological systems at the various border sites.

Keywords Borders • ICTs • Digital systems • Governance • Mobility • Migration • eu-Lisa

---

This chapter is based on research and insights for my dissertation that completed a master of science degree in political sociology at the London School of Economics and Political Science (2015). I would like to thank my supervisor Michael McQuarrie.

P. Trauttmansdorff (✉)
Austrian Institute for International Affairs (oiip), Vienna, Austria
e-mail: p_trauttmansdorff@msn.com

C. Günay, N. Witjes (eds.), *Border Politics*, DOI 10.1007/978-3-319-46855-6_7

1 Introduction

In February 2013, the European Department of Migration and Home affairs issued a press release stating that modern and efficient border management must 'speed up, facilitate and reinforce border check procedures' (MHA 2013). This responds to what is considered one of the most contentious issues in Europe these days: border controls and the mobility of people. The proliferation of international travel and migration increasingly challenge states to cope with cross-border mobility and border control. Europe's recent history of the implementation of a common market zone and the development of the 'Four Freedoms' (free movement of capital, goods, services and people), a key component of EU governance, has triggered the gradual abolition of checks and borders among Schengen members while simultaneously demanding the strengthening of border controls with non-Schengen states. In this context, EU governance has been promoting the so-called *harmonization* of external border control (and visa policy). The common management of migration and mobility is 'now firmly at the top of the European Union's political agenda', according to the European Commission (CEC 2011a: 2).

One of the most crucial components of today's complex European border regime, which encompasses various actors and institutions, is the constant and extensive use of new technologies. In particular, the rapid proliferation and growing influence of databases and information and communication technologies (ICTs) can be regarded as key mechanisms and tools to govern travellers and visitors of all kinds, both wanted and unwanted, at the borders and within them. Three main large-scale databases and a number of information sharing mechanisms have been developed since the Schengen Agreement came into force. European state authorities cooperate on border management mainly through the Schengen Information System (SIS II), the Visa Information System (VIS) and Eurodac, a large-scale fingerprint database. In 2011, these systems were centralized by the newly established European Agency for the operational management of large-scale IT systems (*eu-Lisa*), responsible for the continuous exchange of data between national authorities. Moreover, a proposed 'Smart Border Package', yet to become implemented on a European Scale, is also being tested to achieve a 'safer Europe' through technology (eu-Lisa 2014a: 4). Generally, the on-going development and massive expansion of ICTs show that they are considered one of the most important factors in challenging the future of mobility management and border control. It is underscored by recent plans to spend roughly one third of the 3.8 billion € Internal Security Fund on further development of 'existing or new IT systems that support the management of migration flows' (MHA 2015). The EU's main agency for external border control operations, Frontex, admits: 'The vision of the future relies to a large extent on technology to improve security, convenience and cost-effectiveness in border control' (Frontex 2013).

This chapter examines how border and mobility management in Europe is continuously technologically mediated, contributing to what can be called a virtualization or digitalization of European borders. Anyone who travels to Europe is increasingly confronted by (digital) technologies that function as 'an obligatory passage point' (Dijstelbloem et al. 2011: 2). Europe's borders are thus not only to be found along a geographical borderline on the map, but rather in the electronic devices of border authorities, in asylum files and visa records, in the digital infrastructure and IT systems. This chapter therefore attempts to explore the relationship between digital technology and European border politics, and highlights the key aspects of these techno-political arrangements. It scrutinizes how ICTs and digital systems are deployed and how they are enacted in order to identify and categorize travellers that attempt to enter Europe. After having presented the main large-scale IT systems in Europe (and their political background), it will go on to identify the key aspects of digital borders. First, the effects of digital systems on mobility governance are put into the context of the EU's border politics of remote control. Second, it attempts to show how the techno-politics of ICTs are supposed to enable border governance that guarantees security, control *and* mobility. The digitization of borders will then be conceptualized by focusing on the identification and categorization of travellers, which increasingly target and rely on the human body. It argues that digital borders are co-produced by the interaction between a wide range of actors, i.e. migrants, border and consular posts or law enforcement bodies, their practices and digital technologies across and beyond the Schengen territory. The chapter employs content analysis drawing on official documents authored by the main (European) actors that are related to the making and use of digital technologies in European border politics. This includes communications, agendas and (legal) regulations by the European Commission and the Council, as well as information brochures and technical reports published by the *eu-Lisa* agency.

2 States Border Populations

2.1 The Border as a Categorizing Institution

A diverse and wide range of literature has emphasized the mechanisms of the border as an institution that selects and categorizes; it has focused on the changing 'nature' of borders in order to grasp political and social change, different power mechanisms and articulations (see Rumford 2006; Walters 2006; Paasi 2007; Johnson et al. 2011; Mezzadra and Neilson 2013). Adopting the border as an object of study has helped to analyze the various and rigorous methods of control that are intended to demarcate the state's territory and sovereignty, while producing knowledge about the movements of population and goods. Clearly, for the state's purpose of controlling population movement—the 'monopolization of the legitimate means of movement' (Torpey 2000), technologies of identification and categorization have been at the center of academic interest. John Torpey's study 'The Invention of the Passport' documents the most uniform state technique of governing mobility by 'embracing' populations, rendering them 'legible', and reading off their bodies for manipulation and control. Only then can borders perform their general double function: they play their role in the surveillance and control of travellers in order to protect the state 'from outside threats', but also enable freedom of conduct and for others to cross them (Van Munster 2009: 108).

2.2 The Securitization of Borders/the Autonomy of Migration

Digital border technologies are sometimes explained as resulting from the European Union's intention to strengthen the borders of Fortress Europe (Broeders 2007; Marin 2011) or to construct a 'Cyber-Fortress Europe' (Guild et al. 2008). Similarly, they have been framed around the issue of the securitization of migration and borders (Bigo 2002; Pallitto and Heyman 2008; Van Munster 2009). The concept of (in)securitization found its profound expression in Didier Bigo's 'critique of the governmentality of unease' (2002). Bigo regards digital technologies as part of 'multiple discursive practices [...] as well as the heterogeneity of the non-discursive practices' (p. 84); he diagnoses a powerful 'dispositif' that engages a wide range of security practices, professional actors and institutions. The digital collection of information or the introduction of biometric data, particularly after the attacks of 9/11, are thus regarded as crucial instruments of the overall securitization (of EU's migration and border policies). Accordingly, digital exchange of information would contribute as a 'primary tool' (Balzacq 2008) to the processes of increasing control, surveillance and exclusion.

Another body of literature conceptualizes new border technologies by drawing on two main concepts: 'the autonomy of migration' and the notion of the (border) 'regime' (see for example Moulier-Boutang 1998; Papadopoulos et al. 2008; Mezzadra and Neilson 2013; Scheel 2013; Heimeshoff et al. 2014). Contrary to most security studies literature, these works insist on avoiding an overly control-biased perspective, which often perceives migrants simply as passive actors and under control. By reversing the perspective, they underline the everyday struggles or subversive actions of migrants, highlighting subjective practices, expectations, behavior and strategies (of mobility) that can create moments of autonomy, extending beyond the limits and goals of migration control systems. Moreover, they emphasize the *regime character* of the Schengen border management system. Accordingly, the control techniques and border technologies of the Schengen area should not be framed as a coherent set of tools, policies or as a seamless system that provides perfect surveillance. Instead, the *regime* is shaped and characterized by a complex interplay of actors and 'nebulous legal formulas applied in the EU's regulation of immigration and asylum' (Balch and Geddes 2011: 34). It comprises assemblages of actors and practices that play a role in the governance of mobility. The regime does constant 'repair work' (Kasparek and Tsianos 2014) while its borders are challenged and contested by migratory action and struggle.

Considering the increasing *technologization* of borders and the 'overall rationale of the securitization' (Scheel 2013: 591), this view is crucial for an adequate understanding of digital border technologies because it refuses to reduce technologies to smoothly functioning control tools. In other words, one can avoid adopting a techno-determinist approach that is often inherent not only in conceptualizations of digital borders, but also in official narratives of their use and implementation.

2.3 The Co-production of Digital Borders

A sufficient account for the extensive resort to (digital) technology in the Schengen regime, however, should neither downplay nor underestimate its key role in European border *securitization*, nor fall back into technological determinism. A co-productionist perspective (Jasanoff 2004) on digital borders can explore the interconnectedness of techno-political developments and the (re-)construction of societal and knowledge orders. By claiming that science, technology and society are co-produced, it highlights the mutual interdependence of humanity and technology (Harbers 2005: 11). Digital technologies should not be understood as mere tools, nor should they represent a passive 'background' for social/political goals. Rather, they are developed, shaped, and enacted by various actors in various contexts or networks. As Jasanoff (2004: 3) maps out, the idiom of co-production offers a useful perspective on (networks of) *power*, on the ways knowledge production is incorporated into governance practices, and how practices of governance influence the making and use of knowledge. It highlights the 'role of knowledges, expertise, technical practices and material objects in shaping, sustaining, subverting or transforming relations of authority [... and] stressing the interconnections between the macro and the micro, between emergence and stabilization, and between knowledge and practice' (Jasanoff 2004: 4). By highlighting the socio-technical arrangements of the processes of border digitalization, this perspective allows us to see how both society and technology (Kuster and Tsianos 2012) emerge or co-produce each other, as well as how power networks enable 'domination at a distance' (Latour 1986, 1989; Van der Ploeg 1999). A co-productionist understanding of digital borders considers how the character of securitization processes European border management, but also lays emphasis on the interaction between specific actors, their practices and digital technologies.

3 ICT Systems in the European Border Regime

> Guaranteeing security [...] can no longer be done through physical resources on the ground. The 'virtual world' of IT is now part of the equation, as authorities are increasingly reliant on data and information. In today's complex and globalised world, a single state cannot look after its security alone.
>
> (Kim Garkov, Executive Director, eu-Lisa 2014a: 1)

As this statement indicates, technological and digital developments are often regarded as being the inevitable processes of a complex, globalized and technologized world. It presents this agenda (of eu-Lisa) in the positive or neutral view of technology, as being a *tool* to deal with political problems that are becoming entangled with an advancing technological reality. A study for the European Commission on the Visa Information System claims for example that the 'power of modern *desktop* technology' (computers, digital photography, scanners) has made (document) falsification faster and cheaper (EPEC 2004: 16). Technology is then also supposed to neutralize risks, which are themselves caused by a complex, digitized world. As the EU Commissioner for Justice, Freedom and Security, Franco Frattini, put it; 'there is no alternative' to digitization (Frattini, quoted in Dijstelbloem and Broeders 2015: 2). However, these narratives of inevitable technological progress overstate its role. They rather obscure the necessary human activities involved, the false starts, the complexities of social *and* technical processes, and thereby rely on a technological determinism that takes technical progress for granted. As a consequence, the advancement of digital systems, especially the concept of their 'interoperability and synergy' in order to improve data and knowledge exchange, has officially been regarded as a *technical* (rather than legal or political) issue (CEC 2005; Brouwer 2008: 133–5). But there also seems to be a 'technological imperative' (Chapman 2009), which drives the massive proliferation of ICTs in order to *maximize* their technological potential instead of simply carrying out policy. As a result, the *political* character of problems that technology is supposed to solve is obscured (Scheel 2013: 584–5).

As previously mentioned, there are three large-scale digital databases that store and enable the exchange of information. First, the Schengen Information System (SIS) is a joint electronic police tracking and information system for immigration and border control. It allows access to data related to persons for arrest or subject to an entry ban and to travel movements under surveillance. Its origins can be traced back to the implementation of the 1990 Schengen Agreement, where it was constructed in order to fight (cross-border) criminality and, explicitly, as a 'compensatory measure [. . .] to [maintain] security' following the abolishment of internal border controls (EU 2006: L381/4). Its development was heavily negotiated and its implementation postponed several times due to technical, political, practical and legal issues. As Brouwer (2008: 55–6) documents, countries delayed the process by failing to forward their lists of authorized end users and due to difficulties of national law amendments. In 2013, the 'simple' reporting system was reformed into *SIS II*, a reporting *and* investigation system with extended use and enhanced data storage capacities (photographs and biometric fingerprints) that sought to foster greater police cooperation (CEC 2001: 7). In December 2013, it contained over 50 million entered alerts as sets of data (eu-Lisa 2014b) mostly on objects such as stolen, lost or misappropriated identity documents. However, the preoccupation with information exchange about irregular migrants is also central to SIS II. The majority of alerts on persons (72 % of 861,900) are about individuals for whom entry or stay into Schengen is denied. What constitutes a 'risk' is decided by national border controls, police or custom checks (CEC 2001: 6). Connected with a central system, they use their own standards and are responsible for data accuracy, which can also result in interpretation discrepancies.[1]

Second, in 2003, the European dactyloscopic (Eurodac) database became operational and can be understood as a reaction to the 'asylum crisis' of the late 1990s when the so-called 'asylum shopping problem', claiming multiple asylums in different countries, attracted much attention (Kuster and Tsianos 2012: 33). Eurodac aims to control the mobility of people who do not have a visa and to improve the application of the Dublin Convention by determining which member states are responsible for a refugee's asylum procedure (CEU 2000). As a central registration system, it stores and enables the comparison of recorded fingerprints, place and time of the prints, as well as details about the application. As asylum seekers would often destroy their identification documents, authorities had difficulties with tracking routes and establishing whether individuals had already applied for asylum. Thus, fingerprints had to become an important element in establishing the exact identity of such persons (CEU 2000: L316/1), thereby aiming to insure the single application principle and prevent 'asylum-shopping'. This 'hit/no-hit-System' compares fingerprints taken off every asylum applicant older than 14 with those of 'every alien [...] irregularly crossing an external border of a participating country' or found illegal in the territory (eu-Lisa 2015a).

Third, the Visa Information System (VIS) became operational in 2011 in order 'facilitate' data exchange between the member states on visa applications and all decision relating thereto (EU 2008). Beside its official tasks to contribute to internal security, preventing and investigating terrorism, it is a system of *re-identification* (Broeders 2007) that collects and stores data of visa procedures in order to foreclose migrants' strategies to stay in the EU after a legal visa has expired, detecting so-called 'overstayers'. Moreover, it thereby supports the 'effective application' of the Dublin Convention and prevents 'visa shopping'; authorities, border control, national police, visa, immigration and asylum authorities (and on request Europol) can access and communicate data through national interfaces connected to a central database (CEU 2008). The VIS has been gradually and regionally rolled out with more than 215,000 end-users including consular and border posts, and should eventually cover the entire world (eu-Lisa 2014e). It collects 'standard' alphanumeric data and contains a system that allows biometric matching (primarily for fingerprints).

The implementations of both SIS II and VIS, both constructed with an interconnected technical architecture and both located in Strasbourg, have a history of budgetary and technical problems, mostly regarding the technical standardization of (national) systems and enormous unexpected costs for the complicated architecture(s).[2] The establishment of the eu-Lisa agency in 2011 is thus a further

---

[1]Kuster and Tsianos' research report (2012: 16) on Eurodac serves as a striking example. For example, one of their interviewees, a German IT specialist, stated he could neither explain nor understand the inordinate use of Eurodac category 2, 'illegal border crossers', by the Greek authorities, which would amount to a much higher figure of entries than using category 3, 'illegal residents'.

[2]See for example Hayes and Vermeulen (2012: 31).

step that centralizes the operational management of all systems. Also, by focusing on reporting statistics and research, it aims to improve cooperation and information exchange between the EU border management and the bodies of law enforcement (eu-Lisa 2014c: 5–6).

4 Technology and Extra-territorialization

The on-going centralization and homogenization of different European IT systems should not distract from the various sites and locations, where acts of bordering take place. Rather, the digitalization of borders can draw attention to how technology decouples functions that originally seemed to be attached to the territorial frontier, such as identification, categorization, and selection processes. This particular role that technology plays is not new. According to Aristide Zolberg (2006), the expansion of global markets and rising political tensions around the world have led nation-states to seek to control in a *remote way*, trying to prevent the increasingly inconvenient and risky *refoulement* at the territorial frontier.[3] Transportation technology, for example, has enabled checks at border-crossings through transportation companies, which function as 'ancillary border police' (2006: 224). Remote control thus 'amounted to a projection of the country of destination's borders into the world at large' (ibid.). In other words, strategies and techniques of mobility government can be found far beyond territorial borders, which draws attention to the 'multiplicity of sites' where the act of bordering aims to govern mobility, where 'detectors and effectors' (Broeders and Hampshire 2013: 1207) operate. Digital technology refines this border work of *pro-active* controls, thus relying less on late *re-actions* to migration flows.

A brief look at the various European communications, agendas or 'global approaches' to migration (CEC 2011a, b, 2015) confirms the tendency of arranging practices that extend border work beyond the Schengen territory, indicating the so-called extra-territorialization of migration control. Most notably, a 'forward-looking policy on mobility', as the Commission calls it (CEC 2011b: 10–11), is illustrated by the EU's visa policy, which has undergone significant change in the last two decades. The introduction of ICTs has played a central role in the harmonization of visa policy under the Schengen refinement and standardization of governance. Visa policy and agreements used to be oriented towards a national level, countries were assessed as being more or less of a *risk* (and then black-listed), whereas today's transnational Schengen cooperation attempts to manage risks that are increasingly *individualized* (Salter and Mutlu 2013: 118). As the EU's 'Security in 2020' paper emphasizes, this has to go far beyond traditional paper documentation, but via 'advanced ICT systems [and] interoperable exchanges of data' (CEC

[3]'Remote control' is defined as the requirement of 'obtaining permission to enter before embarking on the journey' (Zolberg 2006: 223).

2014: 16). In order to enter the Schengen area today, a valid travel document, a (required) visa and a justification of the purpose of the stay are required. Moreover, it is checked whether an *alert in a database* has been issued and if the border crosser poses an *individual threat* to public policy, internal security, internal relations or public health (EU 2008: L218/67). Digital storage and the technical exchange of personal information allows checks for these requirements, thereby facilitating the *disengagement* of border controls and visa conditions from the level of nationality, to an increasing focus on the individual:

> The decision to issue a visa should gradually move from the presumption of risk associated with the applicant's nationality to an assessment of individual risk. This development will be made possible by the introduction in the long term of systems that allow collection of advance information on individuals [. . .]. (CEC 2009: 19)

A technical report on the use of biometrics, tasked by the European Commission, describes the importance of technology, not only for visa policy, but for European border control in general: 'It is perceived that knowing who is entering the European territory is one of the key elements of an area of freedom, security and justice' (Goldstein et al. 2008: 1). Crucially, knowing *that* people cross the border legally is now less important than knowing *who* crosses it and who may cross it in future.

Storing information and potentially establishing profiles through identification means enabling the tracing of individuals and populations at *various locations* that are not only to be found at the territorial border point. Rather, it is a 'network of various border sites' (Broeders and Hampshire 2013: 1205), which allows for the reinforcement and refinement of control, aiming to cover more categories of individuals and, moreover, strengthening the link between pre-entry border and internal control measures of travellers/migrants. This 'embracement' (Torpey 2000) of a (mobile) population through large-scale information collection aims for effective regulation and profiling. It is not so much about confronting each individual in a systematic way but rather about categorizing in preventive terms, enabling what Broeders/Hampshire call 'pre-emptive mobility governance' (2013: 1207). Its goal is not simply to prevent movement and extradite migrants, but to map and codify *different* flows of mobility through digitalization, categorizing and sorting subjects into various types, for which inclusion and/or exclusion is facilitated. Border functions such as monitoring and surveillance, administration and registration, identification, verification and categorization form part of a *zone* that is no longer strictly defined by the state's territory.[4] The construction of *digital borders* thus seeks to enable efficient *bordering* for a smooth and secure zone, which does not stick to the traditional image of the territorial, geographical frontier. As the example of *Smart Borders* will illustrate, digital borders rely on the idea of

---

[4]Certainly, Andrew Barry's term 'technological zone' can help to grasp the (non-territorial) character of these arrangements for governance. It is defined as a set of diverse regulations, socio-technical arrangements and processes, technical infrastructures that render objects or flows governable (Barry 2001: 37ff.).

governing movement by guaranteeing *both* security/control and mobility through the effective control of information, ideally, about people before they move.

5 Mobility, Security, Smart Borders

5.1 Smart Borders: Is IT All About Moving?

The 'Smart Borders package', proposed by the Commission in 2013, is a good example of the gradual and extensive deployment of digital technologies, which is considered a central ingredient of the EU's 'Integrated Border Management' strategy (IBM). IBM's overall objective is described for example in the Stockholm Programme 2010, which interlinks cross-border crime, terrorism and irregular migration, establishing what Van Munster calls an 'immigration/security nexus' (2009: 46). It emphasizes the necessity of an open and secure Europe, for example, with the help of an 'extensive toolbox for collecting, processing and sharing information between national authorities and other players' (CEU 2010: C115/ 18). Similar to IBM, the 'Global Approach to Migration and Mobility' (CEC 2011a: 15) stresses a 'broader understanding of security', which not only links *irregular* migration to crime (and trafficking), but also *regular* migration to economic benefit and growth. In this sense, the process of digitalization no longer concerns only the policies of irregular migration, but aims to encompass different forms of mobility, increasingly including all types of border crossing. As borders become crossing points of rapidly increased travel flows, they are supposed to be managed in effective and credible, but also in 'efficient' ways.[5] This means not only preventing 'irregular migration and maintaining public security', but also making those goals 'compatible with the objective of increased mobility' (CEC 2011b: 11). Hence, the Smart Borders package involves the next move towards what is called a more 'modern and efficient border management by using state-of-the-art technology' (eu-Lisa 2015b). Smart borders therefore aim to strike a balance between control, security and facilitation in pursuit of a 'harmonized approach to European border security' (eu-Lisa 2014d: 19). The package contains a 'Registered Traveller Programme' that aims to implement automated visa and border mechanisms, speeding up border-crossings for pre-registered 'low-risk', 'bona fide travellers' or 'persons travelling on business', and an Entry-Exit-System, which should automatically register time and place of entry and exit, issuing alerts in case of irregularities.[6] As travel flows at the EU's external borders will continue to increase

[5]See the Stockholm Programme: '[A]ccess to the Union's territory has to be made more effective and efficient. At the same time, the Union and its Member States have to guarantee security for their citizens' (CEU 2010: C115/5).

[6]Consequently, an 'Entry-Exit-System' would also be connected with other databases like the VIS (CEC 2008: 69).

in future, these projects, heavily reliant on standardized technology, are envisioned to 'prove essential for smoothing EU travel and security' (eu-Lisa 2014a: 12).[7] Digital borders should govern in a way that guarantees mobility in a secure environment, allowing freedom (of movement) and security.

5.2 *Filtering Mobility for a Secure Environment*

On the one hand, an open Europe requires guaranteeing and facilitating mobility, but on the other, increasing flows demand tightened controls and for movement to be restricted. Technology is thereby put forward as the key to easing this 'facilitation and control dilemma at the heart of border management', as Broeders and Hampshire (2013: 1203) call it. There is a strong belief that digital technology would reconcile these tensions between securitization and mobility, between the restriction of movement and enabling mobility in (neo)liberal globalization (Pallitto and Heyman 2008). ICTs are thus advocated as being vital factors in the Schengen zone and its market, for a politics of *harmonization*. For the EU, harmonized border management should regulate access to Europe in a globalized world, ideally governing *mobility in a secure environment* (CEC 2011a: 3). It is important to note that freedom (in this environment) is not necessarily opposed to security. As Didier Bigo (2011) clarifies, freedom is rather reframed as freedom of speed and movement, and transformed into 'dataveillance'. Mobility is ensured with increasing speed, circulation and comfort for normalized categories of *low risk* or *bona fide travellers*, but must be conditioned by intensified control and the potential banishment of travellers that are classified as belonging to high-risk categories (Scheel 2013: 592). Information gathering thereby becomes the prerequisite in order to make all types of border (crossings) become subject to digitalization that aims to both facilitate and control mobility (harmonized less by border guards but rather by specialists in charge of large-scale IT systems).

Borders (and their work) are here imagined as smart, seamless, efficient; not as barriers but rather as a filtering multiple-state process. William Walters' metaphor of a 'firewall' (2006: 5) can grasp this character of ICT-mediated border control as a non-linear, non-territorial form of border, which aims to solve the task of reconciling 'high levels of circulation, transmission and movement'. Governing mobility in efficient ways does neither require a border as a wall or a fence, nor does it attempt to arrest movement entirely, but aims to function rather as a *filter*: 'The task of the firewall is to perform a kind of traffic control at the interface between what network security language calls different "zones of trust" [.... It] scans the flow of

[7]Future Smart Border systems in the Schengen zone suggest that data from more than 250 million third country nationals could be stored (eu-Lisa 2015c: 29).

information entering and leaving the system' (2006: 4–5).[8] Ideally, a 'continuous, uninterrupted exchange of data', as the eu-Lisa report (2014d: 6) formulates it, will guarantee constant production and sharing of information about individuals, leaving their digital traces when they travel; not just at the territorial entry point but also long before the territorial frontier. Mobility is governed by constructing *technologically dependent* types and categories of travellers, from 'low risk', 'bona fide' travellers or 'persons travelling on business', to 'high risk' travellers, data banned or 'new irregulars' (Bigo 2011). Technology should smoothly facilitate and/or restrict movement to different degrees, with mobile subjects being remotely *registered and identified*, ideally, at a distance.

6 Identification and Informatization: Acting at a Distance on Data Subjects

> With an ever-increasing range of uses and ever-evolving need for accurate and reliable personal identification, the field of biometrics is evolving rapidly. Software and hardware for biometric sample enrolment and comparison have advanced significantly in recent times, resulting in improved performance in identification, authentication and verification transactions. (eu-Lisa 2015c: 39)

The historical process of states gaining a monopoly on the 'legitimate means of movement' (Torpey 2000) has associated migration and identification closely with each other. In today's context of migration and the digitalization of identification through ICTs, the *body* is increasingly at the center of identification practices (Van der Ploeg and Sprenkels 2011). The extensive digital registration of migrants and travellers thus includes the deployment of biometrics, the 'automated recognition of individuals by means of physical characteristics' (2011: 73). The proliferation of biometrics is most pronounced in areas relating to border control (eu-Lisa 2015c: 25). Unsurprisingly, the further advancement of biometric identifiers is also a key element of the 2015 European Agenda on Migration (CEC 2015) and the Smart Border Package. Up to date, all databases store personal information about migrants and link it to biometric identifiers, which indicates its crucial role when elaborating *how* digital technologies are enacted. With regards to the concept of remote control, the categorization and sorting of travellers, it is worth pointing out how digital technology *interacts* with the body of the migrant/traveller, how authorities use biometric identification by regarding the body *as* information about the traveller's identity.

[8]Didier Bigo similarly explains the visions of IT and database experts on how borders should not represent 'lines', but function by being 'gaseous [and] constructed via a multitude of points' (2014: 217).

6.1 The 'Data Subjects'

All digital systems collect data from a so-called 'data subject'. The VIS, for example, contains alphanumeric data, such as the application number, status information, names, places and dates of new or prior applications and of biometric information (EU 2008: Article 5). In the EU regulations, the coded 'data subject' is defined as an 'identified or identifiable natural person' (EU 2006, 2008). Accordingly, the processing of personal information through digital networks, 'the free movement of such data' (EU 2006: L381/5), should be guaranteed. These definitions have typically been used and discussed in relation to data protection issues.[9] It is worth, however, considering the role of biometrics beyond privacy/personal information issues that rely on a standard distinction: between the virtual representation, or the abstract information about the body taken through technological/biometric means, and the 'natural' body itself. This distinction fails to see the specific way through which the body is targeted and 'liquefied' (Kuster and Tsianos 2013), how identity is not simply better *read* via new technologies but *established*. As van der Ploeg (1999) notes with regard to Eurodac, fingerprinting and processing information in digital systems, so widely used for border control and law enforcement purposes, is not simply about checking a pre-existing identity, but in fact the establishment of an 'embodied identity' (1999: 300). Thus, unlike identification documents, the use of biometric identification does not make the migrant more legible, but makes his/her body 'machine-readable': 'It transforms the body's surface into digital codes and ciphers to be read by a machine' (1999: 295). Through ensuring identity based on biometric data, the body can be treated as information and included in digital networks and information databanks. The subtle but also invasive and precarious character of this 'informatization of the body' (van der Ploeg and Sprenkels 2011: 99) can also be understood if we consider migrants' resistance to these practices. To avoid the enrolment in one of the systems (and the likelihood of deportation), illegalized migrants sometimes damage their fingers or cut off fingerprint ridges instead of just destroying their identification documents.[10] The informatization of the body thus becomes a crucial mechanism to control a mobile, undifferentiated population by relying less on travel identification documents. Biometric information depends on the *inscription* of identity on the migrant's body.

---

[9]For example, the position of a European Data Protection Supervisor, who is concerned with subject's privacy and the use of personal information, was established.

[10]See for example Van der Ploeg and Sprenkels (2011: 74–87). With regard to Eurodac and the Dublin Convention, see Kuster and Tsianos's report (2012).

6.2 Creating Immutable Mobiles

In the context of the aforementioned refined mode of remote control and the informatization of the body, *digitized governance of mobility* can be characterized as a way of 'dominating at a distance'. As Latour (1986, 1989) defines it, this is enabled through the production of *inscriptions* and the construction of *centers of calculation*. They bring elements:

> from far away [...] without bringing them in for good [...]. This paradox is resolved by devising inscriptions that retain simultaneously as little as much as possible by increasing either their mobility, stability or combinability. This compromise between presence and absence is often called information (1989: 241).

What the data subjects in the European digital databases do is 'present absent things' (1989: 8). Through digitalized forms of identification and the transformation of the migrant's body into a 'data double' (Haggerty and Ericson 2000), numbers and categories in the digital systems like the SIS, VIS or Eurodac can be regarded as inscriptions. They establish an embodied identity of migration in the Schengen area. As inscriptions, they are held immutable or stable by being stored in the databanks, but also made mobile when the data doubles are circulated and exchanged with increasing speed through these networks.[11] Moreover, they can be combined, matched with or compared to other information, made presentable and readable: *mobilized* 'while keeping them at a distance' (Latour 1989: 235). These data subjects or doubles as 'immutable mobiles' characterize the networks of digital border control and surveillance. Border functions such as the categorization of individuals can be projected far away from the territorial frontier and into digital space through their technologization. 'Detector tools' (Broeders and Hampshire 2013: 1207) interact with mobility flows and feed data information into networks with increasing speed that may be accessed in many places, not only by state authorities but also by non-state actors, from law enforcement bodies, embassies, border guards to airline companies or private security agencies.

Thus on the one hand, the VIS or SIS databanks are 'multiple-user scenarios' (Goldstein et al. 2008: 26). An assemblage of actors, enacting and interacting with these digital networks, monitoring mobility, accessing data systems and issuing alerts to border controls, police and customs, national judicial authorities, or authorities responsible for issuing and examining visa application and residence permits (see EU 2006: Art. 27). Issued alerts in databases like the SIS II, for example, can be 'coupled with an action [...] so that officers in other countries can act on the information' and that there are 'better linking options' between different entries at different locations (eu-Lisa 2014a: 8). On the other hand, digital networks can reach far beyond the Schengen territory but also remain at the center:

[11] The VIS will have a processing power of up to 450,000 transaction per hour; in the SIS database 4000 entries are created, updated or deleted per hour (eu-Lisa 2014b).

They act at a distance, collecting information from far away and reassemble it in their central databases, constantly updating and exchanging.

With the help of ICTs the mobile individual can be screened out of a larger flow of mobility as data subject/double, 'individualized, disassembled and reassembled' (Bigo 2014: 211), and ideally categorized long before the arrival at the territorial border. By acting at a distance the subjects can be targeted for intervention and their movement potentially predicted or anticipated by and in the (Eurodac, SIS, VIS) centers of calculation. As Kuster and Tsianos (2013) emphasize, the decisive point is that the numbers and categories in these digital networks do not simply describe or represent, but visualize, project and monitor mobile individuals or streams. Thus, 'totally new phenomena emerge', as Bruno Latour puts it elsewhere (1986: 30). In this sense, digital systems and networks are neither virtual representations of the Schengen borders, nor are they simply technical tools of border securitization. Rather, technology and society, technological control systems and (migrant) mobility are co-produced with the digital border. The digital border(s) thus emerge out of the interplay of different assemblages of actors and their interaction with digital technologies, networks and devices. The co-production of the digital border deterritorializes the Schengen border and is both liquefied and portable through its biometric identifiers—'carried by mobile bodies' as Amoore (2006: 338) observes. This implies a multiplication of borders, but also, as Kuster and Tsianos insist (2013), that borders are challenged in multiple ways and found deep within their territory. The border is *re-territorialized* every time at the many locations where digital control becomes possible, beyond the territory, at the territorial frontier or at the airport, on a bus or train, at stations, or even on the city streets.

7 Conclusion

The ongoing projects of Smart Borders in the EU as well as the continuing general shift toward the integration of ICT functionality into almost all aspects of daily life suggest that processes of digitization in the European border and the migration regime are far from completed. One can hardly ignore the technological imperative that is embedded in the diverse European projects of border securitization. As the border agency Frontex (2013) expressed it, the 'vision of the future' of border control lies in the deployment of new technologies. This includes the use of digital systems and the rapid proliferation of biometrics that respond to the needs for reliable and accurate personal identification. This chapter has explained how these technologies are deployed and enacted throughout the governance of European border to identify and categorize mobile individuals. First, it demonstrated how large-scaled ICT networks contribute to the refinement of remote control through the extra-territorialization effects that ideally perform bordering processes across and beyond the territory. Second, it argued that digital borders are deployed in order to guarantee mobility in a secure environment; technologically mediated European borders are not only envisioned to facilitate control, but also to allow circulation and movement. Finally, the chapter examined the enactment of ICTs and the crucial effects of *biometric* identification, through which the targeted body is used as a source of information. It argued that ICT supported border control functions like 'centers of calculation' (Latour 1989) that gather, interpret and categorize knowledge and use it for programs and practices of governance. The socio-technical processes of identification, data collection and categorization, in which human actors and technology interact at the various border sites and entry points, bring about the co-production of the digital border.

IT systems and digital networks in the European border regime should not be seen as the sum of a smooth running machine that controls and categorizes people with perfect efficiency according to the dichotomy of inclusion and exclusion. Although technologies (of control) are often presented as being successful tools, their political context and (often unintended) effects are also called into question. The digital storage of information regarding the first country rule of the Dublin Convention, for example, has led to serious questions and doubts about the border regime's rationality and efficiency, as countries are unwilling *and* incapable of registering all migrants, and so essentially ignore the convention. Accordingly, the Schengen area is currently experiencing a deep crisis through which states increasingly opt out of the Schengen agreement.

Focusing on the socio-technical arrangements of actors, networks and systems can illustrate the unstable processes of information collection and processing, and show how classifications or categories emerge that are increasingly dependent on these new technologies. More than ever, the treatment and distinction between trusted and distrusted, bona fide travellers, low-risk and high-risk groups, documented and undocumented migrants are decided and made by ICT mediated border control, conditioned by digital information, biometric data and images. It is clear that the technical challenges of these quickly advancing fields lead to a deeper specialization and, increasingly, require specialized knowledge of expertise. Bordering and border management is no longer performed solely by border guards but also by experts, programmers and computers in and through centers of calculation, trying to circulate information and control about travellers and migrants, contributing to the ongoing and complex constructions of digital borders.

References

Amoore, L. (2006). Biometric borders: Governing mobilities in the war on terror. *Political Geography, 25*, 336–351.

Balch, A., & Geddes, A. (2011). The development of the EU migration and asylum regime. In H. Dijstelbloem & A. Meijer (Eds.), *Migration and the new technological borders of Europe* (pp. 22–39). Hampshire, England: Palgrave Macmillan.

Balzacq, T. (2008). The policy tools of securitization: Information exchange, EU foreign and interior policies. *JCMS, 46*(1), 75–100.

Barry, A. (2001). *Political machines. Governing a technological society*. London: Athone Press.

Bigo, D. (2002). Security and immigration: Toward a critique of the governmentality of unease. *Alternatives, 27*, 63–92.
Bigo, D. (2011). Freedom and speed in enlarged borderzones. In V. Squire (Ed.), *The contested politics of mobility. Borderzones and irregularity* (pp. 51–73). London: Routledge.
Bigo, D. (2014). The (in)securitization practices of the three universes of EU Border control: Military/navy—Border guards/police—Database analysts. *Security Dialogue, 45*(3), 209–225.
Broeders, D. (2007). The new digital borders of Europe. EU databases and the surveillance of irregular migrants. *International Sociology, 22*(1), 71–92.
Broeders, D., & Hampshire, J. (2013). Dreaming of seamless borders: ICTs and the pre-emptive governance of mobility in Europe. *Journal of Ethnic and Migration Studies, 39*(8), 1201–1218.
Brouwer, E. (2008). *Digital borders and real rights. Effective remedies for third-country nationals in the Schengen information system*. Leiden: Martinus Nijhoff.
CEC (Commission of the European Communities). (2001). *Communication from the Commission to the Council and the European Parliament. Development of the Schengen Information System II (COM (2001) 720 final)*. Brussels: Commission of the European Communities.
CEC. (2005). *Communication from the Commission to the Council and the European Parliament on improved effectiveness, enhanced interoperability and synergies among European databases in the area of Justice and Home Affairs (COM(2005) 597 final)*. Brussels: Commission of the European Communities.
CEC. (2008). *Communication from the Commission to the European Parliament, the Council, the Economic and Social Committee and the Committee of the Regions. Preparing the next steps in border management in the European Union. (COM(2008) 69 final)*. Brussels: Commission of the European Communities.
CEC. (2009). *Communication from the Commission to the European Parliament and the Council. An area of freedom, security and justice serving the citizen (COM(2009) 262 final)*. Brussels: Commission of the European Communities.
CEC. (2011a). *The global approach to migration and mobility (COM(2011) 743 final)*. Brussels: Commission of the European Communities.
CEC. (2011b). *Communication on migration (COM(2011) 248 final)*. Brussels: Commission of the European Communities.
CEC. (2014). *Security in 2020: Meeting the challenge*. Luxembourg: Publications Office of the European Union. Retrieved from http://ec.europa.eu/dgs/home-affairs/financing/fundings/research-for-security/docs/security_research_brochure_2014_en.pdf
CEC. (2015). *A European agenda on migration (COM(2015) 240 final)*. Brussels: Commission of the European Communities.
CEU (Council of the European Union). (2000). Council Regulation (EC) No 2725/2000 of 11 December 2000 concerning the establishment of 'Eurodac' for the comparison of fingerprints for the effective application of the Dublin Convention. *Official Journal of the European Union*, L361.
CEU. (2008). Council Decision 2008/633/JHA of 23 June 2008 concerning access for consultation of the Visa Information System (VIS) by designate authorities of Member States and by Europol for the purposes of the prevention, detection and investigation of terrorist offences and of other serious criminal offences. *Official Journal of the European Union*, L218.
CEU. (2010). The Stockholm Programme—An open and secure serving and protecting citizens. *Official Journal of the European Union*, C115.
Chapman, G. (2009). Shaping technology for the 'good life': The technological imperative versus the social imperative. In D. G. Johnson & J. M. Wetmore (Eds.), *Technology and society. Building our sociotechnical future* (pp. 445–459). Cambridge: MIT Press.
Dijstelbloem, H., & Broeders, D. (2015). Border surveillance, mobility management and the shaping of non-publics in Europe. *European Journal of Social Theory, 18*(1), 21–38.
Dijstelbloem, H., Meijer, A., & Bester, M. (2011). The migration machine. In H. Dijstelbloem & A. Meijer (Eds.), *Migration and the new technological borders of Europe* (pp. 1–21). Hampshire: Palgrave Macmillan.

EPEC (European Policy Evaluation Consortium). (2004). *Study for the extended impact assessment of the visa information system. Final report.* Brussels: European Policy Evaluation Consortium.

EU. (2006). Regulation (EC) No 1987/2006 of the European Parliament and of the Council of 20 December 2006 on the establishment, operation and use of the second generation Schengen Information System (SIS II). *Official Journal of the European Union,* L381.

EU. (2008). Regulation (EC) No 767/2008 of the European Parliament and of the Council of 9 July 2008 concerning the Visa Information System (VIS) and the exchange of data between Member States on short-stay visas (VIS Regulation). *Official Journal of the European Union,* L218.

eu-Lisa. (2014a). *EU-LISA in action. IT in the service of a more open and secure Europe.* Luxembourg: Publication Office of the European Union.

eu-Lisa. (2014b). *SIS II—2013 statistics.* European Agency for the operational management of large-scale IT systems in the area of freedom, security and justice. Retrieved from http://www.eulisa.europa.eu/Publications/p_reports/Pages/default.aspx

eu-Lisa. (2014c). *eu-LISA annual activity report 2013.* Luxembourg: Publications Office of the European Union.

eu-Lisa. (2014d, October 1). *1st eu-LISA international conference. Smart borders: A faster and safer way to Europe.* Tallinn: Conference Report. Retrieved from http://www.eulisa.europa.eu/Publications/p_reports/Pages/default.aspx

eu-Lisa. (2014e). *Report on the technical functioning of VIS, including the security thereof, pursuant to Article 50(3) of the VIS Regulation.* European Agency for the operational management of large-scale IT systems in the area of freedom, security and justice. Retrieved from http://www.eulisa.europa.eu/Publications/Reports/eulisa_Report%20VIS%20en.pdf

eu-Lisa. (2015a). *Annual Report on the 2014 activities of the Central System of Eurodac pursuant to Article 24(1) of Regulation (EC) No 2725/2000.* European Agency for the operational management of large-scale IT systems in the area of freedom, security and justice. Retrieved from http://eulisa.europa.eu/Publications/Pages/default.aspx

eu-Lisa. (2015b). *Testing the borders of the future. Smart borders pilot: The results in brief.* European Agency for the operational management of large-scale IT systems in the area of freedom, security and justice.

eu-Lisa. (2015c). *Biometrics in large-scale IT. Recent trends, current performance capabilities, recommendations for the near future.* European Agency for the operational management of large-scale IT systems in the area of freedom, security and justice.

Frontex. (2013). Border control in the information age. *Frontex, Feature Stories.* Retrieved from http://frontex.europa.eu/feature-stories/border-control-in-the-information-age-udh57L. Accessed 15 January 2015.

Goldstein, J., Angeletti, R., Holzbach, M., Konrad, D., & Snijder, M. (2008). Final report. Large-scale biometrics deployment in Europe. Identifying challenges and threats. *JRC Scientific and Technical Reports.* Seville: Office for Official Publications of the European Communities.

Guild, E., Carrera, S., & Geyer, F. (2008) The commission's new border package: Does it take us one step closer to a 'cyber-fortress Europe'? *CEPS Policy Brief, No.145.*

Haggerty, K. D., & Ericson, R. V. (2000). The surveillant assemblage. *British Journal of Sociology, 51*(4), 605–622.

Harbers, H. (Ed.). (2005). *Inside the politics of technology. Agency and normativity in the co-production of technology and society.* Amsterdam: Amsterdam University Press.

Hayes, M., & Vermeulen, M. (2012). *Borderline. EU Border Surveillance Initiatives. An assessment of the costs and its impact on fundamental rights.* Berlin: Heinrich-Böll-Stiftung.

Heimeshoff, L., Hess, S., Kron, S., Schwenken, H., & Trzeciak, M. (Eds.). (2014). *Grenzregime II: Migration—Kontrolle—Wissen. Transnationale Perspektiven.* Berlin: Assoziation A.

Jasanoff, S. (Ed.). (2004). *States of knowledge. The co-production of science and social order.* London: Routledge.

Johnson, C., Jones, R., Paasi, A., Amoore, L., Mountz, A., Salter, M., et al. (2011). Interventions on rethinking the 'border' in border studies. *Political Geography, 30*, 61–69.

Kasparek, B., & Tsianos, V. S. (2014). Whatever works! Kontinuität und Krise des Schengener systems. In L. Heimeshoff, S. Hess, S. Kron, H. Schwenken, & M. Trzeciak (Eds.), *Grenzregime II: Migration—Kontrolle—Wissen. Transnationale Perspektiven* (pp. 41–57). Berlin: Assoziation A.

Kuster, B., & Tsianos, V. (2012). Thematic report 'border crossings' (WP 4). *MIG@NET transnational digital networks, migration and gender*, Deliverable No. 6. Retrieved from http://www.mignetproject.eu/wp-content/uploads/2012/10/MIGNET_Deliverable_6_Thematic_report_Border_crossings.pdf

Kuster, B., & Tsianos, V. (2013). How to liquefy a moving body: Eurodac und die Digitalisierung der Europäischen Grenze. In Arbeitsgruppe Informatik in Bildung und Gesellschaft (Ed.), *Biometrische Identitäten und ihre Rolle in den Diskursen um Sicherheit und Grenzen* (pp. 19–36). Berlin: Humbold-Universität.

Latour, B. (1986). Visualisation and cognition: Drawing things together. In H. Kuklick (Ed.), *Knowledge and society. Studies in the sociology of culture past and present* (Vol. 6, pp. 1–40). Greenwich, CT: JAI Press.

Latour, B. (1989). *Science in action. How to follow scientists and engineers through society*. Cambridge, MA: Harvard University Press.

Marin, L. (2011). Is Europe turning into a 'technological fortress'? Innovation and technology for the management of EU's external borders: Reflections on FRONTEX and EUROSUR. In M. A. Heldewegg & E. Kica (Eds.), *Regulating technological innovation: A multidisciplinary approach* (pp. 131–151). Hampshire, England: Palgrave Macmillan.

Mezzadra, S., & Neilson, B. (2013). *Border as method. Or, the multiplication of labor*. London: Duke University Press.

MHA (Migration and Home Affairs). (2013). 'Smart borders': Enhancing mobility and security. *European Commission, Migration and Home Affairs Funds 2014-20*. Retrieved from http://ec.europa.eu/dgs/home-affairs/what-is-new/news/news/2013/20130228_01_en.htm

MHA. (2015). Investing in an open and secure Europe. Two funds for the 2014-20 period [online Infographic]. *European Commission, Migration and Home Affairs Funds 2014-20*. Retrieved from http://ec.europa.eu/dgs/home-affairs/e-library/multimedia/infographics/index_en.htm#080126248ec451b7/c_

Moulier-Boutang, Y. (1998). *De l'esclavage au salariat: économie historique du salariat bride*. Paris: Presses Universitaires de France.

Paasi, A. (2007). Boundaries as social processes: Territoriality in the world of flows. *Geopolitics, 3* (1), 69–88.

Pallitto, R., & Heyman, J. (2008). Theorizing cross-border mobility: Surveillance, security and identity. *Surveillance & Society, 5*(3), 315–333.

Papadopoulos, D., Stephenson, N., & Tsianos, V. (2008). *Escape routes. Control and subversion in the twenty-first century*. Ann Arbor, MI: Pluto Press.

Rumford, C. (2006). Introduction. Theorizing borders. *European Journal of Social Theory, 9*(2), 155–169.

Salter, M. B., & Mutlu, C. E. (2013). Asymmetric borders: The Canada-Czech Republic 'visa war' and the question of rights. In D. Bigo, S. Carrera, & E. Guild (Eds.), *Foreigners, refugees or minorities? Rethinking people in the context of border controls and visas* (pp. 113–130). Farnham, England: Ashgate.

Scheel, S. (2013). Autonomy of migration despite its securitisation? Facing the terms and conditions of biometric rebordering. *Millennium: Journal of International Studies, 41*(3), 575–600.

Torpey, J. (2000). *The invention of the passport: Surveillance, citizenship and the state*. Cambridge: Cambridge University Press.

Van der Ploeg, I. (1999). The illegal body: 'Eurodac' and the politics of biometric identification. *Ethics and Information Technology, 1*, 295–302.

Van der Ploeg, I., & Sprenkels, I. (2011). Migration and the machine-readable body: Identification and biometrics. In H. Dijstelbloem & A. Meijer (Eds.), *Migration and the new technological borders of Europe* (pp. 68–104). Hampshire, England: Palgrave Macmillan.
Van Munster, R. (2009). *Securitizing immigration. The politics of risk in the EU*. London: Palgrave Macmillan.
Walters, W. (2006). Rethinking borders beyond the state. *Comparative European Politics, 4*, 141–159.
Zolberg, A. R. (2006). Managing a world on the move. *Population & Development Review, 32*, 222–253.

Paul Trauttmansdorff studied Philosophy at the University of Vienna and socioeconomics at the Vienna University of Economics. He holds a master's degree in political sociology from the London School of Economics and Political Science. His master thesis examined technological change in the European border regime. Paul's research interests are related to democratization theory, security studies, transitional justice and conflict studies, nationalism, and social movement theory.

Politics of the Schengen/Dublin System: The Case of the European Migrant and Refugee Crisis

Marko Lovec

Abstract The Schengen/Dublin system requiring the first EU member state of entry to take full responsibility for migrants and applicants for asylum has placed an asymmetrical burden on EU border states, resulting in an emphasis being placed on the fight against illegal migration and the reduction of protections for refugees. The system has been explained in terms of intergovernmental decision-making and the dominance of security discourse which enabled member states to block the sharing of burdens. This chapter argues against this approach, grounded in mid-range theory, and finds that the regulatory framework is not due to a particular institutional-discursive setting as such but rather due to deeper causes such as the absence of community policies in areas relevant to migrations and asylum. Research into the interaction between issues, positions, decision-making rules and rhetoric applied on the EU level during the European migrant and refugee crisis of 2015 demonstrates that (a) the sharing of burdens as such was in fact not a disputed issue, (b) that there is broad support for the existing policy among member states and (c) that departure from a veto setting triggered nationalist security rhetoric that deepened the crisis suggesting the role of causes at a deeper level.

Keywords Migration • Asylum • European Union • Migrant and refugee crisis • Border • Intergovernmental • Securitization

1 Introduction: Fortress Europe

In the European Union (EU) migrant and asylum policy is regulated by the Schengen/Dublin system. This consists of the Dublin regulation which requires the first member state of entry to take full responsibility for migrants and refugees, and the Schengen agreement, which removed internal border controls in return for the standardization of controls on external borders (Poptcheva 2015: 3). The system has placed substantial burden on border countries, resulting in an emphasis on the fight against illegal immigration and the reduction of international standards for

---

M. Lovec (✉)
Centre of International Relations (CIR), University of Ljubljana, Ljubljana, Slovenia
e-mail: Marko.Lovec@fdv.uni-lj.si

C. Günay, N. Witjes (eds.), *Border Politics*, DOI 10.1007/978-3-319-46855-6_8

refugee protection (ibid.). In 2015, Europe faced growing immigration pressures, with the number of applications for asylum reaching one million. The Dublin regulation was subsequently suspended, due to the inability of member states to agree on sharing the burden via refugee quotas, resulting in the rise of secondary migration. In order to manage migrant flows, controls were re-established on internal borders, thus placing Schengen on hiatus.

The distribution of responsibilities for migrants and refugees under the Dublin/ Schengen system has been explained in terms of (a) an intergovernmental mode of decision-making which has enabled each government to block any decision that would make its position worse in terms of its share of burdens, and (b) with the dominance of a security discourse that has legitimized the role of high politics in this field by depicting migrants as a national security threat (Huysmans 2000; Guild 2006; Thielemann et al. 2010; Mouzourakis 2014). The existing explanatory framework suggests that the political deadlock resulting in the 2015 European migrant crisis was a consequence of the failure of an intergovernmental decision-making setting and a security discourse that acted as an institutional-discursive trap. Against this argument, which is based on a 'mid-range' theory approach towards European integrations (Wiener and Diez 2009), this chapter would like to argue that the crisis was not a result of the particular setting as such, but was rather due to deeper causes, especially the absence of common policies in other areas relevant to migrations and asylum, such as social support and labour market policies. To test the argument the current political decision-making process in the EU was explored, observing how key issues, the positions of governments and EU institutions, and decision-making rules and rhetoric interacted and were applied. The research draws on official documents and media reports referring to the EU-level decision-making process.

The chapter begins by explaining the Schengen/Dublin system in the context of the EU's migrant and asylum politics. It elaborates the role of the intergovernmental-security setting as seen by the mid-range theory of European integration and puts forward an alternative view that points out the possible role of deeper-level causes. In the empirical section the European migrant and refugee crisis is studied. The research first takes a narrative approach to two distant stages of the 2015 crisis: the crisis of the system in the first half of the year, and the suspension of regulations in the second half. This is followed by an analytical examination of the crisis.

2 The Conceptual Framework: The Intergovernmental-Security Trap Revised

According to Meyers (2000: 1247), migration policy has often been equated with immigration regulation policy or border control policy, which refers to rules and procedures governing the admission of different categories of foreign nationals crossing borders, thus pointing at the central role of controlling immigration.

Following the increase of immigration since the 1980s, and the unwillingness of developed countries to take further economic immigrants, the fight against illegal immigration gained importance (Düvell 2011). Another important aspect related to migration has been migrant integration policy, which refers to the specific rights and obligations of immigrants within the receiving country (Meyers 2000). While nation states have kept migration policies firmly in their hands, refugees, representing a special category of migrants, have been an exception. Following the 1951 Geneva Convention and the subsequent protocol, refugees were defined as people facing the risk of persecution and inhumane treatment in their home countries. According to the obligations assumed, they should be provided international protection and should, in line with the 'non-refoulement' principle, not be returned (ibid.). In practice, refugees cross borders illegally and the line between economic and political causes for migration has become increasingly blurred, with all migrants typically trying to apply for asylum. Thus, the fight against illegal immigration and international protection have, in spite of their opposite objectives, become enmeshed (King 2012).

There is no common migrations and asylum policy in the EU since member states have not been willing to transfer their authority to the supranational level. A framework of agreements, however, regulates individual aspects of migrations, supported by a set of Community instruments to make the implementation of agreements more efficient. The EU has enabled member state citizens to move freely, to study, work and enjoy related benefits in other member states. This 'internal mobility' is not considered as being a part of the migrations policy but rather as a right based on EU citizenship (Weinar 2011; Sommer 2013). In order to remove the obstacles related to internal border controls, these controls were removed under the Schengen agreement of the 1990s, in return for common standards of control on external borders. With the removal of internal border controls, the issue of the distribution of responsibility for applicants for asylum emerged. By being able to move freely within the Schengen area, migrants could decide in which country to apply for asylum. This 'asylum shopping' could result in a 'moral hazard' situation in which border countries that were not target countries for migrants themselves, would not implement border controls effectively. Furthermore, asylum seekers could submit multiple applications in different countries, which would result in 'asylum orbiting' in terms of increased administrative burdens for the countries involved and a prolonged 'legal' stay (Poptcheva 2015: 3). In order to address these issues, the Dublin regulation was agreed upon. It requires the country of entry to take full responsibility for the applicant, including the processing of applications and, if so decided, the provision of asylum. In cases of secondary migration to another member state, migrants could be returned, except for humanitarian reasons such as family reunification.

The regulation, which has 'put a lot of weight on countries located at [Europe's] border' (Poptcheva 2015: 3–4), has been criticized from the very beginning. The border countries, in trying to reduce their burdens have placed greater stress on fighting illegal immigration, thus affecting the chances of refugees entering the EU as part of mixed migration flows being dealt with appropriately (Guild 2006: 637).

The overall international protection standards in the EU have declined as a result (Thielemann et al. 2010: 33). What is more, some authors (Mouzourakis 2014: 12) suggest that the system has not really been efficient since illegal migration within the EU has strengthened. The approach was not limited to the relations within the EU. In their relations with third countries, individual members and the EU as a whole have prioritized the fight against illegal migration and, in turn, often supported non-democratic regimes that were the cause of migrations in the first place (Kostakopoulou 2000: 512–13; Demmelhuber 2011; Weinar 2011: 15). Following the fall of the Berlin Wall, a lot of pressure was placed on the newly emerged countries, who later became candidates for EU membership, to implement strict border controls and prevent illegal immigration (Grabbe 2000).

The Schengen/Dublin system became part of Community law with the Amsterdam treaty (Kostakopoulou 2000). To improve its functioning, it received several upgrades, including the introduction of new instruments: the EU asylum directive limiting the asylum procedure to maximum 6 months; the Frontex[1] agency coordinating external border protection; the fingerprint regulation and the Eurodac fingerprint system; the European Asylum Support Office (EASO) supporting and overviewing the procedures; and a special fund financing the integration (Weinar 2011: 2–3; Thielemann and Armstrong 2013: 154–155). There was also a discussion of a more comprehensive approach towards migrations involving legal migration and cooperation with third countries (Weinar 2011: 4; Poptcheva 2015: 5, 7). The Lisbon treaty established a basis for enhanced coherence and consistency in foreign policy and introduced the EU External Action Service to support it.

2.1 The Intergovernmental-Security Nexus

The Schengen/Dublin regulation, and its implications in terms of the high burden carried by border countries and resulting stress on the fight against illegal immigration, has been related to the intergovernmental decision-making framework and the dominance of security concerns in the field, with the two being considered mutually reinforcing. The intergovernmental framework refers to the setting in which individual governments cooperate only to the extent to which this directly improves their position, under the condition that their interests are relatively well defined and strong. The agreements thus correspond to the minimum common denominator of the individual interests of governments. Such a setting is typically institutionalized in a form of decision-making by consent that prevents the community institutions from enforcing decisions against the interests of individual governments (Keohane and Nye 1977; Moravcsik 1997, 1998; Moravcsik and Schimmelfennig 2009). In the particular case of the Schengen/Dublin system, the

[1]Frontext stands for *Frontières extérieures*.

intergovernmental framework, characterized by a veto-player setting, is considered to enable individual member states to block decisions on sharing the burdens.

The roots of an 'intergovernmental mode' go back to cooperation between ministers of interior affairs over the fight against illegal immigration and on border control which began in the 1980s as the issue emerged (Düvell 2011). This cooperation took place outside the community framework since the internal affairs were not part of community competences at the time. This kind of cooperation setting, which was under weak community influence, is considered to have 'structured' the approach (Bigo 1996; Guiraudon 2000). The Amsterdam treaty communautarized the Schengen and Dublin regulation and established Justice and Home Affairs (JHA) as a part of the 'third pillar' policies that were based on coordination between member states, meaning that pressure for an EU policy was still weak (Kostakopoulou 2000). The Lisbon treaty introduced certain changes (see Espinoza and Moraes 2012 for details) by subjecting the JHA to the ordinary decision-making procedure, meaning that decisions in this field could now be taken by qualified majority vote (QMV), thus preventing individual ministers from blocking them. Secondly, the European parliament was given the right to co-decide, which could strengthen the democratic control of the process and the sense of community interests. In addition to that, European courts, by rejecting transfers of migrants back to individual countries for humanitarian reasons, eroded the logic of the Schengen/Dublin system and contradicted the interests of national governments (Mouzourakis 2014: 13–14). The effects of these changes have, however, been limited. The QMV only theoretically increased the opportunity for a proposal to be passed. In practice, ministers of interior affairs continued to decide upon consent. The European parliament could only veto the new proposals but could not change the existing laws. The judicial authorities merely operated within the limits of the existing system (Mouzourakis 2014: 14, 26).

The intergovernmental framework has been related with the dominant role of the security discourse in the field. The security discourse has established migrations as an issue of cross-border smuggling operations, organized crime and terrorism, thus subjecting migrations policy to the authority of ministers of interior affairs and police (Huysmans 2000: 760).[2] By depicting migrants as a security threat, security discourse has put this issue into the domain of high politics that has typically been related with the exclusive politics of national interests (Weaver 1996; Huysmans 2000: 757). According to Huysmans (2000: 753), presenting migrants as a 'destabilizing factor or dangerous challenge as opposed to cultural homogeneity makes the inclusion of immigrants, asylum seekers and refugees more difficult and has implications for the chances of [...] solidarity and distribution of rights and duties [on the EU level] that is not determined by cultural identity.'

The security discourse has been challenged by economic and humanitarian discourses (Sommer 2013: 46). Economic discourse is not necessarily reserved

---

[2]The central role of the ministries of interior affairs, police and security experts has been both the cause and consequence of the dominance of the security issues.

for the ‘low politics’ (Keohane 1984). In the field of EU’s migrations policy, it re-emerged in the 2000s as a part of discussions on unsustainable social security systems due to the ageing of European society, the need to make home labour markets flexible and to enter the ‘global fight for brains’ (Castles 2006; Sommer 2013: 47, 50, 56–58). Human rights or humanitarian discourses, pointing out the importance of basic rights and responsibility for providing them (Sommer 2013: 68, 70), criticized the Schengen/Dublin system in terms of the reduction of international protection standards and argued for a solidarity approach, and more open border regimes, as well as for changed policy towards third countries (Demmelhuber 2011).

2.2 *Bringing National Interests Back in*

As presented above, the majority of authors working in the field hold that the intergovernmental institutional setting of the Schengen/Dublin system, and the prevailing security discourses are responsible for the lack of solidarity and the reduction of international protection standards, resulting in ‘Fortress Europe’. This argument is in line with the so-called ‘mid-range’ theoretical approach towards the European integration that looks into the socio-institutional contexts in which a political process is embedded. The ‘long-range’ approach focuses on the question of why certain socio-institutional forms of cooperation evolve, that is it is concerned with the EU polity. The ‘short-range’ approach focuses on explaining/understanding the outcomes of the political process, such as EU policy while ‘mid-range’ theory focuses on how socio-institutional forms interfere with power struggles, such as the way rules and identities promote or inhibit individual interests, or in other words EU politics (Wiener and Diez 2009). The general problem with mid-range approaches is that, based on their theoretical assumptions, they often take the role of particular institutional-discursive factors as being decisive causes (Moravcsik and Checkel 2001) when in fact they are merely consequences of more basic or deeper level causes. The fact that agencies act in accordance with certain frameworks and ideas does not imply a causal relationship with certain types of actions.

As seen in the above discussion, the Schengen/Dublin system is not much more than a common border policy, while a number of other issues relevant to migration such as legal migration, mobility and integration of migrants, as well as social and labour market policies to which these issues refer, are not being addressed on a community level. As a result, member states have not been willing to let go of the powers requiring agreement to any changes concerning the intake of third country nationals. According to Meyers (2000) and Hollifield (2008), there has been a lack of discussion of the national politics of migrations.[3] Existing research implies that

[3]More recently Tichenor (2015) has addressed this issue for the USA.

migrations policy is affected significantly by socio-economic factors. Following Weaver et al. (1993, in Meyers 2000: 1265), 'in Western Europe, societal insecurity has replaced state sovereignty as the key to success or failure of European integration, pushing concerns about identity and immigration to the top of the political agenda.' Migrants have been used as scapegoats to 'remedy declining political legitimacy' (Huysmans 2000: 769). Nationalism, including its extreme version in terms of xenophobia and chauvinism, has been considered as a way of reclaiming political authority through high politics in response to poor governance (Mouzourakis 2014: 24).

3 The Case of the European Migrant and Refugee Crisis

Critics of the mid-range approaches argue that a methodology of research that aims to establish the role of a particular institutional-discursive setting as such should be applied in a way that also enables rejection of the given argument, for example, by pointing at a possible alternative explanation (Moravcsik 1998, 1999; Moravcsik and Checkel 2001). In order to test the role of an intergovernmental-security setting for the European migrant and refugee crisis against an alternative explanation, such as the absence of community policies in areas relevant to migration, this chapter looks into the interaction of (a) the main issues, (b) positions of governments and EU institutions and (c) the decision-making rules and rhetoric applied during the course of the crisis. In particular, it is interested in what were the key issues discussed, which positions governments took and what was the role of decision-making rules and rhetoric for the outcomes of the process. The main issues, positions, rules and rhetoric are established based on an analysis of formal documents issued by EU institutions and media reports. A number of mainstream international media has been consulted to exclude any important differences in reporting. The presentation of the results begins with an overview of the political process divided into two stages the crisis of the first half of 2015 and the suspension of the regulation in the second half of the year.

3.1 The Crisis of the Schengen/Dublin System

Illegal immigration to Europe has been on the rise since the crises that arose in the Middle East and North African region following the 'Arab Spring' of 2011. Italy and Greece, typically the countries of first entry, faced dramatic growth in immigration pressures. The scope of secondary migrations as reflected in applications for asylum in inland EU member states also increased. The Mediterranean Sea took on a growing death toll. After the sinking of a ship in April 2015 that resulted in over 800 deaths, European leaders brought migration and border policy onto the agenda (BBC 2015a). On 20 April 2015, the European Commission published a proposed

10-point plan which, apart from strengthening the fight against smugglers, proposed considering the emergency relocation of refugees within the EU according to Article 78 (3) of the Lisbon treaty, and a voluntary resettlement programme to take refugees directly from camps in third countries (European Commission 2015a). At the European Council of 23 April 2015, German Chancellor Angela Merkel pushed for 'objective' relocation criteria (Huggler and Marszal 2015). David Cameron the prime minister of the UK, which is not a Schengen member,[4] declined his country's participation. In spite of arguments set out by the European Council President Donald Tusk on the need to sacrifice some national interests in these extraordinary circumstances, the meeting ended without a concrete agreement (European Council 2015a). In its subsequent statement, the European Parliament (2015) criticized leaders of member states for displaying a 'lack of solidarity.'

In May 2015, the Commission laid out its plan in more concrete terms (European Commission 2015a–c). It proposed relocating 40,000 migrants; 24,000 from Italy and 16,000 from Greece. The number corresponded to 40 % of migrants who had arrived since the beginning of the year and who were 'in clear need for protection' in terms of coming from nationalities for which the rate of recognition of refugee status was above 75 %. Relocation would take place over 2 years, with member state allocations based on an 'objective key' consisting of the total population (40 %), GDP (40 %), unemployment rate (10 %) and existing efforts (10 %). The target number for voluntary resettlement was 20,000. After consulting the European Parliament, the Council would take the final decision on relocation using QMV. The proposal triggered criticism with a number of governments. The Prime Minister of Hungary, Victor Orbán called the plan 'mad and unfair' (Euractiv 2015). At the time, Hungary was itself facing a rapid growth of applications for asylum and the government feared that the relocation would act as a 'pull factor' (ibid.). At the European Council on 25–26 June 2015, all EU leaders agreed to participate in the relocation. Exceptions were Ireland and Denmark, which have special positions in regard to Schengen/Dublin regime, and with the UK, which was explicitly not taking part. The relocation quotas were, however, to be agreed by consensus and not by QMV (European Council 2015b). Italian Prime Minister Matteo Renzi, commenting on the latter said that: 'If this is Europe, you can keep it' (Graham-Harrison et al. 2015). On 20 July, the JHA Council reached agreement on relocation quotas. Compared with 'objective quotas', the quotas that were agreed corresponded more to the actual intake taking place due to secondary migration (JHA Council 2015a).

Reflecting on the early crisis stage, it can be seen that the main issue was with the asymmetrical pressures on the two border member states, resulting in the failure of Dublin/Schengen system in terms of growing secondary migration. Emergency

---

[4]At the time, 22 out of 28 EU member states participated in Schengen; the UK and Ireland had opt-outs while Bulgaria, Croatia, Cyprus and Romania would join after fulfilling the criteria. In addition, four European Free Trade Agreement (EFTA) countries participated: Iceland, Lichtenstein, Norway and Switzerland. The Dublin regulation applied to all EU member states but Denmark and was applied in EFTA members.

relocation, which was addressing the issue, was only objected to by some of the member states that were not part of the Schengen/Dublin system. And even in the case of the UK, which was the only member state that was explicitly against participation, its position was perhaps more related with the coming referendum on the British membership of the EU rather than with the issue as such, since the British government did not want to provide supporters of the leave vote with an additional grievance. Other member states were rather opposed to the 'objective key' which tried to enforce additional redistribution of migrants between the target and non-target member states. The agreement by leaders of member states to make the decision upon consent, corresponding to an intergovernmental framework, enabled them to bring the final decision on quotas closer to the actual intake based on the secondary migration. The fact that each member state was able to weight the proposal against what would happen in case of a non-decision helped to save the Schengen/Dublin system. The humanitarian concerns were raised in support of the relocation and objective quotas. While from a humanitarian perspective, taking the burden off the shoulders of the border countries was important in terms of maintaining asylum standards, the latter did not have much to do with the particular redistribution of migrants within the rest of the EU. Furthermore, the voluntary resettlement target, which was much more important from a humanitarian point of view, was met.

3.2 The Schengen and Dublin Regulation Suspended

Since May 2015, the migrant wave on the West Balkans route had been strengthening. Migrants who first entered the EU/Schengen area in Greece continued onto Macedonia and Serbia, and re-entered the EU/Schengen area in Hungary. The Hungarian government responded by announcing rigorous measures to fight illegal immigration, including building a border fence. The German Chancellor Angela Merkel criticized Hungarian authorities, arguing that there was 'no legal limit to refugee numbers' (Graham-Harrison et al. 2015). In August 2015, Germany announced that it was suspending Dublin unilaterally with regard to the migrants from Syria. It was expecting to receive 800,000 applications for asylum by the end of the year (ibid.). Simultaneously, internal border controls were established, thus temporarily suspending Schengen (Martin and Macdonald 2015).[5] After the death of a 3-year old migrant on a Greek beach in early September 2015, which was widely reported by the media and became a cause célèbre, Germany decided to suspend Dublin in general. Together with France, it called upon the Commission to come up with a new, permanent, binding and objective regime of relocation (Graham-Harrison et al. 2015). Hungarian Prime Minister Orbán was highly critical

[5]The Schengen agreement allows for a temporary re-introduction of border controls for up to 2/6 months.

of this 'German' policy, saying that it was 'inviting migrants' and thus exposing the Christian Europe to 'Muslim threat' (ibid.). He also said that his country would not take part in any relocation and that the migrants were a 'German, not a European problem' (ibid.). Since they were not able to hold the influx back at its border before the fence was built, Hungarian authorities were, nevertheless, left with no other choice but to direct migrants to Austria. Leaders of Poland, Hungary, Czech Republic and Slovakia, known as the Visegrád group, at a meeting in September 2015, jointly declared that they would not accept any compulsory long-term quota (ibid.).

In the new plan announced on 9 September 2015, the European Commission proposed the relocation of a further 120,000 migrants, 15,600 from Italy, 50,400 from Greece and 54,000 from Hungary (European Commission 2015d). The number corresponded to 62 % of people 'in clear need of international protection' who entered Italy and Greece irregularly between July and August 2015, and in Hungary since the beginning of the year 2015. The relocation quotas were based on the objective key rejected in spring (ibid.). In addition, the proposal included a permanent relocation mechanism that could be triggered at any time by the Commission (European Commission 2015e). At the JHA Council meeting on 14 September 2015, there was, in principle, agreement on the second relocation package, but not on the distribution key, and the permanent mechanism was widely opposed (JHA Council 2015b).[6] In response, German Chancellor Merkel and her Austrian colleague Werner Faymann pushed to take a decision based upon QMV in order to outvote individual 'troublemakers'. On 22 September 2015, following the procedure in the European parliament, the objective key was approved by the JHA Council, with the Czech Republic, Hungary, Romania and Slovakia voting against and Finland abstaining (JHA Council 2015c). Slovakian Prime Minister Robert Fico who was facing elections at the time said that as long as he was in charge they would not take a single migrant. Slovakia immediately announced that it would fight relocation by legal means (BBC 2015b).

In October 2015, after Hungary finished construction of the fence on its southern border and tightened its border regime, the migrant flow was diverted, re-entering the EU/Schengen in Slovenia. In October attitudes towards migrants started to turn negative in a number of member states. Internal border controls were increasingly used as a way of keeping migrants out of territories and distributing pressure towards neighbouring countries. The Dutch government proposed the establishment of a 'mini-Schengen' that would consist of the Benelux countries, Germany and Austria. The new Polish government argued that it would not accept a migrant quota. At the European Council Summit in La Valletta in early November 2015, the re-establishment of Schengen and protection of the external borders re-emerged as a priority over humanitarian concerns (European Council 2015c).

In comparison with the early stage of the crisis, the second stage saw greater divergence in views between member states with Germany and, initially, some other member states, placing humanitarian need at the forefront and arguing for an

[6]At the Council, the June 2015 agreement on the first relocation package was formally approved.

'open doors' policy while individual Eastern member states argued in favour of a more restrictive regime. Since changes to the Schengen/Dublin regime required for consent that would be difficult to attain, Germany made the decision to suspend it unilaterally and to take in migrants directly. The signal of a changed EU policy attracted further migration. In the absence of internal borders, the migrant wave spilled into other EU member states as well. Simultaneously, a new relocation package was proposed involving objective quotas. This time, the decision was to be made using QMV, thus enforcing it on individual members. Perceiving that they were being pushed into a corner, governments, who had previously only objected to the 'objective' quotas began to reject the relocation altogether. Moreover, to legitimize nationalist reaction, a security discourse was increasingly utilised, resulting in growing hostility towards migrants. By the end of the 2015, the escalation of nationalist responses took the focus away from humanitarian issues completely. Thus, the departure from the Schengen/Dublin system, and the intergovernmental framework on which it was based, in fact produced negative effects on the humanitarian concerns that were used as a reason for the departure in the first place. Consent re-emerged on the need to re-impose the Schengen/Dublin system.

3.3 Positions of the EU Governments

The positions of member states on the issues concerning the Schengen/Dublin system demonstrate to what extent the specific decision-making setting was responsible for the crisis by influencing proposals for possible changes to the existing regulation. As seen above, there were two major issues of concern: (a) the distribution of burdens in terms of balancing between solidarity and responsibility and (b) the balance between humanitarian and security objectives (Table 1). With regard to the distribution of burdens (columns in the Table 1), the proposals of 'objective relocation' and 'relocation' can be considered to be 'strongly pro-solidarity' oriented and 'pro-solidarity' oriented while 'joint border operations' and 'own responsibility for border protection' stress more the 'responsibility for migrants' and 'full individual responsibility'. Considering the alternative objectives (rows in Table 1), proposals to 'increase absorption of migrants' and 'keep existing asylum standards' can be considered 'strongly pro-humanitarian' and 'pro-humanitarian', while the ideas of 'external' and 'internal border protection' are more 'security oriented' and 'strongly security oriented'. The policy proposals of introducing relocation quotas and joint border operations as a means of striking a balance between solidarity and responsibility; ensuring the provision of certain asylum standards while maintaining external border controls, and thus also balancing humanitarian and security objectives, correspond to the existing Schengen/Dublin system in legal and policy terms (depicted by bold-formatted area in the Table 1).

As seen from the preceding discussion of the political process during the crisis, a large majority of member states supported relocation quotas and joint border

Table 1 Positions of selected EU member states on the Schengen/Dublin system

Distribution of burdens/ objectives	Solidarity + ('objective' redistribution)	**Solidarity (relocation quotas)**	**Responsibility (joint border operations)**	Responsibility + (individual)
Humanitarian + (maximum capacity)	Germany^{II-III}, Austria^{II}			
Humanitarian (asylum standards)	**France, Italy**	**Slovenia^{II}**	**Finland^{II}**	
Security (external border control)		**Hungary^{I}, Slovakia^{I}, Czech Republic^{I}, Poland^{II}, Slovenia^{III}**	**Hungary^{II}, Slovakia^{II}, Czech Republic^{II}, Poland^{III}**	
Security + (internal border control)	Denmark^{II}, Netherlands^{III}, Austria^{III}			UK^{I}

Columns: positions on the distribution of burdens; *rows*: positions on policy objectives. Position categories correspond to the issues disputed during the negotiations process. *Bold-formatted area*: current Schengen/Dublin system. The positions, which were marginal for the Schengen/Dublin system during the course of the crisis, are also presented. Numbers indicate time periods during the crisis: ^{I}April–July 2015; ^{II}July–October 2015; ^{III}November 2015. Estimated positions by individual member states are based on the evidence presented in the research part such as statements on record from political representatives and votes (see Sects. 3.1 and 3.2)

operations as a way of balancing solidarity and responsibility. A large majority of member states also supported maintaining certain asylum standards and external border controls as a means of balancing humanitarian and security objectives. As already mentioned, these positions corresponded to the characteristics of the existing regulatory framework (the bold-formatted area in Table 1). The first exception was the UK which stressed the individual responsibility of member states (see UK^{I}) but the UK is not part of the Schengen system. The second exception was Germany and, initially, Austria, which departed from the Schengen/Dublin regulation in August 2015 for the humanitarian objectives of maximizing the absorption of migrants (see Germany^{II-III}, Austria^{II}). During the September 2015 vote, a number of other member states supported the objective distribution key, but their aims were more related with redistribution than with the absorption capacity of the EU. Towards the end of the 2015, Denmark, the Netherlands and Austria began to argue in favour of re-establishing internal border controls as a reaction to the collapse of the Schengen/Dublin system (see Denmark^{II}, Netherlands^{III}, Austria^{III}). Furthermore, as a reaction to the unilateral actions taken by Germany and the employment of the communitarian method during the September 2015 vote on objective quotas, the positions of individual Eastern member states became more conservative, now rejecting relocation altogether and refocusing on security (see Hungary^{II}, Slovakia^{II}, Czech Republic^{II}, Poland^{III}, Slovenia^{III}). Thus, an intergovernmental framework was not in contradiction with the positions of most member states. In fact, it was the departure from the framework that resulted in the radicalization of positions and crisis of the Schengen/Dublin system.

4 Conclusion: A Softening of the Edges of Theory and Policy

The purpose of this chapter was to engage with the argument holding the intergovernmental-security institutional and discursive setting responsible for the European migrant and refugee crisis by hindering the sharing of burdens, and to propose an alternative explanation pointing to the role of the absence of policies in other areas relevant to the integration of migrants. The former argument is based on mid-range theoretical approaches towards the Schengen/Dublin system suggesting that the particular setting is responsible for the emphasis placed on the fight against illegal migration and reduction of refugee protection standards. The proposed argument of this chapter suggests the opposite, that since the Schengen/Dublin system is merely a common border policy, more should be done to establish community policies in other areas relevant to migration, such as social rights and labour market.

Key issues, positions, types of vote and rhetoric were researched in order to assess the role of particular institutional-discursive settings on the making of the cooperative agreements during the course of the crisis. Research demonstrates that during the early stage of the crisis, there was broad agreement on the relocation of migrants which was, together with the fight against smugglers, expected to reduce pressures on border countries, thus helping to preserve the Schengen/Dublin system. The disagreement was rather on the relocation quotas, with individual member states pushing for an 'objective' key. The latter was, however, not related to a basic policy objective, but rather to additional redistribution between the target and non-target member states. The vote by consent, as is characteristic of the intergovernmental framework, enabled each government to weigh the proposal against what would happen if no decision was reached, and enabled them to agree on the relocation quotas. In contrast, during the second stage of the crisis, the divergence of basic objectives became much more elaborated. In an attempt to enforce an open doors policy for humanitarian reasons, Germany departed from an intergovernmental framework that would require consent on any change in the policy. Soon afterwards, a communitarian method based on QMV was applied to enforce objective quotas. In response to this departure from community policy, nationalist reactions followed, in terms of the re-imposition of internal border controls. Eastern member states felt policy was being imposed upon them and now began to reject relocation altogether. National politics and the securitization of the issue strengthened negative attitudes towards migrants, contradicting the humanitarian objectives, which were the reason for the departure from the setting in the first place.

The overview of government preferences, demonstrating that Germany supported the open doors policy and that Eastern members were against it, can be linked to specific differences between the countries, such as economic trends, labour market conditions, even multiculturalism. More importantly, research demonstrates fairly limited differences in the positions of member states, which implies that the conditions on the EU level are much more important. Limited differences in member state preferences suggest that the role of the intergovernmental veto-player setting for the Schengen-Dublin system is much less important than has been argued by the mainstream theory.

References

BBC. (2015a, April 19). As it happened: Migrant boat disaster. Retrieved from http://www.bbc.com/news/live/world-32372351

BBC. (2015b, September 25). Migrant crisis: Why EU deal on refugees is difficult. Retrieved from http://www.bbc.com/news/world-europe-34324096

Bigo, D. (1996). *Polices en réseaux. L'expérience européenne*. Paris: Presses de Sciences Po.

Castles, S. (2006). *Back to the future? Can Europe meet its labour needs through temporary migration?* (Working paper). Oxford: International Migrations Institute.

CEC (Commission of European Communities). (2015a, April 20). *Joint Foreign and Home Affairs Council: Ten point action plan on migration* (IP/15/4813). Luxembourg. Retrieved from http://europa.eu/rapid/press-release_IP-15-4813_en

CEC. (2015b). *European agenda on migration 2015—Four pillars to better manage migration*. Retrieved from http://ec.europa.eu/dgs/home-affairs/what-we-do/policies/european-agenda-migration/background-information/docs/summary_european_agenda_on_migration_en

CEC. (2015c). *Proposal for a council decision establishing provisional measures in the area of international protection for the benefit of Italy and Greece* (COM (2015) 286 final). Brussels.

CEC. (2015d). *Proposal for a council decision establishing provisional measures in the area of international protection for the benefit of Italy, Greece and Hungary* (COM (2015) 451 final). Brussels.

CEC. (2015e). *Proposal for a Regulation [...] establishing a crisis relocation mechanism* (COM (2015) 450 final).

Demmelhuber, T. (2011). The European Union and illegal immigration in the southern Mediterranean: The trap of competing policy concepts. *The International Journal of Human Rights, 15* (6), 818–819.

Düvell, F. (2011). Irregular migration. In A. Betts (Ed.), *Global migration governance* (pp. 78–108). Oxford: Oxford University Press.

Espinoza, S. A., & Moraes, C. (2012). The law and politics of migration and asylum: The Lisbon Treaty and the EU. In D. Ashiagbor, N. Countouris, & I. Lianos (Eds.), *The European Union after the Treaty of Lisbon* (pp. 156–184). Cambridge: Cambridge University Press.

Euractiv. (2015, May 8). Hungary's PM Orban calls refugee quota plan 'mad'. *Euractiv*. Retrieved from http://www.euractiv.com/sections/migrations/hungarys-pm-orban-calls-eu-refugee-quota-plan-mad-314457

European Council. (2015a, April 23). Special meeting of the European Council [Statement]. Brussels. Retrieved from http://www.consilium.europa.eu/en/press/press-releases/2015/04/23-special-euco-statement/

European Council. (2015b). European Council meeting conclusions (22/15 CO EUR 8 CONCL 3). Brussels, 26 June. http://data.consilium.europa.eu/doc/document/ST-22-2015-INIT/en/pdf. Accessed December 2015.

European Council. (2015c). Action plan and political declaration. Valletta summit on migration, 11–12 November. Retrieved from http://www.consilium.europa.eu/en/press/press-releases/2015/11/12-valletta-final-docs/. Accessed December 2015.

European Parliament. (2015). Resolution on the latest tragedies in the Mediterranean and EU migration and asylum policies. 2015/2660 (RSP).

Grabbe, H. (2000). The sharp edges of Europe. *International Affairs, 76*(3), 519–538.

Graham-Harrison, E., Kingsley, P., Waites, R., & McVeigh, T. (2015, September 5). Cheering German crowds greet refugees after long trek from Budapest to Munich. *The Observer*. Retrieved from http://www.theguardian.com/world/2015/sep/05/refugee-crisis-warm-welcome-for-people-bussed-from-budapest

Guild, E. (2006). The Europeanisation of Europe's asylum policy. *International Journal of Refugee Law, 18*(34), 630–651.

Guiraudon, V. (2000). European integration and migration policy: Vertical policy-making as venue shopping. *Journal of Common Market Studies, 38*(2), 251–271.

Hollifield, J. F. (2008). The politics of international migration: How can we bring the state in? In C. B. Brettell & J. F. Hollifield (Eds.), *Migration theory. Talking across disciplines* (pp. 183–237). New York: Routledge.

Huggler, J., & Marszal, A. (2015, April 24). Angela Merkel calls for new rules for distributing asylum seekers in Europe. *Daily Telegraph*. Retrieved from http://www.telegraph.co.uk/news/worldnews/europe/germany/11561430/Angela-Merkel-calls-for-new-rules-for-distributing-asylum-seekers-in-Europe.html

Huysmans, J. (2000). The European Union and the securitization of migration. *Journal of Common Market Studies, 38*(5), 751–777.

JHA Council. (2015a, July 20). *Outcome of the council meeting. Provisional version, press*. 11097/15 3405th Council meeting, Justice and Home affairs. Brussels.

JHA Council. (2015b, September 14). *Council decision establishing provisional measures in the area of international protection for the benefit of Italy and of Greece*, 2015/1523. Brussels.

JHA Council. (2015c, September 22). *Council decision establishing provisional measures in the area of international protection for the benefit of Italy and Greece*, 2015/1601. Brussels.

Keohane, R. O. (1984). *After hegemony: Cooperation and discord in the world political economy*. Princeton, NJ: Princeton University Press.

Keohane, R. O., & Nye, J. S. (1977). *Power and interdependence: World politics in transition*. Boston: Little, Brown.

King, R. (2012). Theories and Typologies of migration: An overview and a primer. Willy Brandt Series of Working Papers in International Migration and Ethnic Relations 3/12. Malmö: Malmö Institute for Studies of Migration, Diversity and Welfare.

Kostakopoulou, T. (2000). The 'protective union'; change and continuity in migration law and policy in post-Amsterdam Europe. *Journal of Common Market Studies, 38*(3), 497–518.

Martin, M., & Macdonald, A. (2015, September 14). Germany re-imposes border controls to slow migrant arrivals. *Reuters*. Retrieved from http://www.reuters.com/article/europe-migrants-idUSKCN0RD0NU20150914

Meyers, E. (2000). Theories of international immigration policy—A comparative analysis. *The International Migration Review, 34*(4), 1245–1282.

Moravcsik, A. (1997). Taking preferences seriously: A liberal theory of international politics. *International Organization, 51*(4), 513–553.

Moravcsik, A. (1998). *The choice for Europe: Social purpose and state power from Messina to Maastricht*. Ithaca, NY: Cornell University Press.

Moravcsik, A. (1999). Is Something Rotten in the State of Denmark? Constructivism and European Integration. *Journal of European Public Policy, 6*(4), 669–681.

Moravcsik, A., & Checkel, J. T. (2001). A constructivist research program in EU Studies? *European Union Politics, 2*(2), 219–249.

Moravcsik, A., & Schimmelfennig, F. (2009). Liberal intergovernmentalism. In A. Wiener & T. Diez (Eds.), *European integration theory*. Oxford: Oxford University Press.

Mouzourakis, M. (2014). *We need to talk about Dublin: Responsibility under the Dublin System as a blockage to asylum burden-sharing in the European Union*. Refugees Studies Centre, Oxford Department of International Development.

Poptcheva, E. M. (2015). *EU legal framework on asylum and irregular immigration 'on arrival' State of play* [Briefing]. European Parliament Research Service.

Sommer, S. (2013). Opening fortress Europe? Constructing a new approach to EU migration policy. *Brussels Journal of International Studies, 10*, 42–92.

Thielemann, E., & Armstrong, C. (2013). Understanding European asylum cooperation under the Schengen/Dublin System: A public goods framework. *European Security, 22*(2), 148–164.

Thielemann, E., Williams, R., & Boswell, C. (2010, January 22). *What system of burden-sharing between member states for the reception of asylum seekers?* European Parliament, Directorate-General Internal Policies, Policy Department C, Citizens Rights and Constitutional Affairs, Civil Liberties, Justice and Home Affairs, PE 419.620. Brussels.

Tichenor, D. (2015). The political dynamics of unauthorized immigration: Conflict, change and agency in time. *Polity, 47*(3), 283–301.

Weaver, O. (1996). European security identities. *Journal of Common Market Studies, 34*(1), 103–132.

Weaver, O., Buzan, B., Kelstrup, M., & Lemaitre, P. (1993). *Identity, migration and the new security agenda in Europe*. London: Pinter.

Weinar, A. (2011). *EU cooperation challenges in external migration policy, EU-US immigration systems 2011/02*. Robert Schuman Centre for Advanced Studies, European University Institute.

Wiener, A., & Diez, T. (Eds.). (2009). *European integration theory* (2nd ed.). Oxford: Hampshire.

Marko Lovec is a Research Fellow at the Centre of International Relations (CIR) and Assistant Professor in International Relations at the University of Ljubljana, Faculty of Social Sciences. The main fields of his research and expertise include International Relations Theory, International Political Economy, Philosophy of Social Sciences and Politics of European Integration.

The Meaning of Borders for National Identity and State Authority

Sybille Reinke de Buitrago

Abstract What do national borders mean today? Can they be effectively maintained in times of massive humanitarian crises and refugee influx? What do such mass movements imply both for the authority and sovereignty of states and how do they affect debates on national identity? This chapter debates these questions on a conceptual level. Premised on the perspectives of critical geopolitics and post-structuralism, it enquires into concepts of bordering, ordering and othering. National borders function to distinguish, demarcate and divide, to protect and maintain a particular socio-political system with specific norms, but they are also points of contact. In a globalized and more populous world, with the possibility of masses of people moving more readily between countries, new processes of identification with and differentiation from an 'other' are likely to emerge. The national sense of belonging may be both diluted and enlarged. Re-definitions of self-other relations in response to events are significant because they likely impact the prospects of constructively dealing with the challenges posed by this migration. In light of the European Union's Schengen regime that has strong external but soft internal borders, this chapter focuses on the nexus of borders, authority and identity, and considers processes of othering, ordering and bordering in the context of the current refugee crisis.

Keywords Borders • National identity • State authority • Self • Other

1 Introduction

The number of people seeking refuge globally is currently estimated as being above 60 million people (UNHCR 2015). Massive migration and refugee flows, while not a new phenomenon, raise significant questions regarding the understanding of national borders, and the effects on state authority and national identity. Europe, the Maghreb and the Middle East, and much of Africa are experiencing a flow of migration that seems to surpass previous movements. European news media have

S. Reinke de Buitrago (✉)
Institute for Peace Research and Security Policy, University of Hamburg, Hamburg, Germany
e-mail: sybille.rdeb@gmail.com

C. Günay, N. Witjes (eds.), *Border Politics*, DOI 10.1007/978-3-319-46855-6_9

showed people *en masse* simply walking across national borders, overburdening border control capacities and questioning their very utility. Responses by European politicians and segments of their societies point to a renewed importance and valorization of national borders; this has led to a call to defend or re-impose national borders. But also elsewhere, though in different forms, national borders have recently been questioned. For example, Russia's annexation of Crimea in 2014, and its support for separatists in Eastern Ukraine, has questioned the authority of the Ukrainian state over its borders. Russia's actions within Ukrainian territory, by inserting soldiers as well as utilizing an internal support base of Ukrainian Russian speakers, has constrained the ability of the Ukrainian government to respond, while the international community has no effective tools to reverse the annexation. These developments call attention to the function of national borders and how borders can be contested. While the cases mentioned above are different in nature, they do raise similar and significant questions: do we live in a world with conditions that (increasingly) weaken the authority of states to control their national borders? Has state sovereignty become diminished? Are the existing tools to both conduct humane border control and safeguard state sovereignty effective? Furthermore, how may national identity in processes of identification with, and differentiation from, the other be affected?

Recognizing the significance of spatial constructions such as national borders and of national identity for international and inter-state relations and political behavior (see, for example, Croft 2012a; van Houtum and van Naerssen 2002; Neumann 1999c) the above crises place a spotlight onto national borders. There seems to be, again, a great need to grapple with what national borders mean today for state authority and national identity. These have been challenged before, for example by processes of globalization or advancing European integration, and one may even argue that state authority and national identity are always under some challenge. But the migrant and refugee crisis, at least regarding its effects on European borders, has developed in a rather short timeframe and therefore has had a much more forceful immediate effect. Furthermore, the crisis comes with violence and human suffering, seen in news every day, and thus demands more immediate response. It should be pointed out that emotional factors are also important in these circumstances. Not only are emotions relevant in the actions carried out and in the media images produced thereof, but also in policy discourse on how to respond. Emotionalizing statements and truth claims add weight to articulations, inform interpretations, obscure political agendas, and shape discussions (yet, without emotion there would be no national identity and no sense of belonging within a society).

The aim of this chapter is conceptual and exploratory, that is, to discuss the concepts of national borders as they relate to state authority and national identity, and to explore these in current developments, in particular by considering the case of massive migration and refugee flows. An underlying aim is to widen conceptual approaches to national borders. Applying a critical geopolitics and post-structuralist perspective that links space, power, identity and discourse, the chapter asks if and how the understanding and function of national borders have changed, and what such changes mean for state authority and the impact on debates on national identity. The chapter proceeds as follows: it first offers a conceptual framework regarding space and spatial constructions and national identity. It then discusses repercussions of the migrant and refugee crisis for state authority and national identity. The concluding section offers ideas that may be helpful in developing measures to deal with the challenges posed and points to areas where further research is needed.

2 Conceptual Framework

2.1 Space, Spatial Constructions, and National Borders

Underlying the existence, maintenance and practice of national borders are certain territorially and legally defined and confined spaces. Space is constructed by bordering practices and events such as war and conflict and their settlement, and thus by various political actors. Some borders have been quite stable over time, while others have been re-drawn and adjusted several times. Borders are then more or less historical, that is, they have a temporal dimension. In some cases, borders surround a somewhat, even if not fully, ethnically or religiously homogeneous societies, while in other cases they enclose multiple ethnicities, languages and religions. Borders also display different degrees of permeability, depending among other things on geographic factors, national law, bilateral state relations, capacities to maintain sovereignty and authority, and border protection policies and practices.

> Borders by definition lead to creating and taking sides, producing and occupying opposing spaces, and to many associated dichotomizations: inside/outside, inclusion/exclusion, we/they. But they also simultaneously invite transgression, a movement beyond the defined limits and enclosures of our lives to open new places and spaces, to search for reconciling alternatives, creative syntheses, resolving hybridities. (Soja 2005: 33)

National borders have their functions: they define who belongs to a certain (political) society/group and who does not. They thus differentiate. For those within a given national border, certain norms and rights apply, which typically differ to those outside. Borders thus enclose a certain set of accepted and enforced norms and rules, thereby marking the difference between distinct normative, political, legal and social orders. State authority is then legally and legitimately exercised only in the territory enclosed by the state's national borders; the term 'state authority' is used here to refer to the state having the legitimacy to exercise power over its own territory based on legal norms, linked with sovereignty as the supreme political authority (see also Lansford 2011: 1580 ff.). Regarding the case of the European Union (EU), national borders still exist between member states, but some of their functions have been adjusted, making national borders inside the EU more permeable (Diez 2006). In terms of understanding who we as humans in our various cultural groups are, borders play an important role. Languages and language application present an easily experienced and noticeable marker of difference and are in many cases also defined by borders. Since borders function as markers of rules, laws and orders, they offer guidance as to which rules to follow and where state authority is located. In today's globalizing world of high fluidity and mobility, national borders continue to have their functions. While on the one side national borders divide self from other and in a way also 'protect' the self from the unknown, on the other side, and at the same time, borders act as places of encounter between the self and the other.

Because national borders, conceived as spatial constructions, enclose a specific group or groups, they are also related to certain imaginations, memories and narratives. Of interest is not only which shared or distinct ideas these are, but also where processes of bordering, ordering and othering may be enabled and, in particular, by whom, against whom, and for what purpose. Here, the perspectives of critical geopolitics and post-structuralism are useful in informing on the discursive construction of self and other in the context of space, identity, and power, and the effects these have. (Spatial) ordering then relates to the ordering of material things, subjects, identities, rules and norms. A linked process is bordering, referring to how space is—both implicitly and explicitly—politically and socially produced and endowed with particular meanings. It involves the construction of dichotomies and boundaries, and similarities and linkages; bordering divides, isolates and delimits as well as connects and encompasses (Soja 2005: 33; van Houtum and van Naerssen 2002: 125 ff.; Neumann 1999c). Borders can thus be acted out and experienced as more or less rigid spatial barriers between the self/inside and a perceived non-threatening/threatening outside. Scholars in this field focus on how political actors articulate self and other, how they articulate threats to security and link these to identity, and how they discursively practice geostrategy and thereby engage in bordering, ordering and othering in international relations (Rumelili 2013; Agnew and Muscarà 2012: 11, 28–29; van Houtum 2012: 415). Spatial boundaries and orders then define both territory and identity by differentiating distinct normative orders and by creating cohesion within a group and differences to other groups (van Houtum and van Naerssen 2002: 125 ff).

2.2 *National Identity, Self and Other, and Difference*

National identity (and its constructions) acts as a powerful force upon the human sense of belonging, upon identification and differentiation, and political action. National identity can be defined as an evolved construct that implies a political community with certain institutions, rights and obligations in a defined and historic territory, shared myths and memories, and a particular way to understand and define the self (Smith 1991: 9 ff). But for identity to form, differentiation from something other and thereby the construction of difference is needed. Scholars point out that this construction of difference can also include the construction of otherness and thereby enable exclusion, something that can also take place at the level of states (Holland 2014: 203); this otherness is then placed opposite to the discursive construction of sameness within the self/in-group. The formation of national identity, and thereby self-other difference, can take a binary form or various other forms of identification with and differentiation from the other, enabling multiple self-other constructions (Croft 2012b: 91; Laclau 1996: 39, 52; Laclau and Mouffe 1985: 128).

How one group is defined and categorized from another is discursively constructed and of a social and political nature (Wagner and Butenschön 2014: 8). National identity then also constitutively affects political actions, as shown by the link of discourse, meaning-making and the production of social reality; political behavior in foreign policy and international relations are co-shaped by national identity (Herschinger and Renner 2014; Diez et al. 2011; Holland 2013: 10–11, 24; Rumelili 2013: 2). In articulating a state vis-à-vis others, decision makers articulate and construct inter-state relations of different qualities and with various elements of amity and hostility. Also national interests are expressed and constructed in discourse. Flint and Mamadouh (2015: 1) argue that national interests are served by articulated claims regarding political space and spatial expansion. Inherent in the development of states, for example as power centers, are processes of ordering and bordering with their effects on the inside and outside (van Houtum 2012). But it is political actors who make truth claims about how political space is organized and how it is connected with national identity. Because such representations have constitutive effects on behavior and political action, the manner in which truth claims are articulated is significant: they can motivate, re-enforce, change or overcome processes of bordering, ordering and othering (see also Allen 2003: 101 ff.; van Houtum and van Naerssen 2002; Laclau and Mouffe 1985). Discourse is then fundamental in such processes. 'Language . . . brings into being that which it claims to deal with but actually constructs' (Holland 2014: 202). Some representations of migrants and refugees point to their construction as possible security threats (see for example Hammerstad 2014; Huysmans 2000). But such articulated/constructed dichotomies—between an apparently threatening migrant/refugee and the kept-to-be-safe new home society—likely produce barriers for humane solutions to the migrant and refugee crisis.

When difference between self and other, a normal process in identity formation, is exaggerated or over-constructed, we may speak of active moves of over-differentiation. Such moves involve the construction of hierarchy and dichotomies, whereby the self is typically represented as overly positive and the other as overly negative. We may speak of processes of essentializing the self and the other, whereby the self becomes the essence of good and the other the essence of bad. Thus, the self is at core good in character, the other is at core bad in character. Situational constraints are, according to Stein Gross (2006: 294), typically not recognized when making negative ascriptions to the other. In doing so, not only new meaning for understanding self and other is created, but also self-other relations are re-defined, typically in a negative manner. A case in point is the aforementioned construction of migrants/refugees as possible security threats to European societies.

Such processes may be described as othering; the concept and process of othering is also often linked with bordering and ordering, in particular, when spatial dimensions are relevant. Othering refers to processes in which the self is making an other into the self's opposed or radical other. Since inter-state relations are self-other relations, states also engage in othering when constructing radical others as well as discursive and social boundaries to that other (Neumann 1999a: 218–219; Neumann 1999b: 20, 35–36). While some argue for the possibility of constructing otherness and still maintaining a neutral position toward that other (Diez 2005: 628–629), other scholars highlight the production of categorical difference between self and other, as well as the construction of hierarchy with superiority claims for the self and inferiority ascriptions to the other (van Houtum 2010: 960; Hansen 2006: 38–41). In the latter view, othering is a negatively oriented process.

Furthermore, in the articulation of threats, there are linked aspects relating to identity and security. (Perceived) threats to a state's power are seen to reduce predictability and to challenge a state's national identity and ontological security (Steele 2008: 12). When current developments regarding the efficacy of national borders are understood by politicians as threats to state authority, both national identity and security may be seen at risk. This can, in turn, motivate and accelerate moves intended to safeguard national identity and security, moves that may have undesired side-/counter-effects. The following section relates the elaborated concepts to current developments in the migrant and refugee crisis.

3 Repercussions of the Migrant and Refugee Crisis

3.1 Borders and State Authority

The questioning of national borders by current events, as well as the responses by governments, are argued here to illustrate that national borders can be a weak physical construct. How weak, of course also depends on the means and amount of force with which national borders are controlled and enforced. In the case of the EU's Schengen agreement, borders were no longer meant to be points of control for people travelling within the Schengen area. The state could therefore withdraw from its otherwise needed border control tasks at inner-Schengen borders and thereby also weaken its exercise of power at these borders. Massive migration and refugee flows are a phenomenon that the Schengen agreement was not made for and thus has difficulty to handle; the failure of the Dublin treaty points to this. Or, arguably, it may be that Schengen is still a useful and important regime, but that the EU has thus far been unable (and perhaps also unwilling) to establish a common border control and a shared refugee policy. As long as refugees mostly arrived at the EU's southern borders and were to stay there according to the Dublin agreement, the EU's northern countries seemed quite content to remain inactive. With the current disagreement and lack of common action by the EU, a situation has arisen where the state is again assuming a larger role vis-à-vis national borders, and the view of borders as a physical barrier has become re-valued. States in Europe and in the EU are increasing border controls again. In doing so, they mark their sovereignty—and this act presents an assertion of authority at borders. Yet, within the Schengen area, EU citizens are no longer accustomed to this and will find it undesirable when they themselves become inconvenienced by controls. Warnings of new costs associated with border controls inside the Schengen area are also voiced in various news media, for example by economists and some politicians, as well as by the European Commission (see for example DIHK 2016; Reuters 2016). But to enable a controlled influx of migrants and refugees, in whatever size and amount, one way to proceed may be to again and temporarily increase state authority at borders within the Schengen area. This, for example, is argued by Judy Dempsey from Carnegie Europe, who in March 2016 called for the temporary suspension of Schengen, as the 'member states have failed' the regime (Dempsey 2016). Schengen also entails intelligence gathering and sharing: Thus, the Schengen Information System is meant to '[allow] national border control and judicial authorities to obtain information on persons or objects', but according to Dempsey, it knowingly underperforms. Dempsey sees lacking or inefficient EU external border control as a risk to security in Europe, yet member states the past have constrained those agencies tasked with external border control, in particular FRONTEX/European Border and Coast Guard Agency. The additional goal of Schengen to motivate the creation of a common EU migration policy has thus far not been reached. Dempsey argues that the high costs associated with suspending Schengen for some time may encourage EU governments to devise a better functioning Schengen regime that will place more concentrated efforts on managing the refugee crisis (ibid). Why though would member states constrain the agencies that they themselves have created to conduct external border control? The reasons for doing so are not entirely clear, but they may relate to state authority/sovereignty and definitions of the other: EU member states, while under a supranational roof, still seem to want to decide themselves who enters their country and who does not. A controlled influx also includes knowing who enters a country and with what motivation. As was noticeable in the summer and fall of 2015, for example, state authorities seemed overwhelmed in performing their function of registering migrants and refugees in the middle of Europe. Greece has long been overwhelmed as well. Aside from greater border controls, and renewed efforts to keep out migrants and refugees, other solutions to overseeing or managing the influx of people may be thinkable. In public discourse, multiple actors in the political and humanitarian sector argue for establishing legal ways of migrating to Europe, as well as dealing more effectively with the root causes of people fleeing their home countries. Concrete plans and a coordinated European/EU approach are, however, still lacking.

Parkes (2015: 2, 4) also points out that in the case of the EU, there are no traditional external borders, rather cooperation agreements with its various neighboring states. With this, the EU pursues a political agenda of functional integration in parts of its neighborhood. According to Parkes, the Schengen area was meant to manage territory in the EU by actually overcoming territorial divisions. He adds that for Schengen to work the EU would have to be somewhat successful in its efforts of spreading good governance and stability in the neighborhood, so that those outside the EU have an incentive to stay in their home countries. Control at Schengen's borders would then be reduced in importance, and within Schengen there would be no need to control borders, thus overcoming territorial divisions within while at the same time making it harder for those from outside to enter the controlled space. The argument is that Schengen, with the freedom of movement within the Schengen area and (some) border control at its borders, can only work when not overwhelmed by massive migrant and refugee influxes.

In view of the migration trends of recent years, the EU's border control management has actually implemented some changes. These relate to an increasing extra-territorialization and externalization of EU border controls, that is, the moving of significant parts of EU border control and jurisdiction beyond the EU's physical borders and beyond EU sovereignty. Border control has been outsourced to other, non-EU countries. The European border management agency FRONTEX is seen to have been playing an important and increasing role in these practices. In effect, EU borders are 'shifted' to territory beyond its legal borders, namely to those non-EU countries that now assume parts of EU border control tasks (see, for example, Casas-Cortes et al. 2014; Mountz and Loyd 2014; Red Cross EU Office 2013). Müller (2014: 50), for example, speaks of EU exterritorial migration control and the 'gradual inclusion of neighboring countries in a variety of community policies', which result in ambiguity regarding the rules that apply and who has authority. A number of NGOs have criticized such extra-territorialization and externalization practices. They argue that the EU is exporting border control equipment, changing migration procedures and entangling migration policies with security policies in order to keep migrants and refugees out (Evangelischer Entwicklungsdienst 2016).

These developments raise several critical questions. For example, how successful has the EU been in spreading good governance in its neighborhood? The massive migration and refugee flows, while also a result of regional conflict, authoritarian regimes and dim economic and social prospects, seem to make a case for the EU not having been successful at spreading good governance to its neighborhood. It is arguable that if the EU had been more successful at it, there would be more stability and better conditions for a good life in the countries south and southeast of the EU—although this is indeed a tall order—and there would likely be less incentive to migrate to the EU. Whatever the reasons for migration and seeking refuge, the current influx places enormous stress on the Schengen agreement, but so do many of the responses by national governments as well as the lack of a coordinated European or EU approach.

Furthermore, the dire situation of refugees waiting in camps to enter the EU makes a case for the stated extra-territorialization and externalization trends not having been successful at effectively and/or constructively addressing migration and refugee movements. It may also be that the influx is too large to be handled by the EU and EU states, or that the EU and EU states have no appropriate, effective and humane instruments to address the influx. Over the years, they have failed to develop a coordinated approach of effective and humane border control. Extra-territorialization and externalization practices also raise questions regarding sovereignty and where border control tasks are best located, as well as relating to spatial constructions and territory in terms of whether or not the EU is perhaps inappropriately expanding its physical presence beyond its physical borders. Responsibility is shifted beyond EU borders, which calls into question how norms of responsible border control and management may then be upheld. The created dis-ownership, and the distancing towards border tasks, may actually enable the inhumane and undesired practices now witnessed. Also, political space is re-drawn; the EU both enlarges its sphere of influence and dilutes its responsibility for managing what occurs in this sphere. In such bordering practices, we may in effect speak of a shifting or re-drawing of borders, or of creating new borders. Such moves introduce new ambiguities and insecurities regarding the actual location of borders and the spaces in-between. Considering the nexus of national borders and state authority, such practices and their effects may actually weaken a state's territorial sovereignty and control, as states hand over responsibility for, and control over, the formulation and implementation of border control to another actor, as stated above, to other non-EU states or to EU agencies. By doing so, they also relinquish their normative influence over what occurs at borders.

3.2 *Identity Processes*

The above mentioned migration/refugee trends and practices of extra-territorialization and externalization of EU border control also impact national identity in multiple ways. They likely create new processes of inclusion and exclusion, along with re-definitions of self and other. Within Europe, there may be a process of diluting common understandings of a European self/an EU self into various national selves again, along with the creation of various others that are linked with various degrees of otherness and perceptions of risk and danger. Outside of Europe, the practical moving of border control beyond the EU's physical border may produce ambiguities regarding the rules for entering Europe. In addition, new processes of identity construction and belongings are enabled.

Studies highlight the difficulty of integrating migrants/refugees, for example the often greater hurdles for migrants in securing good employment and a good living standard (see for example Aiyar et al. 2016; OECD/EU 2015; MPI 2014). Migrants and refugees also face processes of identity re-construction, typically linked with (more or less) distress involved in adjusting to the new society (La Barbara 2015; Golden and Lanza 2013; Bhugra 2004). For example, as migrants and refugees come with other identities and other cultural, ethnic and religious backgrounds to their new home country, they are at first foreign and unfamiliar and need to find their place in society. This unsettles their identity, until a new, enlarged identity is produced, or, in other cases, the original one is strengthened (for such processes, see for example Logemann et al. 2014). The process of adjustment can become even more difficult when there is uncertainty as to whether or not asylum status will be granted; such uncertainty creates ambiguities in the process of identity re-construction. In addition, the foreign and unfamiliar can, depending both on how it is lived and acted out by newcomers and on how it is viewed and dealt with by the new home societies, to some degree unsettle existing belief systems of parts of the population. It can make the home society feel insecure in their identity vis-à-vis their state and society. Fears may develop that national identity will become blurred and/or weakened. The more this feeling of identity-at-risk is shared within a population, the greater the backlash may be towards those perceived to be the source of risk. While it depends to a large degree on the type of political and media discourse and on how successful newcomers are integrated, integration is a challenging and long-term matter that varies in its levels of success; in addition, what successful integration means may be contested. Discourse regarding migrants and refugees can of course contribute to whether or not national identity is felt at risk. When such discourse is conducted without strong self-other differentiation and without othering, that is, when migrants and refugees are not pitted against home societies and not portrayed as potentially threatening, the national identity of home societies would likely be considered less at risk. That there are distinct discourses with distinct effects can be seen when looking at various EU states and their internal debates on the refugee crisis, and on migration in general.

Impact on identity will also depend on the strength and impact of those groups and of far-right political parties that proclaim to 'protect' national identity, as seen in recent examples in Austria, France, Germany, and the UK. Developments likely vary depending on the degree to which such nationalist movements and political parties gain more legitimacy and leverage over policy formulation, for example, when elected into state or national parliaments, such as the recent success of the German far-right party AfD. But also those movements and initiatives that favor multiculturalism and work towards inclusion will arguably impact national identity. The latter efforts, when successful, may result in a broadening of national identity, perhaps also some sort of dilution, to the benefit of a more cosmopolitan and fluid identity. Populations may also be divided in how they feel (about) their national identity—the case of Germany, with both strong anti- and pro-migrant/refugee movements, points in that direction. Movements with followers that fear a loss or weakening of national identity, that see their identity at risk, may also react with a narrowing of their sense of national identity—the opposite of broadening. Those that fear identity loss may, in addition, also react to moves of identity broadening with a retreat into their narrower sense of identity. This may again result in some division within society. Since identity formation is a long-term process, it is still too early to make any concrete conclusions on how exactly national identity is impacted. Possible identity re-constructions are also a complex process, in which ethnic-religious nationalists and multiculturalists present the two opposing poles of a continuum. It would be a constructive step to recognize also the many nuances in between these poles and work towards overcoming such dichotomies and either-or positions.

In dynamics relating to identity maintenance, processes of ordering and othering by state, society and individuals are likely. For example, there may be intentional or unintentional, explicit or implicit moves of pitting inhabitants against newcomers, underpinned with discursive constructions of superiority and inferiority, and the creation of otherness. Some will welcome newcomers but may turn against those in their societies that are against increased migration and the offering of increased asylum. Others will not welcome newcomers and instead retreat and narrow their sense of national identity. At different societal levels, some will be included and others excluded. Public discourses in Europe are already heated and emotionalized. Furthermore, the fact that EU states promote distinct positions vis-à-vis migrants and refugees also adds ambiguities, in terms of offering distinct interpretations on the crisis, its causes and effects, and on policy needs. Simply put, everyone can pick and cite a particular position that fits own viewpoints. This does not seem helpful in generating or agreeing on ways of how to proceed jointly.

Thus, how migration and refugee flows are handled by the EU and EU member states may initiate or motivate multiple processes of othering—within a society and, even more likely, against migrants and refugees as newcomers to a society. Even if not actually intended, such processes make migrants and refugees into the other/others that must be kept out of EU territory or in some manner managed when already within EU territory. Migrant and refugee agency is thereby minimized. Preventing processes of othering, and effects of marginalization and exclusion, seems difficult in current circumstances and without a coordinated EU or even a global approach. There is a need for border control and management, but this need must be balanced with humanity. In such efforts, benefit can come from generating new perspectives of self and other. A differentiation of both what the self and the other means, that is, the differences within, may be helpful. As Nabers and Shim (2011: 23) argue, recognizing the heterogeneity of collective identities, as well as the danger in hegemonic representations can lead to alternative thinking about the other. The migrant or refugee other can then come to be seen more like the self. Similarities and the nature of being human can be more fully recognized and, in actual interactions with the other, also experienced. A felt distance to the other is thereby reduced, and potential views of threat vis-à-vis the other can be weakened.

4 Conclusion and Further Implications

This chapter has delved into concepts of space, national borders, state authority and national identity to elaborate current challenges directed at national borders. It has explored how our understanding of national borders impacts upon state authority and national identity, particularly in the case of the current migrant and refugee crisis. In doing so, it has referred to the constitution of self and other, and to processes of bordering, ordering and othering. In approaching this subject matter in a conceptual and exploratory manner, the chapter has sketched out preliminary insights that may be useful when formulating policy measures, as well as identified further research needs.

To address the enormous challenges, it seems important that the legal principle of sovereignty and a state's control of its borders should be upheld. In terms of the migrant and refugee flows into Europe, it is both national governments and the EU that are called to act. They may need to find ways to temporarily change how EU-internal borders are controlled without questioning the Schengen agreement altogether. Controlling the EU's external borders, in a humane way, is another task. For this, it seems counterproductive to outsource border control tasks. The control of EU borders should stay within the clear and direct responsibility of the EU. Mechanisms need to be developed within the EU, and in cooperation with member states, for conducting efficient registration of incomers and for then integrating them in a manner that does not overburden states. Some sort of fair sharing of the associated costs of integration is needed, and policy makers may need to find innovative and flexible ways of sharing and distributing costs. Regarding the EU, ties with other regional organizations/bodies, in particular with those in the Middle East, may need to be strengthened. These regional bodies should be motivated to play a larger role in assuring growth and prosperity as well as border management in their regions. Allowing for more legal ways of immigration into Europe may be helpful in reducing some of the pressure, but this will neither end the migrant and refugee flows nor solve the conflicts in countries that people flee from. In addition, since the migrant and refugee crisis is actually a global one, the UN is also an important player; perhaps only a global approach is able to deal with this crisis.

Furthermore, it appears necessary to build and maintain a cohesive national identity that can withstand minor shocks and risks from an outside, and that is still somewhat inclusive to newcomers—thus, to balance between cohesion and openness. Moves of utilizing national identity for very limited policy agendas, or of exploiting national identity by national governments, are not helpful in building a cohesive sense of identity. Governments should then work towards the inclusion of newcomers as well as a safeguard identity, in order to maintain societal cohesion. Perhaps it is societal actors such as educational institutions and civil society that are best able to foster a cohesive identity with a degree of openness. Regarding self and other, processes of essentializing self and other should be attended to. When portrayals of self and other recognize existing complexity, and both the good and bad in self and other, the other can become less important in defining the self. Self and other can be de-essentialized again. This can buffer societies against easily engaging in othering. Regarding national identity, regional and supranational institutions may be of lesser import, although it should be mentioned that the EU for example makes certain efforts to foster a larger-than-national, European identity. This presents a broadening of identity—the inclusion of elements from other identities may be eased here. At the same time, if overstretched, identity's cohesive force is weakened, and the sense of identity may be put at risk again. Thus, also here a careful balance between inclusion and safeguarding seems needed.

Finally, while not a focus of this chapter, the influence of media should not be ignored when considering identity processes. That media play an important role in shaping public discourse and in part influencing a country's political agenda has been amply shown (see, for example, Entman 2010; Cook et al. 1983; Nacos et al. 2011; Puglisi 2004; Sutter 2010). Regarding migrants and refugees coming to new countries, and in light of technological advances in communication, there should be an awareness of the continuing influence of the home media of migrants and refugees. With newcomers continuing to speak their native languages, they also continue to rely on media in their own tongue. But the content and interpretation of issues and of political action by perceived friends and foes likely differ from their new home countries' media. Opposing truth claims are difficult to verify. Furthermore, there can also be the active spreading of non-facts and false information. Especially with social media, quick verification of truth claims is nearly impossible. How to deal with these problems? A short answer must suffice here. Overall, it is important to promote responsible journalistic coverage of events, in terms of comprehensive, non-inflammatory reporting. Both journalists and readers should be wary of fostering or falling for a discussion that is full of simplified ascriptions and dichotomous portrayals of actors according to good-versus-bad stereotypes. Strong emotional content and claimed value oppositions should prompt a second, closer look. It also seems advisable to attend to the strong divide between those that define national identity in a narrow and more nationalistic sense and those that see it as being broader and more inclusive, as well as to the arguments brought forward by each.

Further research needs have also become apparent, not least because factual developments are still unfolding. Further empirical studies are needed regarding the effects of current changes in border control and management, in particular the impact of extra-territorialization and externalization. More such studies and their generated data should further enrich our understanding of borders and their functions, and of policy effects and policy needs regarding borders and migration. Also the impact of EU policy on third countries such as states in the Maghreb and Middle East should be better understood. In addition, more empirical data on how national government responses impact on their own societies, including constructions of national identity and moves to protect or to broaden it, are needed. Further research on national identity should then also focus on particular dynamics in identity maintenance such as how people/societies collectively react when feeling their national identity to be at risk.

References

Agnew, J., & Muscarà, L. (2012). *Making political geography* (2nd ed.). Lanham, MD: Rowman & Littlefield.

Aiyar, S., Barkbu, B., Batini, N., Berger, H., Detragiache, E., Dizoli, A., et al. (2016). *The refugee surge in Europe*. IMF Staff Discussion Note. Retrieved from https://www.imf.org/external/pubs/ft/sdn/2016/sdn1602.pdf

Allen, J. (2003). Power. In J. A. Agnew, K. Mitchell, & G. Ó. Tuathail (Eds.), *A companion to political geography* (pp. 95–108). Malden, MA: Blackwell.

Bhugra, D. (2004). Migration, distress and cultural identity. *British Medical Bulletin, 69*(1), 129–141.

Casas-Cortes, M., Cobarrubias, S., & Pickles, J. (2014). 'Good neighbours make good fences': Seahorse operations, border externalization and extra-territoriality. *European Urban and Regional Studies*, 1–21.

Cook, F. L., Goetz, E. G., Gordon, M. T., Leff, D. R., Molotch, H. L., Protess, D., et al. (1983). Media and agenda setting: Effects on the public, interest group leaders, policy makers, and policy. *Public Opinion Quarterly, 47*(1), 16–35.

Croft, S. (2012a). Constructing ontological insecurity: The insecuritization of Britain's Muslims. *Contemporary Security Policy, 33*(2), 219–235.

Croft, S. (2012b). *Securitizing Islam: Identity and the search for security*. Cambridge: Cambridge University Press.

Dempsey, J. (2016, March 3). Suspend Schengen to rescue Europe. *Carnegie Europe*. Retrieved from http://carnegieeurope.eu/strategiceurope/?fa=62954

Diez, T. (2005). Constructing the self and changing others: Reconsidering 'normative power Europe'. *Millennium. Journal of International Studies, 33*(3), 613–636.

Diez, T. (2006). The paradoxes of Europe's borders. *Comparative European Politics, 4*, 235–252.

Diez, T., Bode, I., & da Costa, A. F. (2011). *Key concepts in international relations*. Los Angeles: Sage.

DIHK (Deutscher Industrie- und Handelskammertag). (2016, January 21). Grenzkontrollen können die Wirtschaft Milliarden kosten. Retrieved from http://www.dihk.de/presse/meldungen/2016-01-21-wansleben-grenzkontrollen

Entman, R. (2010). Media framing biases and political power: Explaining slant in news of campaign 2008. *Journalism, 11*(4), 389–408.

Evangelischer Entwicklungsdienst. (2016). *Aus den Augen, aus dem Sinn: Externalisierung und Regionalisierung von Migrations- und Flüchtlingspolitik*. Background paper. Retrieved from https://www.medico.de/fileadmin/user_upload/media/aus-den-augen-aus-dem-sinn.pdf

Flint, C., & Mamadouh, V. (2015). The multi-disciplinary reclamation of geopolitics: New opportunities and challenges. *Geopolitics, 20*(1), 1–3.

Golden, A., & Lanza, E. (2013). Metaphors of culture: Identity construction in migrants' narrative discourse. *Intercultural Pragmatics, 10*(2), 295–314.

Hammerstad, A. (2014). The securitization of forced migration. In E. Fiddian-Qasmiyeh, G. Loescher, K. Long, & N. Sigona (Eds.), *The Oxford handbook of refugee & forced migration studies* (pp. 265–277). Oxford: Oxford University Press.

Hansen, L. (2006). *Security as practice: Discourse analysis and the Bosnian War*. Oxon: Routledge.

Herschinger, E., & Renner, J. (2014). Einleitung: Diskursforschung in den Internationalen Beziehungen. In E. Herschinger & J. Renner (Eds.), *Diskursforschung in den Internationalen Beziehungen* (pp. 9–35). Baden-Baden: Nomos.

Holland, J. (2013). *Selling the war on terror: Foreign policy discourses after 9/11*. London: Routledge.

Holland, J. (2014). The elusive essence of evil: Constructing otherness in the coalition of the willing. In D. Pisoiu (Ed.), *Arguing counter-terrorism. New perspectives* (pp. 201–220). Abingdon, Oxon: Routledge.

Huysmans, J. (2000). The European Union and the securitization of migration. *Journal of Common Market Studies, 38*(5), 751–777.

La Barbara, M. C. (Ed.). (2015). *Identity and migration in Europe: Multidisciplinary perspectives* (International perspectives on migration, Vol. 13). Dordrecht: Springer.

Laclau, E. (1996). *Emancipation(s)*. London: Verso.
Laclau, E., & Mouffe, C. (1985). *Hegemony and socialist strategy. Towards a radical democratic politics*. London: Verso.
Lansford, T. (2011). Sovereignty. In G. T. Kurian (Ed.), *The encyclopedia of political science* (pp. 1580–1584). Washington, DC: CQ Press.
Logemann, J., Donna, G., & Gregory Kohlstedt, S. (Eds.). (2014). *Europe, migration and identity. Connecting migration experiences and Europeanness*. New York: Routledge.
Migration Policy Institute. (2014, November). *Aiming higher: Policies to get immigrants into middle-skilled work in Europe*. Retrieved from http://www.migrationpolicy.org/research/aiming-higher-policies-get-immigrants-middle-skilled-work-europe
Mountz, A., & Loyd, J. M. (2014). Constructing the Mediterranean region: Obscuring violence in the bordering of Europe's migration "crises". *ACME: An International E-Journal for Critical Geographies, 13*(2), 173–195.
Müller, A. (2014). *Governing mobility beyond the state. Centre, periphery and the EU's external borders*. Houndmills: Palgrave.
Nabers, D., & Shim, D. (2011). *North Korea and the politics of visual representation* (GIGA Working Paper 164). German Institute of Global and Area Studies.
Nacos, B. L., Bloch-Elkon, Y., & Shapiro, R. (2011). *Selling fear: Counterterrorism, the media, and public opinion*. Chicago: University of Chicago Press.
Neumann, I. B. (1999a). Conclusion: Self and other after the death of the sovereign subject. In I. B. Neumann (Ed.), *Uses of the other. "The East" in European identity formation* (pp. 207–228). Manchester: Manchester University Press.
Neumann, I. B. (1999b). Uses of the other in world politics. In I. B. Neumann (Ed.), *Uses of the other. "The East" in European identity formation* (pp. 1–37). Manchester: Manchester University Press.
Neumann, I. B. (Ed.). (1999c). *Uses of the other. "The East" in European identity formation*. Manchester: Manchester University Press.
OECD/EU. (2015). *Indicators of immigrant integration 2015: Settling in*. OECD, Paris. Retrieved from http://www.oecd.org/els/mig/Indicators-of-Immigrant-Integration-2015.pdf
Parkes, R. (2015). *20 years on: Rethinking Schengen* (Issue Brief 36). European Union Institute for Security Studies. Retrieved from http://www.iss.europa.eu/uploads/media/Brief_39_Schengen.pdf
Puglisi, R. (2004). *Being the New York Times: The political behavior of a newspaper* (Working Paper). Retrieved from http://ssrn.com/abstract=573801
Red Cross EU Office. (2013). *Shifting borders: Externalizing migrant vulnerabilities and rights?* Retrieved from http://redcross.eu/en/upload/documents/pdf/2013/Migration/Shifting_Borders_Externalizing_migrant_vulnerabilities_rights_Red_Cross_EU_Office.pdf
Reuters. (2016, February 10). *EU-Kommission- Grenzkontrollen kosten bis zu 18 Mrd Euro pro Jahr*. Retrieved from http://de.reuters.com/article/fl-chtlinge-eu-kosten-idDEKCN0VJ1YG
Rumelili, B. (2013). Identity and desecuritization: The pitfalls of conflating ontological and physical security. *Journal of International Relations and Development, 18*, 52–74.
Smith, A. D. (1991). *National identity*. London: Penguin Books.
Soja, E. W. (2005). Borders unbound. Globalization, regionalism, and the postmetropolitan transition. In H. van Houtum, O. Kramsch, & W. Zierhofer (Eds.), *B/ordering space* (pp. 33–46). Aldershot: Ashgate.
Steele, B. (2008). *Ontological security in international relations: Self-identity and the IR state*. London: Routledge.
Stein Gross, J. (2006). Psychological explanations of international conflicts. In W. Carlsnaes, T. Risse, & B. A. Simmons (Eds.), *Handbook of international relations* (pp. 292–308). London: Sage.
Sutter, T. (2010). *Medienanalyse und Medienkritik. Forschungsfelder einer konstruktiven Soziologie der Medien*. Wiesbaden: VS.

UNHCR. (2015). *2015 mid-year trends*. Retrieved from http://www.unhcr.org/statistics/unhcrstats/56701b969/mid-year-trends-june-2015.html
van Houtum, H. (2010). Human blacklisting: The global apartheid of the EU's external border regime. *Environment and Planning D: Society and Space, 28*, 957–976.
van Houtum, H. (2012). Remapping borders. In T. M. Wilson & H. Donnan (Eds.), *A companion to border studies* (pp. 405–418). Malden, MA: Wiley-Blackwell.
van Houtum, H., & van Naerssen, T. (2002). Bordering, ordering and othering. *Tijdschrift voor Economische en Sociale Geografie, 93*(2), 125–136.
Wagner, U., & Butenschön, C. (2014). Zur Entwicklung des Gegenübers. Sozialpsychologische Ursachen von Intergruppenkonflikten. *W&F Wissenschaft und Frieden, 32*(1), 6–9.

Sybille Reinke de Buitrago holds a doctorate in Political Sciences. She is a researcher at the Institute for Peace Research and Security Policy at the University of Hamburg (IFSH) and the Institute for Theology and Peace (ITHF) in Hamburg, Germany. Her research focuses on international relations, peace and conflict resolution, and security policy, in particular on identity, perception and discourse. She has published in Global Affairs, the Journal of Terrorism Research, Journal of Strategic Security and Asian Politics & Policy. She also lectures at the Leuphana University in Lüneburg, Germany.

Part IV
Borders Beyond the Nation State

Beyond Borders: Subcultural Theory and the Transnational Jihadi Identity in Europe

Reem Ahmed and Daniela Pisoiu

Abstract The contemporary discourse on terrorism has largely evolved in terms of the unit of analysis from organizations and networks to include 'movements', 'communities', 'milieus', or indeed 'subcultures'. In general, subcultures have been for a long time considered as economically and politically marginal, emerging out of frustration with the impossibility to adapt to mainstream standards and to more generally be successful. Recent scholarship has acknowledged the autonomous, rather than deterministic nature of the jihadi subculture and, more importantly, their increasingly strong political involvement drawing on a transnational identity. Individuals living in various European countries relate less to their national or ethnic identity but see themselves more as part of a global community of believers. This chapter traces back the emergence of social movement and subcultural approaches to radicalization and illustrates how the jihadi subculture is driven by the need to resist the Western mainstream norms and values and the perceived notion that the West is attempting to manage the conduct of Muslims.

Keywords Transnational jihad • Subcultures • Radicalization

1 Introduction

In recent years, radicalization research has witnessed a dramatic increase in both the sheer number of works dedicated to the field and the types of approaches applied to it. Immediately after the infamous 9/11 attacks, quick and practical solutions were needed. Thus, the initial texts dealing with the topic usually tried to model a process of radicalization in several phases or steps, or looked for simple explanatory variables at the macro-level, in which engagement in terrorism was explained as a consequence of broader socio-economic and political phenomena. Especially in the

R. Ahmed
Institute for Peace and Security Research, University of Hamburg, Hamburg, Germany
e-mail: ahmed@ifsh.de

D. Pisoiu (✉)
Austrian Institute for International Affairs (oiip), Vienna, Austria
e-mail: Daniela.pisoiu@oiip.ac.at

C. Günay, N. Witjes (eds.), *Border Politics*, DOI 10.1007/978-3-319-46855-6_10

context of jihadi radicalization, a number of 'root-causes' such as deprivation, alienation and marginalization, coupled with religious seeking, have been identified (see for example, Khosrokhavar 2005; Korteweg et al. 2010). As the discipline matured—and given the difficulty of matching theory with empirics—other theories, concepts and models were developed at the meso- and micro-levels, most prominently those drawing on social movement research, psychology and criminology. Building on the issue of grievance, approaches unfolding at the meso-level looked at various types of social interaction, and at various levels: within the group, between the group and the broader social environment, between the group and the state, and so on. Many of them had already been used to explain other types of political violence, including terrorism, while others were 'borrowed' from neighboring areas such as criminology. From this perspective, radicalization is explained as a process of gradual socialization into particular worldviews and attitudes. Namely, movements or networks frame and construct an unjust 'reality' that successfully taps into individual grievances and persuades individuals to engage (Wiktorowicz 2005). A further meso-level approach draws on subcultural theory. The concept of 'subculture' alludes to the way in which some minority groups differentiate themselves from the 'mainstream' by adopting specific alternative norms and style (Cohen 1997a; Gordon 1997). Proponents of this approach argue that individuals are radicalized and drawn to subcultural values through status frustration (see Cottee 2011).

The underlying assumption in the approaches outlined above is that structural factors and socio-economic status play a deterministic role in the radicalization process. However, we know that this is not the case as violent extremists are not confined to the same structural processes and not all individuals affected by grievance radicalize. More recent contributions to the study of subculture have moved away from the traditional notion of deviance/strain and incorporated elements of the micro-level of analysis, which considers the particularities of individuals. The focus has thus shifted to the role of agency rather than structural constraints. In other words, such individuals have a strong desire to resist the mainstream and adopt new values regardless of their social background or prior grievances or failures (see Hemmingsen 2015; Pisoiu 2015).

This chapter traces back the emergence of social movement and subcultural approaches to radicalization and seeks to demonstrate that violent jihadis are not necessarily confined to one social grouping, nor do they react to the structural constraints around them. Rather, they are driven by the need to resist Western norms and values and the perceived notion that the West is attempting to manage the conduct of Muslims. Furthermore, over the last decades, the Internet has eased the communication and international outreach of ideas and propaganda, and reinforced a transnational jihadi identity that actively resists the Western mainstream.

2 Political Violence, Jihadism and Social Movement Theory

In the contemporary political and academic discourse on terrorism a recent change has become noticeable; namely, the emergent inclusion of conceptualizations such as 'movements', 'communities', 'milieus', or indeed 'subcultures', alongside or replacing the more traditional approaches focusing on 'organizations' or 'networks'. These 'new' concepts have been used for various purposes: to depict the units of radicalization—i.e. who radicalizes, their explanations, as well as attempts to control them. They are also a symptom of an evolution away from initial macro-level explanations of radicalization, which usually identified macro-level factors such as economic or social status, discrimination, foreign policy, etc. This evolution is traceable in part to the more recent interest social movement scholars have shown towards the study of radicalization. Similar to other disciplines that have applied their knowledge and instruments to this incipient area of inquiry, these scholars also brought in specific theories and concepts, such as the ones developed in earlier scholarship on left-wing terrorism (Della Porta 1992), but also more general social movement theories on mobilization mechanisms. One prominent example is Quintan Wiktorowicz (2005), who created a model for Islamist radicalization based on a case study and extensive field research (including interviews) with members of the now banned group Al Muhajiroun in the UK. His model includes established concepts of social movement—in particular framing theory, such as 'frame alignment', but also innovative concepts such as 'cognitive opening' and 'religious seeking'; namely, the point at which an individual becomes susceptible to new ideas and starts to look towards religious reasoning. Della Porta herself went on to apply her initial model to other types of political violence, including Islamist violence (Della Porta 2013).

Applying social movement theories to radicalization not only necessarily involved a broader conceptualization of the unit of analysis as 'movement'; it also opened the way towards more sophisticated inquiries into the relationship between the 'hard core' radicalized groups and the broader social movement. One such inquiry has been undertaken around the concept of 'milieu'. Milieu has been defined as the immediate social environment, which 'shares their perspective and objectives, approves of certain forms of violence, and (at least to a certain extent) supports the violent group morally and logistically'. Malthaner and Waldmann (2014) devised three ways in which a terrorist organization can relate to its 'milieu': during a process of gradual radicalization, the terrorist group can arise from the radical milieu; both the terrorist group and the radical milieu can materialize at the same time, independently of one another; or as a result of the creation of support groups the radical milieu emerges after the terrorist group. Although it has not been explicitly named as such, terrorist groups arising out of radical milieus have been empirically explored within studies on social movements and terrorism. In Della Porta's examination of the left-wing terrorism of the 1970s (1992: 261), she found that 'those who joined the armed struggle had already been involved, often for many years, in legal radical Left organizations'. Similarly, past research on right-wing extremism detected transitions from subcultural right-wing milieus, such as Skinheads, towards more extreme Neo-Nazi movements and terror groups (Bjørgo 1993; Sprinzak 1995; Dobratz and Shanks-Meile 1997; Van Dyke and Soule 2002; Schäfer-Vogel 2007). In the case of jihadis, transitions of individuals from non-violent Islamic organizations such as Hizb ut-Tahrir or Tabligh, who later became involved in violent jihad has also been explored (Barnes 2006; Beyler 2006; Hoffman 2009).

Apart from the various types of dynamics occurring between the organization (or the group) and the milieu, the two also share certain features, namely social networks and 'experiences, symbols, narratives, and frameworks of interpretation' Malthaner and Waldmann (2014: 7). These ideational elements, along with the more complex aspect of 'style', constitute the core content of another concept, namely 'subculture'. In classic social movement research, 'subculture' was regarded as another depiction of the social environment surrounding the emerging terrorist group. In its original criminological formulation, and its later development, the concept is however, significantly more complex. In the area of political violence, and particularly jihadism, subculture has only recently found a more sophisticated application.

3 Subculture and Political Violence

The concept of 'subculture' originates from criminology and refers to an autonomous normative system and social values distinguishing certain minority groups, a way of life which somewhat draws on, but is fundamentally different from, the 'mainstream' (Cohen 1997a; Gordon 1997). Subculture has usually been conceptualized as a relatively isolated subdivision of culture, with various content features, such as (deviant) norms and values versus style (dress, music, argot, and ritual) (Cohen 1997b: 545). Opening the way towards later, less isolationist approaches to subculture, Hebdige (1979: 122) raised the important point that, while involvement in subcultures can be 'a major dimension in people's lives', individuals bring 'different degrees of commitment to a subculture'. Thus for some, it may merely be a 'slight distraction' or a 'means of escape' from the tedium of day-to-day life. A contemporary and arguably realistic depiction of the relationships between subculture and 'mainstream' is that of interaction. Subculture emerges as a protest and resistance against the mainstream, and creates its own different style, norms and values, to be then continuously assimilated in the mainstream.

In the general subcultural literature, subcultures have for a long time been considered economically and politically marginal, emerging out of frustration with the impossibility to adapt to mainstream standards and to more generally 'make it'. Both the older American tradition (the Chicago School's urban ethnography, or deviance and strain), and the initial British school (Centre for Contemporary

Cultural Studies—CCCS) conceptualized an initial situation of (mostly economic) need and/or cultural hegemony giving rise to subcultures.

Regarding situational factors that give rise to subcultural groups, both the American and the CCCS schools are based on the premise that subcultures draw on disadvantaged groups. Namely, both schools solicit a structural approach that assumes that the working class does not have the same possibilities or opportunities to reach middle-class goals and thus, according to these schools, subcultures most likely emerge within disadvantaged population groups. Cohen (1997a) and Cloward and Ohlin (1963) drew on Merton's (1938) strain theory, which argued that 'actual advance toward desired success-symbols through conventional channels is . . . relatively rare and difficult for those handicapped by little formal education and few economic resources. . . On the one hand, they are asked to orient their conduct toward the prospect of accumulating wealth and on the other, they are largely denied effective opportunities to do so institutionally' (Merton 1938: 679). In terms of economic positioning, Cohen depicted the situation of the working class as being 'the worst of all possible worlds' (1997b: 93). However, in contrast to the deviance/strain school, which perceives middle-class goals as a 'natural development', the CCCS considers cultural dominance and an exercise of hegemonic power relationships as part of the problem. For example, Hebdige (1979) argued that 'it should be obvious that access to the means by which ideas are disseminated in society (i.e. principally the mass media) is not the same for all classes. Some groups have more say, more opportunity to make the rules, to organize the meaning, while others are less favorably placed, have less power to produce and impose their definitions of the world on the world' (2004: 122).

This dichotomy regarding the cultural element also gives rise to different theories surrounding motivational factors. In correlation with Merton's (1938: 678) thesis of cultural homogenization where 'the individual has assimilated the cultural emphasis on success', Cohen (1997a) and Cloward and Ohlin (1963) argue that structural strain prohibits working class individuals from reaching middle-class goals. From this, A. Cohen thus conceptualized that subcultures emerge as a solution to this situation of 'status frustration', and create an alternative 'frame of reference', with criteria that deliberately go against mainstream values and norms (1997a: 51). According to the assumption of the CCCS, by not assimilating into mainstream norms and values, individuals attempt to resist middle-class dominance. This resistance to hegemony ensures preservation of working class values and is executed in the cultural realm through appearance and style: 'the challenge to hegemony which subcultures represent is not issued directly by them. Rather it is expressed obliquely, in style' (Hebdige 1979: 17).

Within the literature on political violence, subculture has also been used to depict the broader activist social environment (Della Porta 1992), but its usage more frequently refers to specific sections or 'scenes' of the radical or extremist spectrum such as the right-wing Skinheads or the left-wing Autonomous. The classic conceptualization of subculture in this context has been that of socially marginal groups, emerging from disadvantaged socio-economic layers, powerfully driven by the pursuit of a certain lifestyle and the enjoyment of particular music and clothing, and only marginally interested in politics. More recent conceptualizations have moved away from this idea in two important ways. In relation to contemporary jihadism in Europe, authors have argued that the very terrorist cells and individuals, rather than some precursors in the radicalization process, can be meaningfully conceptualized as 'subcultures'. Currently, in the context of political violence, resistance is conceptualized in a different fashion, as strong, autonomous, and not necessarily against a background of need or cultural hegemony, but due to the wish to have and especially be something different.

4 The Jihadi Subculture

In the study of jihadism, subculture has been approached from various perspectives. One is similar to the original use in the 1990s to generally depict the social environment. For example, Sageman (2011: para. 3) stated that 'Terrorism emerges out of a political subculture . . . Just as these terrorists emerge from a neo-jihadi subculture rejecting the values of the West, so did Breivik emerge out of an Islamophobic subculture rejecting the immigration of Muslims to the West'. A second perspective draws on the aforementioned deviance school and sees jihadism as an autonomous system of norms and values radically opposed to the mainstream as a reaction to status frustration (Horsburgh and Jordan 2004; Cottee 2011). A third perspective outlines the prevalence of aesthetics, style and lifestyle in the self-understanding of individual activists and the strategies groups use to attract new adherents (Crone 2014; Hemmingsen 2015; Pisoiu 2015). This research at the same time challenges the more 'traditional' arguments surrounding the processes of radicalization.

Crone (2014) sets out to dispute the notion that religious radicalization is primarily a cognitive process. Based on Foucault's 'care of the self', Crone (2014: 292) argues that the physical body plays an important role in the process of radicalization as the body is 'transformed', and violence is often carried out by and inflicted on bodies. Thus, theories of violence that only consider the cognitive aspects of religious interpretation and worldviews overlook a 'critical dimension of violence'. Crone asserts that the whole human being goes beyond rationality and intellect and other factors such as habits, emotions, tendencies and aspirations should be considered. In the context of jihadi youth violence, Crone argues that religious violence is enabled by 'aesthetic technologies of the self', such as jihadi propaganda and media available on the Internet. These aesthetic technologies, in contrast to intellectual technologies, create 'frames' of violence that appeal to bodily emotional functions such as fascination and pleasure. As a result, traditional intellectual technologies such as religious scripture or doctrine become less significant. Through 'imagination, identification, and mimetic practice', youths transform their body techniques and succumb to violence (Ibid.: 303).

Similarly, Hemmingsen (2015) argues that in addition to the more typical religio-political dimension, jihadism should also be viewed through the perspective of counterculture. While Hemmingsen acknowledges that the countercultural perspective cannot be used in a vacuum, this approach has the ability to shed some light on why individuals choose to go down the path of jihad. Through assessment of five terrorism trials and personal interviews, Hemmingsen suggests that there are a number of reasons why individuals may be attracted to jihadism. These include: being taken seriously as a threat; a way to reject traditional norms and free oneself from authority; feeling a sense of superiority; forming strong social bonds and joining a community; and the promise of thrill and adventure (Ibid.).

Through assessing the applicability of subcultural theories to both individual cases of jihadi and right-wing extremists in Germany, Pisoiu (2015) found that individuals were neither driven by status frustration nor by situational factors, but rather that they were very much agents of their own actions. Here, the argument is that contemporary jihadis in Europe are not marginal; they cut across all socio-economic layers; are not frustrated with failure, but actively resist mainstream definitions of norms, values and lifestyle more generally. Significantly, their political involvement is visible not only in the soft areas of music or graffiti, but also through more serious acts of damage against property, arson and even terrorist attacks. In the case of the jihadis, the individuals sought alternative values not because they had failed to achieve a particular status, but because they were unhappy with their current values, or their way of life had been questioned by someone they had come into contact with. In terms of cultural aspects, jihadis successfully use and 'occupy' mainstream and other subcultural elements to promote their political agenda and appeal to their 'audience'. For example, elements of hip-hop and rap are evident in the jihadi 'battle-Nasheeds' (Pisoiu 2015). In light of this, Pisoiu argues that research on radicalization should incorporate the concept of subculture as an analytical tool, which focuses on aspects such as norms and style, and what emotional and cognitive effects subcultural elements and products have on political violence.

5 The Transnational Identity of the Jihadi Subculture

A particularity of the jihadi subculture is its transnational identity. Individuals living in various European countries relate less to their national or ethnic identity, and see themselves more as part of a global community of believers (Al Rasheed 2009; Meijer 2009). The term refers to the manner in which jihadi ideology transcends borders promoting norms through global communication networks. Peter Nesser (2004: 20) defines transnational jihadist movements as: 'clandestine revolutionary movements, which are committed to the use of violence to force the infidels (kuffar) to withdraw from the Arab lands, and to reestablish a worldwide Islamic community, the Umma, based on God's law (al-Sharia). They are intolerant and moralistic, and claim that violent jihad against the "forces of global unbelief" is an individual duty for every Muslim'. Transnational jihad is by no means a strictly uniform movement as divergent beliefs and contradictions are apparent (Al Rasheed 2009).

Thomas Hegghammer (2011) traces the roots of jihadi transnational identity back to the 1970s pan-Islamist movement in Hijaz, Saudi Arabia. This movement, which unlike the preceding Caliphates that predominantly sought to establish an Islamic state, aimed instead to ally Muslims worldwide and raise awareness of the perceived plight of Muslims globally. The movement was centered in the Hijaz because, as Hegghammer argues, this region of Saudi Arabia housed the highest number of Islamic religious institutions in the world. These institutions ranged from Islamic universities to charitable organizations. With communist and secular governments cracking down on Muslim Brotherhood activists and radical Islamists from Egypt, Iraq, and Syria from the mid-1950s onwards, the Hijaz became a sanctuary for these exiles. Having based his findings on primary evidence, Hegghammer provides a credible account of how Sayyid Qutb and Muhammad Ibn Abd-al-Wahhab's ideas on jihad were circulated and reinforced among the Hijazi community. Through the structure and global nature of these charitable and educational institutions, the Hijazi pan-Islamists sought to construct a discourse of inter-Muslim solidarity, which not only focused on unity, but also on threats that Muslims faced around the world. With a combination of oil money, developing technology, institutional support, and soft power, these activists were able to spread their message globally through magazines and journals. The messages often depicted suffering women and children and a call for donations for fellow Muslims in need. The conflicts in Lebanon, Afghanistan, and Israel and Palestine during the 1970s and 1980s provided ample propaganda material for a global audience (Ibid.). Thus, Hegghammer believes that this pan-Islamist movement was highly influential in spreading Islamic norms and solidarity to Muslims all over the world.

The turning point of 'global' jihad, namely the visible shift of jihad from the local to transnational level, took place during the 1979–89 Afghanistan war. The religious ideologue Abdallah Azzam played a central role in this mobilization as he reinforced the pan-Islamic discourse to which individuals had been exposed to for over a decade (Al Rasheed 2009; Hafez 2009; Hegghammer 2011; Nesser 2011). In the early stages of the Afghan war, volunteers were sent from a number of international Islamic charities to help refugees and provide humanitarian assistance, and by 1984, volunteers started to come to Afghanistan to fight in the conflict. The 'Arab Afghans' were the first mujahedeen involved in a foreign conflict (Hafez 2009).

While Hegghammer looks to the Islamist exiles in Saudi Arabia, Nesser (2004, 2011) examines the rise of transnational jihadism in the context of radical religious exiles from the Middle East and North Africa region who found refuge further afield in Europe during the 1980s and 1990s. Among these exiles were also 'jihad veterans' from the war in Afghanistan. The aim of these individuals was to mobilize the Diaspora to support jihad in their home countries or support jihad in Afghanistan and Chechnya. Furthermore, in the open societies of the West, these groups were able to operate relatively freely in regards to recruitment and propaganda. In addition, the European-based groups formed alliances and networks with other radical Islamist groups worldwide. Like the pan-Islamists in the Hijaz region, the exiles living in Europe established international NGOs centered on Muslim politics, such as al-Muhajirun, and Hizb ut-Tahrir. These organizations and advocacy networks intended to reach out to individuals in the Diaspora.

Regardless of the specific origins of the transnational jihadi identity, there are also differing arguments surrounding why individuals are drawn to these movements in the first place. One of the more traditional arguments stipulate that Salafi identity in general—whether violent, or non-violent—offers discontented individuals a sense of superiority, empowerment and religious purification. Armed with the alleged 'Truth', Salafi-jihadis begin to challenge their parents, friends, communities, the state and the cultural values of the West (Meijer 2009; Wiktorowicz 2001). According to Olivier Roy (2002), the fundamentalist pan-Islamist movement has had a lot of success constructing a universal religious identity that goes beyond culture and territory and attracts those desperately seeking identity and new (transnational) communities. Crucially, Roy additionally points out that the movement does not necessarily only attract the impoverished, as 'the reconstruction or recasting of a lost identity' is more important 'than the expression of a depressed social or economic situation' (Roy 2002: 315). The 'identity crisis' narrative especially taps into issues faced by second- and third-generation Muslim immigrants in the West, who feel neither European nor any significant ties to their parents' and grandparents' homelands. Thus, Salafism offers these youths a purpose and identity along with the perception that they are superior to others (see for example studies by Adraoui 2009; de Koning 2009). Identifying with transnational jihad is by no means confined to second- or third-generation Muslim immigrants as it is clear that jihad has also attracted a number of Muslim converts. This argument would still hold for those who prior to their conversion were faced with social anomie and seeking meaning and purpose in their lives.

On the other hand, within the context of foreign fighters, Hegghammer (2011) and David Malet (2010) argue that individuals are most likely attracted to the jihadi transnational movement through the so-called 'victim narrative', rather than complex theological reasoning. According to Hegghammer (2011), the identity discourse constructed by the Hijazi pan-Islamists was alarmist and effectively presented Muslims as victims, which in turn successfully played on individuals' sense of solidarity and humanity. By visually and verbally portraying Muslims in danger, the pan-Islamist movement was appealing to Muslims worldwide to help their brothers and sisters in need. Similarly, Malet (2010) argues that successful mobilization of foreign fighter recruits is possible through targeting relevant transnational identity groups and framing the local conflict as one that threatens this group. Thus, in the context of jihadi foreign fighters, framing local conflicts as an attack against Muslims urges the wider community to defend the Umma. This is evident when looking to publications from terrorist groups such as al-Qaeda's *Inspire* and the so-called Islamic State's (IS) magazine, *Dabiq*, which often portray the West as 'crusaders' killing and harming the 'brothers and sisters' of Islam. This powerful rhetoric and framing has been used in the last decades to mobilize individuals to fight jihad and defend the Umma. Hutson et al. (2009) have also explored the effect of the victim narrative—especially on those who are not directly victims themselves—and call the adoption of others' victimization 'tertiary victimization through the Umma' (TVU). The authors take it further by suggesting that it is not only jihadi terrorist groups who utilize this narrative, but also Arab satellite channels, which tend to have a strong focus on the Israel-Palestine conflict and the wars in Afghanistan and Iraq. Such exposure can unconsciously reinforce perceptions of victimization in the viewer, and thus individuals may as a result start to identity with the jihadi identity.

Whether individuals are attracted through theological reasoning, a search for meaning, or altruism, the impact of globalization on the transnational nature of jihad should not be understated. Transnational jihadi discourse is what Al Rasheed (2009) terms a 'hybrid construction' of rhetoric from the last 30 years, which seeks to preserve Islamic tradition but at the same time functions as a product of Western globalization and modernity. Thus, in line with the subcultural tradition, this 'rebel' movement takes elements from the (Western) mainstream. Globalization has facilitated communication between these transnational groups allowing global outreach of publications, ideas and propaganda. The Internet has further accelerated this outreach and has allowed the jihadi ideologues to transcend borders using the Internet to establish a virtual community where individuals can feel more in touch with the Umma (Nesser 2004). An analysis of global jihadism by the National Coordinator for Security and Counterterrorism (NCTV 2014) in the Netherlands, argues that the cyber aspect of transnational jihad is important because, as individuals break away from their physical communities, the 'virtual Umma' provides a transnational community where the individual can ultimately feel a sense of being part of a global identity movement.

While the above approaches necessarily focused on the 'beyond the state' nature of the jihadi transnational identity, de Koning (2013) 'brings it home' and at the same time links it to a central subcultural concept, namely 'resistance'. He does not focus necessarily on the commonalities with other nations or the blurring of differences among Muslim nations in terms of ethnicity. Rather, his analysis focuses on the relationship with the state. In this case, the jihadi identity is transnational in the sense of beyond state, or escaping the given existence criteria provided by the concept of nation and what it implies in everyday life: 'their transnational engagements stand in sharp contrast to the increasingly inward-looking governmental practices of the Dutch state' (2013: 104). De Koning's perspective is furthermore deeply subcultural, as he conceptualizes this identity as a form of 'resistance'. His thesis is that the actions of the Hofstad network 'denote a form of resistance which is not just aimed at changing oppressive structures in society, but at escaping the attempts of the Dutch state to manage the conduct of Muslims' (Ibid.: 93). The ensuing identity emerges through the appropriation of the negative stereotype of terrorism, 'a strong deterrent identity by the re-appropriation of the negative connotations of Muslims and converting them into signs of strength'; 'warrior-like, tough, manly and dedicated to God (instead of democracy)'. This is a form of 'secondary deviance', as it involves the appropriation of the deviant label proposed by the state, while at the same time contesting its negative connotation: 'terrorism was not morally wrong at all, it was simply given a bad name by the United States and their allies' (Ibid.: 100).

De Koning's broader theoretical framework draws on Foucault and his concept of 'governmentality', for the case in point 'the techniques which the government uses to try to monitor and discipline Muslims into being liberal subjects' (Ibid.). Starting with the 1990s, the argument goes that the Dutch government had begun to promote the integration of immigrants, which involved several mechanisms and labels: one is the so-called 'culturalization of citizenship', whereby integration meant adopting certain cultural values such as secularism and sexual freedoms. Another is the predominance of religion and culture as features for foreigners, and finally negative connotations attached to 'Muslim'—namely 'violence' and 'threat'. Finally, a category of 'good' versus 'bad' Islam was created, with 'good' referring to 'liberal'. Against this backdrop, resistance emerged, but one that does not only refuse the official model. Again drawing on Foucault, de Koning argues that this move away from the mainstream as it were continues towards yet another mode of being governed: 'It is not only about moving away from the governmentality of, in this case, the Dutch government, but it is also about seeking to be conducted differently, by other leaders, with other objectives and ambitions, other modes of salvation and other means ... Counter-conducts, according to Foucault ... are to be distinguished from revolts against power by their emphasis on disciplining the self as the ultimate goal of their resistance' (Ibid.: 96). This is an innovation or an addition to the subcultural concept of resistance, which usually 'only' means rejection of the mainstream, without the wish for a replacement thereof. This more 'traditional' approach does not entirely fit the case of jihadis, Salafis, and in fact all types of political radicalization. This is because in the course of the radicalization process—in the Islamist case from the very beginning, ideological (and religious) precepts reflect on, shape and constrain private life to a significant extent. There is little freedom left in the choice of food, clothing, as well as the kinds of social contacts one entertains. That is, private life is submitted to a process of 'rules directed re-designing' (Pisoiu 2011). The concept of 'counter-conduct' in this sense is an appropriate depiction and theoretical handle. Counter-conduct unfolds against Dutch policies, in particular the idea of a liberal Islam, and going against the mainstream Muslim institutions which emphasized Islam as a religion of peace; 'small and devoted pure vanguard'. Counter-conduct is put in practice through various types of behavior such as wearing beards and the niqab. Importantly, the Dutch integration discourse is not the cause of this resistance, it just shapes the form of this resistance.

6 Conclusion

The application of subcultural theory to the study of radicalization is relatively new. With its roots in social movement literature, this concept offers much promise in terms of understanding various pathways to political violence. While traditional literature on the topic tended to rely on the assumption that subcultures emerge from disadvantaged groups and are a reaction to status frustration, marginalization, and domination by the middle-class; more recent scholarship has challenged this claim, particularly in the context of the jihadi transnational subculture. As this chapter has shown, violent jihadis are not confined to one social group and the structural forces at play do not necessarily affect their actions. They reject mainstream norms and values because they are driven by a strong desire to be different. The global nature of the jihadi movement has particularly attracted second- and third-generation Muslim immigrants who feel neither Western, nor an attachment to their parents' home countries. Transnational jihad allows these individuals to forge an alternative identity that is against the (Western) mainstream, while, at the same time, to acquire instant perceived religious purification and superiority. Regardless of whether an individual originates from a disadvantaged social standing, or a privileged middle-class background, this transnational subculture attracts individuals who seek a virtual community that is worlds apart from the one in which they have been brought up in. This transnational jihadi identity is an autonomous resistance to Western values and norms, as well as a resistance to the perceived notion of Western attempts to manage the conduct of Muslims.

References

Adraoui, M. A. (2009). Salafism in France: Ideology, practices and contradictions. In R. Meijr (Ed.), *Global Salafism: Islam's new religious movement* (pp. 363–383). New York: Columbia University Press.

Al Rasheed, M. (2009). The local and the global in Saudi Salafi discourse. In R. Meijr (Ed.), *Global Salafism: Islam's new religious movement* (pp. 301–320). New York: Columbia University Press.

Barnes, H. (2006). *Born in the UK: Young Muslims in Britain.* London: Foreign Policy Centre.

Beyler, C. (2006). The jihadist threat in France. In H. Fradkin, H. Haqqani, & E. Brown (Eds.), *Current trends in Islamist ideology* (Vol. 3, pp. 89–113). Washington, DC: Hudson Institute.

Bjørgo, T. (1993). Militant neo-Nazism in Sweden. *Terrorism and Political Violence, 5*, 28–57.

Cloward, A. K., & Ohlin, L. E. (1963). *Delinquency and opportunity: A theory of delinquent gangs.* New York: Free Press of Glencoe.

Cohen, A. K. (1997a). A general theory of subcultures. In K. Gelder & S. Thornton (Eds.), *The subcultures reader.* London: Routledge.

Cohen, P. (1997b). Subcultural conflict and working class community. In A. Gray, J. Campbell, M. Erikson, S. Hanson, & H. Wood (Eds.), *CCCS selected volume 1* (pp. 536–559). New York: Routledge.

Cottee, S. (2011). Jihadism as a subcultural response to social strain: Extending Marc Sageman's 'bunch of guys' thesis. *Terrorism and Political Violence, 23*(5), 730–751.

Crone, M. (2014). Religion and violence: Governing Muslim militancy through aesthetic assemblages. *Millennium Journal of International Studies, 43*(1), 291–307.

De Koning, M. (2009). Changing worldviews and friendship: An exploration of the life stories of two female Salafis in the Netherlands. In R. Meijr (Ed.), *Global Salafism: Islam's new religious movement* (pp. 404–423). New York: Columbia University Press.

De Koning, M. (2013). 'We reject you'—'Counter-conduct' and radicalisation of the Dutch Hofstad Network. In M. Herding (Ed.), *Radikaler Islam im Jugendalter—Erscheinungsformen, Ursachen und Kontexte* (pp. 92–109). Halle/Saale: Deutsches Jugendinstitut.

Della Porta, D. (1992). Political socialization in left-wing underground organizations: Biographies of Italian and German Militants. In D. Della Porta (Ed.), *Social movements and violence: Participation in underground organizations* (pp. 259–290). Greenwich, London: JAI Press.
Della Porta, D. (2013). *Clandestine political violence*. Cambridge: Cambridge University Press.
Dobratz, B. A., & Shanks-Meile, S. L. (1997). *The white supremacist movement in the United States: 'White Power, White Pride!'*. Baltimore, MD: John Hopkins Unviersity Press.
Gordon, M. M. (1997). The concept of the sub-culture and its application. In K. Gelder & S. Thornton (Eds.), *The subcultures reader*. London: Routledge.
Hafez, M. M. (2009). Jihad after Iraq: Lessons from the Arab Afghans. *Studies in Conflict and Terrorism, 32*(2), 73–94.
Hebdige, D. (1979). *Subculture: The meaning of style*. London: Routledge.
Hegghammer, T. (2011). The rise of Muslim foreign fighters: Islam and the globalization of Jihad. *International Security, 35*(3), 53–94.
Hemmingsen, A. S. (2015). Viewing jihadism as a counterculture: Potential and limitations. *Behavioral Sciences of Terrorism and Political Aggression, 7*(1), 3–17.
Hoffman, B. (2009). Radicalization and subversion: Al Qaeda and the 7 July 2005 bombings and the 2006 airline bombing plot. *Studies in Conflict and Terrorism, 32*, 1100–1116.
Horsburgh, N., & Jordan, J. (2004). Jihadist subculture of terrorism in Spain. In *5th Global Conference Interdisciplinary.net*.
Hutson, R., Long, T., & Page, M. (2009). Pathways to violent radicalisation in the Middle East: A model for future studies of transnational Jihad. *The RUSI Journal, 154*(2), 18–26.
Khosrokhavar, F. (2005). *Suicide bombers. Allah's new martyrs*. London: Pluto Press.
Korteweg, R., Gofel, S., Heisbourg, F., Ranstorp, M., & De Wijk, R. (2010). Background contributing factors to terrorism. In M. Ranstorp (Ed.), *Understanding violent radicalisation: Terrorist and jihadist movements in Europe*. London: Routledge.
Malet, D. (2010). *Why foreign fighters? Historical perspectives and solutions*. Philadelphia: Foreign Policy Research Institute.
Malthaner, S., & Waldmann, P. (2014). The radical milieu: Conceptualizing the supportive social environment of terrorist groups. *Studies in Conflict & Terrorism, 37*(12), 979–998.
Meijer, R. (2009). Introduction. In R. Meijr (Ed.), *Global Salafism: Islam's new religious movement* (pp. 1–31). New York: Columbia University Press.
Merton, R. K. (1938). Social structure and anomie. *American Sociological Review, 3*(5), 672–682.
National Coordinator for Security and Counterterrorism. (2014). *Global jihadism: Analysis of the phenomenon and reflections on radicalisation*. The Hague: NCTV.
Nesser, P. (2004). Jihad in Europe—A survey of the motivations for Sunni Islamist terrorism in post-millennium Europe. *FFI/RAPPORT-2004/01146*.
Nesser, P. (2011). Ideologies of Jihad in Europe. *Terrorism and Political Violence, 23*(2), 173–200.
Pisoiu, D. (2011). *Islamist radicalisation in Europe. An occupational change process*. New York: Routledge.
Pisoiu, D. (2015). Subcultural theory, jihadi and right-wing radicalization in Germany. *Terrorism and Political Violence, 27*(1), 9–28.
Roy, O. (2002). *Globalized Islam: The search for a new Ummah*. New York: Columbia University Press.
Sageman, M. (2011). Why do extremists like Breivik turn to violence? *CNN* [Online]. Retrieved from http://edition.cnn.com/2011/OPINION/08/01/sageman.norway.terror/
Schäfer-Vogel, G. (2007). *Gewalttätige Jugendkulturen—Symptom der Erosion kommunikativer Strukturen*. Berlin: Duncker & Humblot.
Sprinzak, E. (1995). Right-wing terrorism in a comparative perspective: The case of split delegitimization. *Terrorism and Political Violence, 7*, 17–43.
Van Dyke, N., & Soule, S. A. (2002). Structural social change and the mobilizing effect of threat: Explaining levels of patriot and militia organizing in the United States. *Social Problems, 49*(4), 497–520.

Wiktorowicz, Q. (2001). The new global threat: Transnational Salafis and Jihad. *Middle East Policy, 8*(4), 18–38.
Wiktorowicz, Q. (2005). *Radical Islam rising: Muslim extremism in the West*. Lanham, MD: Rowman & Littlefield.

Reem Ahmed is a researcher at the Institute for Peace Research and Security Policy at the University of Hamburg (IFSH). She works within the framework of the EU FP-7 funded VOX-Pol Network of Excellence, which focuses on researching the prevalence, contours, functions, and impacts of violent online political extremism and responses to it. Her main research interests include: terrorism, jihadi and right-wing extremism, foreign fighters, and Middle Eastern politics.

Daniela Pisoiu is senior researcher at the Austrian Institute for International Affairs—oiip. Her fields of research are: terrorism, radicalisation, extremism, comparative regional security, American and European foreign and security policy. She completed her PhD at the University of St Andrews, Centre for the Study of Terrorism and Political Violence. She has conducted fieldwork on the topic of radicalisation in Austria, Germany and France, as well as other European countries. She is the author of Islamist Radicalisation in Europe: An Occupational Change Process (2011/2012), and editor of Arguing Counterterrorism: New Perspectives (2014), both with Routledge.

The Depth of Borders Beyond the State: Analytical, Normative and Epistemic Challenges of Study

Helena Rytövuori-Apunen

Abstract Borders, with reference to the dividing lines between different states, are one of the most heavily institutionalized concepts in the practice of international relations. A whole range of other borders escape our attention if we frame questions with conceptual *a priori* such as the state-centered view of the world and its normative parallels in the b/ordering principles of sovereignty and territorial integrity. This chapter reflects on three interrelated aspects of this problem. First, it discusses analytical perspectives for examining how the bordering practices of non-state actors, internationally unrecognized but internally functioning *de facto* states, as well as state agencies, challenge and consolidate internationally recognized borders. Second, it argues that the erosion of international law relating to state borders has made these principles susceptible to political uses and that these discussions have left in their shadow the dynamic social processes in which borders are contested, created and confirmed in international relations. The third argument is that inquiries into the reality of borders in relation to the concepts that define them with practical implications must have a place in research in order to address this problem and to be able to proactively contribute to the prevention of destructive outbursts of border-related conflicts. The chapter proposes a pragmatist interpretation of reality for unfolding the depth of borders beyond the state.

Keywords Borders • Practices • Pragmatism • European Union • Russia • Nagorno-Karabakh • Transnistria • Gagauzia

1 Introduction

Borders create orders of qualitative difference. Examples include boundaries between mine and yours, right and wrong, normal and deviatory. Borders are signs of inclusion and exclusion; they are not always linear but, more generally, delimitations that mark boundaries and difference. Borders in international relations denote, in the first place, territory or geo-space while also marking frontiers of

H. Rytövuori-Apunen (✉)
Tampere Peach Research Institute, University of Tampere, Tampere, Finland
e-mail: Helena.Rytovuori-Apunen@staff.uta.fi

C. Günay, N. Witjes (eds.), *Border Politics*, DOI 10.1007/978-3-319-46855-6_11

power and boundaries of identity. 'Border problems' appear in two basic ways. The first is that the institutions of the border fail to perform their task as 'filters' that separate legal and acceptable flows of people, goods and information from the illegal and not-acceptable; the second is when the border itself is not recognized. European border problems are primarily of the first type, whereas the problems to be found outside the Western world are of both kinds and, consequently, far more complex. The borders drawn by colonial administrations are fused with layers of historical affiliations, family connections in blood or in purpose, and livelihood practices. States are often mutually interpenetrated with the existence of trans-boundary communities, and borderlines between them are weak or non-existent. Thus, borders are not only 'porous' and 'leaking' but also contested by practices which more or less systematically evade their rules and regulations, or confront these openly in the form of insurgent movements and separatist pursuits. When the problem arises that the borderline is so artificial in relation to local inhabitants' life-practices, the concentration of efforts on more efficient border management merely focuses on some symptoms while remaining unable to cure the problematic condition.

This chapter does not pretend to propose a remedy but tries to aid in the diagnosis of the problem. The goal is, first, to unfold the notion of border in the multiplicity of its practical meanings and to lay out a research agenda relevant to the study of international relations.[1] Second, it emphasizes that research must advance from the point of arguing that borders and identities are constructed in multiple ways. Research must also contribute to counteracting the erosion of the norms of the international community that is manifest in the politically instrumental uses of concepts such as respect of sovereignty and territorial integrity. The discussion of these issues leads us towards our third and main goal, which is to argue for the relevance of the study of borders in a way that includes the pursuit of truth by inquiring what is real.[2] In the pragmatist perspective applied in this chapter this is not detached from but, rather, logically entails the aim of facilitating solutions to border-related conflicts. We argue that the habitual reality of borders (the border-related life-processes of different groups of people) is an area of research which deserves serious attention in the study of international relations, because a focus on the state border cannot increase our knowledge and understanding of how all these

---

[1]We use 'international relations' as a general description of the empirical area of study that is multidisciplinary in its origins. The term 'IR' (International Relations) again is more specific and refers to the discussions that seek to develop a field with its own identity (the Great Debates, IR Theory, etc.). 'International Affairs' is a traditional description of the area of study where diplomatic relations and international organization are the main focus. All such terms are discursive and have emerged with different foci in the history of the field of study.

[2]Although it can be said that ideas become 'true' when they are 'proved' by events and processes, this is seldom a simple matter of fact but depends also on attitudes and perspectives (Searle 1995, pp. 1–13), and consequently does not represent anything like the whole truth or the final truth. For these reasons we prefer to speak about truth as being the pursuit and the idea(l) of an ultimate consensus, as a pursuit that is present in the questioning of reality.

other b/ordering practices consolidate or challenge the borders between the states and, consequently, strengthen or bring into question the normative order of international relations. Although the limitations of state-centric conceptualizations and approaches have been recognized in the study of international relations, the study of borders is predominated by the concepts of the border as state border and the state border as institution. The constructivist and state-building approaches that typically are used to formulate problems examine borders as institutions and ask how they are, or should be, set up, while the epistemic doubt that we would like to emphasize (questioning how real borders are) is left to the side. We would like to argue that the pragmatist perspective, which inquires how different b/ordering practices resist the state- and nation-centric concepts through which they are conventionally framed, provides a relevant approach to examine the experience of borders beyond the institutional reality of the states and thus has a contribution to make in complementing these approaches. The chapter is organized in three sections, which in their respective discussions correspond to the aforementioned three aspects of the problem in the study of borders.

2 Borders as Multiple Ordering Practices in International Relations

Although the concept of the state and corresponding normative discourses about sovereignty and territorial integrity are central to the study of borders, framing border problems from this perspective limits our knowledge and understanding of the sheer variety of border-related processes. From such a one-dimensional, state-centric perspective these problems appear as sporadic events ('incidents' at the border) that must be managed in order to restore stability in and around state borders: their continuity, and the problems that they represent, are left in the shadow. A more comprehensive approach is made possible by examining borders as practices. Activities are practices when they recur with some regularity and demonstrate a pattern that not only describes the past but also anticipates the future. They become practices about borders when they claim control of some geo-space or establish normative hierarchies of inclusion and exclusion: they are 'b/ordering' practices. 'B/ordering'—a term coined by Van Houtum et al. (2005)—emphasizes that practices that set up borders are also ordering practices. These authors relate such practices primarily to identity-construction, arguing that collective identities are constructed in multiple ways. While we agree with this, our aim is to contribute to making such a 'practice turn', which is critical of theory-centered discourses and epistemic idealism,[3] more nuanced in the analytical sense, and to bring out normative and epistemic problems in the study of borders in international relations.

[3]Epistemic idealism refers to the assumption that 'idea' and 'practice' are different categories and that the first is primary in relation to the second. Theory-centered discourses are an example

The practices that claim control of some geo-space may be institutionalized and bear corresponding symbolic markers (state flags, official stamps, etc.); yet, they may also claim legitimacy based on other social conventions. These claims may be explicit in policies or demonstrated through recurrent action. A state's efforts to consolidate its borderlines are one example of such bordering practices; other examples include claims (by states and other actors) about spaces of operation on territory that formally belongs to another state. Such transboundary spaces may, for example, include military presence, grazing rights for cattle or access to water resources. Transboundary spaces might also entail historical places that play a role in the construction of identities or provide contemporary construction sites and routes of access for economic activity. They may connect communities inside one state to another state through citizenship and ties of ethnicity including language and religious belief. Symbolic markers of the agents performing bordering practices range from state flags to private fences and from letters of law to codes for clandestine action. All this can be relevant for relations between states but it certainly demands a focus which goes beyond the state-centric framework of study. Conflicts between transboundary communities involving disputes over the use of resources and mobility are not always considered to be of sufficient importance to involve the authority of the state. The communal conflicts in the Ferghana Valley, where the borders between Uzbekistan, Tajikistan and Kyrgyzstan intertwine, provide numerous examples of these governments' reluctance to pay attention to growing problems when they do not threaten the state's central power (Rytövuori-Apunen and Usmonov 2016). The processes that make border-related conflicts 'international' tell much about the structures of authority and the conditions of state legitimacy in countries.

Non-state agencies and groups of people are not the only challengers of state borders. States themselves also engage in bordering practices other than those dealing with the formal boundaries of sovereignty. They pursue spaces of defense outside their legal borders, economic access for markets and resources, and they seek to expand their cultural and ideological frontiers. The borderlines between states, viewed as being bounded by sovereignty and fenced in their territorial integrity, are thus permeable for two different reasons: first, because they intertwine with and are challenged by historical and habitual affiliations and, second, because in the institutional relations between states interference in each other's affairs has a considerably wider register than that conveyed by the normative dualism embedded in the legal perspective (for instance, the idea that a line is either held or crossed, a rule respected or breached). Economic integration, with exclusive zones of cooperation, set up their own borders, which are institutionalized through agreements and joint institution-building between the participating states, as do energy grids and regional cross-border development projects. Scholars in the field of International Relations have explored the interpenetration of orders rather than states

because they outline problem formulations independently of context (Toulmin 1990). Rytövuori-Apunen (2005) discusses theory-centered approaches in the study of International Relations.

(see the contributions in Marlin-Bennett 2012)[4] and examined how states inside their bounded spaces have 'nesting' societies representing other polities than those of the state (Ferguson and Mansbach 1996).

B/ordering practices described in this way are about geo-graphing power as presence and as control. They are about gaining influence and establishing identity in relation to a space, which may denote a bounded territory (from pieces of land up to entire countries) or a more diffuse functional space (such as information and networking spaces). While flows of people, goods and information may be signs of the diminishing importance of state borders, they also can create their own borders by bringing forth transboundary spaces and creating outwardly dynamic frontiers. Borders are shaped by the processes of globalization and they also reignite sentiments of historical belonging (Parham 2016b).[5] The interactions and the accumulation of transactions by one state or its citizens or inhabitants in another state do not in themselves create borders; they only do so as bordering activities—when claims of privileged access and efforts to control political outcomes are attached to mobility (Rytövuori-Apunen 2016).

Bordering practices take many forms, and taxonomies make little sense in the flux of developments where borders are constantly fading or evolving. In relation to this actual pulse of life, the conventional map of the world as a map of states is largely an ideational grid which shapes reality through the heavily institutionalized practices of the modern state. In relations between states, which seldom are equal in power and position, issues are more complex and nuanced in their context and can be explained—and explained away when norms are breached—with reference to contractual relations between states or a larger frame of international cooperation. The principled legal perspective on international relations is also blurred by the fact that in the contemporary world the presence of one state within another relates less to the pursuit of domination over territory than it does to the interest in controlling specific political outcomes, such as decisions about access for mobility and integration with other states. Correspondingly, practices of power are subtle and persuasive and operate through mutually conditional collaborative relations instead of being directly coercive. As suggested by the initially U.S.-specific but nowadays widely applied idea of 'soft power' (Nye 2004), the power that can change borders also operates with the attraction of values and normative discourses. Hence, this also means that borders have become an increasingly contested concept in the normative battles of international relations: a border-related conflict is less about a specific border than it is a symbol of an order.

---

[4]The Dialectics of World Orders theoretical approach of Hayward Alker, Thomas Biersteker, Tahir Amin, and Takashi Inoguchi is an example. See their contributions in Marlin-Bennett's edited volume (2012).

[5]Parham (2016b) is an insightful discussion of these processes in the context of Central Asia and China.

3 International Relations: A Field Trapped in Its Concepts

The normative dualism embedded in the concept of the state border is easily politicized and becomes part of the political contests between states. For example, the conflict in Eastern Ukraine became deadlocked when the Ukrainian parliament in January 2015—subscribing to a practice that already existed in the government—defined the insurgents and separatists in the self-proclaimed Donetsk and Luhansk people's republics as 'terrorists' and thereby criminalized not only their military methods but also their voices concerning the issues that had ignited the conflict (USA Today 2015). This is not to argue for, or against, one or the other of the parties but, instead, to stress that the normative dualism of concepts serves to polarize conflicts. The state border is a good example of the '(quasi)legal approach' which, in the argument of John W. Burton (1979) represents the 'win-lose' framework logically opposed to conflict resolution. Burton's aim is not to undermine the importance of law but to emphasize that in those cases where consensus and legitimacy have already crumbled there is little to be gained from imposing one-sided definitions on the conflict and pointing out who the 'culprits' are. The resolution of a conflict is a process that can only be started once the parties to the conflict start taking steps towards agreeing upon what it is that the conflict holds as its content.

In border-related conflicts diplomacy and efforts to solve these conflicts are frequently trapped in approaches that create the categories of 'right' and 'wrong' and use them to support one or the other party in the conflict. Such normative battles are seen in the way in which the U.S., in the case of the Federal Republic of Yugoslavia in 1999, justified NATO's infringement of the principle of the inviolability of borders that had been agreed in the Helsinki Final Act (1975), and the way in which Russia used a similar argumentation in its recognition of the independence of South Ossetia and Abkhazia in 2008, as well as in its annexation of Crimea in 2014. After the ideological confrontation of the Cold War ended, it was reasonable to expect that the respect for international law that had been recreated after World War II would be solidified, but within a decade developments had taken the opposite direction. While E. H. Carr, in his realist critique of idealist politics, argued that the League of Nations crumbled due to political values that were seemingly universal yet disguised particular interests (Carr 1939), in the present day such a politically instrumental role is being played by abstract legal principles corrupted in their political usage.

Governments in conflicted states have also learned to use legal norms to 'freeze' their position in negotiations over conflicts. Azerbaijan and Moldova are examples of how the stance on a disputed issue (Nagorno-Karabakh and the existence of a Russian military base in Transnistria, respectively) can be made into law and, in this way, used to support fixed positions ('a law is a law') in negotiations. A provision, which Azerbaijan introduced into its Constitution in 1995, requires that any change of the state's borders requires a nation-wide referendum. Popular opinion provides the possibility to avoid any compromises that the negotiations may achieve. More specifically, it strengthens Baku's argument that a referendum on the status of Nagorno-Karabakh would have to include the entire population of Azerbaijan or, alternatively, take the form of a plebiscite in the territory of Nagorno-Karabakh after the return of Azerbaijani displaced persons and refugees to their former places of residence. Moldova, again, has made permanent neutrality a constitutional provision (Article 11 of the Constitution adopted in 1994), and by doing so it has not only chosen a security policy that, in the 1990s, seemed the best option for the then newly independent state. This political move also increased the justification of its political stance in negotiations over Transnistria: Neutrality as the chosen path makes it a matter of principle to demand that foreign military troops dispersed over its territory, which includes Transnistria, must be removed. This approach was developed with international interaction and, among other things, expressed later in the OSCE 'Istanbul requirements' of 1999, which made the ratification of the Adapted CFE treaty dependent on the removal of all Russian troops from Moldova and Georgia.[6] The result was that the knot became tighter for both issues, the CFE and the resolution of these conflicts.

The geopolitical processes and global power relations, which have made it possible to change state borders through military force, have weakened the normative order by affecting its key principle of the respect of sovereignty and territorial integrity. When the normative international community was embodied in the United Nations and gained new authority over the decades following World War II, military intervention and, thus, the breaching of a member state's territorial integrity became legitimate in only two cases, that is, under the authority of the UN Security Council, and as a measure of self-defense against an occurred aggression (UN Charter Chapter VII). But while the new rule was being solidified in principle, the domain of exceptions was extended from the original stipulations of the Charter. The question of the conditions and circumstances in which military intervention can be legitimate, even if the role of the Security Council is reduced, has opened the sluices for discussions of norms (extended forms of self-defense, humanitarian intervention, Responsibility to Protect, national self-determination and self-determination of peoples as defined in the UN Charter).[7] In the study of international relations, the preoccupation with issues of the normative international order is not unconnected to the study of borders: Because the principled legal perspective, and the politicized argumentation around it, has taken over the majority of the agenda of research and policy discussions, questions about borders in any other sense than their formal state boundaries have remained at the margins of interest. This can no longer remain so because the challenges to state borders threaten to destroy the normative order of international relations.

---

[6]At the OSCE Summit in Istanbul in November 1999 the Western states pressed for Russia's complete withdrawal from Moldova and Georgia to be made a condition for signing the Adapted Treaty on Conventional Armed Forces in Europe (CFE).

[7]'To develop friendly relations among nations based on respect for the principle of equal rights and self-determination of peoples, and to take other appropriate measures to strengthen universal peace;' (The Charter of the United Nations, Article 1(2)).

The study of International Relations and especially the disciplinary mainstream, which may be identified through the 'IR Theory' debates, is not well equipped to meet this challenge. The reasons for this lie less in the influence of international law than in the ideals of modern social science adopted by the discipline in the decades following World War II. The central idea was to formulate 'models', and the state-centric view of the world was established as such a model. The levels-of-analysis discussions, which were begun by Kenneth N. Waltz, James N. Rosenau and J. David Singer, and which were continued by the Neorealists in their many proliferations, Alexander Wendt's constructivist theory among them, have had much significance in establishing the predominance of state-centered approaches to IR in the disciplinary mainstream.[8] Overcoming the problem of the predominance of this model requires adopting an approach that does not privilege conceptual *a priori* ('models'). Our starting point on this issue is pragmatic and emphasizes the practical implications of concepts: Whenever b/ordering practices other than those of the state become reality with real effects, the reluctance of state authorities to admit their existence will exacerbate the conflict between state and non-state agents and embed it deeper in state–society relations. This is the dilemma of building the borders of a modern state in entire regions, such as Central and South-Central Asia. Stories of people who for decades have sold their agricultural products across the borders that more recently have gained new significance in terms of state security, and who now are exposed to border guards' suspicions that they in fact smuggle drugs, proselytize Islam, and are potential terrorists, are just some examples (Parham 2016a).

Ways to alleviate such conflicts include, for example, simplified border crossing procedures for the residents in the border districts and setting up joint border markets and Free Economic Zones, such as those that the UNDP and the EU (BOMCA) have helped to establish on the border between Afghanistan and Tajikistan.[9] Similarly in the conflict over South Ossetia, the relatively flexible attitude expressed by Georgian authorities on the issue of opening a market, which is comparable to the one closed down by President Saakashvili in Ergneti in 2004 on the border with the separatist region, is a positive sign although the

---

[8]Exemplary works are J. David Singer's 'The Level-of-Analysis Problem in International Relations' in James N. Rosenau's edited opus *International Politics and Foreign Policy* (New York: The Free Press, 1969) and Kenneth N. Waltz's *Man, the State and War: A Theoretical Analysis* (New York: Columbia University Press, 1959). Much of the later discussion in the disciplinary mainstream arises from these works, including Waltz's *Theory of International Politics* (Reading: Addison-Wesley, 1978) and the abundance of research that it has inspired by its further elaboration, as well as its constructivist criticism. The works by Alexander Wendt worth mentioning in this context are 'Anarchy is what States Make of it: The Social Construction of Power Politics' *International Organization*, Vol. 46, No. 2. (Spring, 1992), and *Social Theory of International Politics*. Cambridge: Cambridge University Press, 1999.

[9]The first joint border market was set up at Ishkashim in 1995. Since 2008, Tajikistan has set up Free Economic Zones (FEZ) in Ishkashim, Dangara and Pyanj. Corruption is a major problem in the implementation of these policies.

conflict as such remains in gridlock.[10] These arrangements reduce the pressures that relate to cross-border livelihood practices and the existence of major transboundary communities. The borders mentioned above also clearly show the dilemma of state policies: while maintaining this cross-border interaction with a controlled flexibility is a formidable security challenge, closing it also deteriorates security because the pursuit of livelihood in this case seeks other ways and strengthens illegal networks. In the pragmatist sense the practices which continue to exist in one form or the other are the 'force' of reality that resists the practical implications of imposed concepts, such as the borderline between states that obstructs habitual interaction. The starting point of research in studying these complex matters is that the state and the principled normative perspectives, which generate legitimacy through international law, must be considered as part of the dynamic social processes in which borders are contested and corroborated by mutually rivaling and collaborative practices.

4 The 'Hard' Reality of 'Deep' B/Orders

The naïve empiricist approach to the question whether borders are real is to ask whether the signs that correspond to our concept—border-crossing points (BCPs), flags, fences, gates and procedures to open these gates, literal and symbolic—exist as objects of our sense experience. For the pragmatist such sense experience does not yet provide enough proof. The pragmatist assumes that physical structures exist irrespective of being observed but that they are, for example, 'BCPs' on the basis of our interpretation which asks if they have the practical consequences that they have been designated to have. While a simple fence proves to be real if it obstructs movement, borders between states exist in their institutional contexts. They are institutional facts; facts that only appear, have some practical meaning, in the context of the institution that they manifest and symbolize (Searle 1995). Correspondingly, where the institution, the state as part of a community of modern states, is not rooted in a tradition that provides it with legitimacy, the 'fact' of state borders is a mere formality and contested by practices which derive their justification from other social conventions, communal practices and symbols of identity; practices which reflect affiliation with region, ethnic group, and family in blood or in purpose, as we have already discussed. Such non-national(izing) practices of belonging become complex when they are also strengthened by the memories of a colonial past and nourished by wider regional and global rivalries for resources and influence.

The structure of a unified state is most burdened in those cases where communities within, or existing in close connection with, a state are also an integral part of

[10]The former market in the village of Ergneti had brought together Georgians, Ossetians and Russians to trade since 1996, and its closure in 2004 immediately reignited the long-lasting conflict between the Ossetians and the central government in Tbilisi (Eurasianet 2012).

the identity of another, neighboring state. Armenia and Azerbaijan are gridlocked in their mutual conflict over Nagorno-Karabakh because the national identity and the project of the state in both cases must be fundamentally revised if Nagorno-Karabakh ceases to be part of it. The structure of the conflict is similar in Moldova, although not because of Transnistria but because of what its separation represents: increased demands for autonomy from Gagauzia, the loss of which would be yet another blow to Moldova's project as a unified state (see, for example, Ursu and Raileanu 2014). The relevant question for study is how the different practices contest or consolidate the borders at which the state's state-building efforts and nationalizing projects for a unified state are manifested. For example in Gagauzia, which is an Autonomous Territorial Unit within the Republic of Moldova, only three out of 55 education units teach in the official state language, Moldovan, which is a variation of Romanian. The main language in the region is Russian, which on the basis of Gagauz internal law (confirmed in Moldovan law) alongside Gagauz and Moldovan has the status of an official language (Bucataru 2015: 148–152).[11] The state-level status of the Gagauz language limits its official use to Gagauzia, whereas in this region the state language (Moldovan) is used in mainly official connections and its dominant status is forestalled by keeping it as one among three official languages. This hierarchy of languages maintains a political border between Gagauzia (where 82 % are ethnic Gagauz) and the other parts of Moldova (excluding Transnistria). The Russian language, which 40 % of Gagauz speak in their homes (ibid.: 151), is the Gagauz' language of communication outside the region. However, the b/order, which the state-level legislation makes between Moldovan, as the only national language, and Russian as a language of 'interethnic communication', restricts the full integration of the Russian-speakers, the Gagauz among them, by privileging Moldovan especially in the higher echelons of state administration.

Transnistria also has three official languages (Russian, Moldovan and Ukrainian). The Russian language is the main language and used in 90 % of schools. About 8 % of schools teach in the official state language of the Republic of Moldova and less than 1 % teach in Ukrainian. The 'school wars' over the closure of the few schools that use the Latin script and the Romanian language on the 'left bank' of the Dniestr signify similar b/ordering practices, which in this case are much more ruthless and dictatorial. Transnistria is a *de facto* state that consolidated its separation from Moldova in a war in spring 1992, whereas Gagauzia has remained within Moldova after narrowly avoiding a violent clash in autumn 1990.[12] An ethno-

[11]The Legal Code of Gagauz-Yeri, Art. 16(1), http://gagauzia.md/pageview.php?l=en&idc=389&id=240. The basic elements of this code, including the three official languages, are confirmed in the law on the status of Gagauzia adopted by the Moldovan Parliament on December 23, 1994.

[12]When Gagauzia organized its own parliamentary elections in October 1990, the possibility that Soviet troops from the 14th Army base in Transnistria could intervene prevented a group of tens of thousands of men representing the militant ranks of the Moldovan National Front from entering Gagauzia. In the preceding summer Gagauzia, and Transnistria, had declared independence from

nationalist discourse is actively maintained to secure the special status, which was negotiated with the Moldovan government in 1994, and that has enabled the Gagauz to develop their own legal code to keep politics in local hands. The message that the Gagauz leaders have sent through a referendum organized in February 2014 is that the region's inhabitants prefer developing closer ties with Russia instead of the EU and support a declaration of independence should Moldova lose or surrender its own independence ('sovereignty') (RFE/RL 2014; Romashov 2014: 60).[13]

The resistance demonstrated by the small Turkic-speaking population[14] against Moldova's European choice presents a tough issue for Moldova's pro-EU forces. Gagauzia's post-Soviet decades show that the protection which it continuously seeks and accepts from Russia is, in the pragmatist sense, 'hard' reality: it does not yield to real-ize—make real in their practical implications—the concepts by which the pro-EU political forces would like to frame Moldovan national unity. The government in Chisinau may try to crush the resistance with generous minority rights and economic benefits, but this may not be enough: Gagauzia may also demand some form of international guarantees for its status, and such arrangements would include Russia, which since the early nineteenth century has been the 'protector state' and main affiliation of this ethnic population. A failure to solve the problems related to this complex reality of borders on behalf of the EU will not only cause the Union's relations with Russia to deteriorate but also harm Moldova, which maintains its European path at the risk of losing not only Transnistria but also Gagauzia.

For more than a decade the EU has invested much in its Neighborhood policies (ENP), including the Eastern Partnership, and a great number of European policy institutes have focused on research to promote institutional change in accordance with European political values in the target countries. In Moldova, 'dialogue' projects have brought benefits to people on both sides of the Dniestr River and the expectation is that such 'soft power', which operates with the mechanisms of attraction that the Union has created through its policies, will draw the two states, one *de jure* and another *de facto*, closer together. Because of the predominance of this approach in policy discussions within the Union, discussion of the question why it is that many residents in Transnistria wish for their small homeland to be a part of Russia rather than any other country is only of marginal interest to research

Moldova and claimed a status that made it subject only to Soviet central authority. See, for example, Chinn and Roper (1998).

[13]The use of the term 'sovereignty' in Gagauzia reflects the region's post-Soviet political vocabulary. Because 'sovereignty' in Russian linguistic practices is synonymous with 'independence' in the sense of having the highest authority in decision-making the words can easily be associated with Moldova's integration with the EU, i.e. they have an indirect meaning that is more comprehensive than a reference to Moldova's formal merger with Romania.

[14]The Gagauz population in Moldova consists of around 155,000 people in 2016. Small Gagauz populations are also present in Ukraine, Turkey and Russia. The majority of the Gagauz are Orthodox Christians. Ethnically they are mixed with Eastern European (mainly Bulgarian) populations.

in the policy-making context. The opinion often expressed by observers in Western countries is that this is the choice that has been made for them by Tiraspol's (the capital city of Transnistria) ruling elites and that popular opinion has also been influenced by Russia's manipulative efforts. Along with the other residents in Moldova, they are persuaded that closer cooperation with the European Union will benefit future generations even if the structural changes that are necessary in the economy and society require sacrifices in the immediate future. Such discursive practices cast aside the element of surprise arising from resistance to the future promised by the EU. They ensure the continuity that follows from our reliance on *a priori* knowledge, habit and authority—reliance on predefined values and models about society, such as the definition of democracy in terms of specific institutions, the habit to consider the EU's Eastern neighborhood from the point of view of the Union's relations with Russia (rather than focusing on the specific development problems of each country), uncritical adoption of concepts of 'best practices' defined by authoritative institutions, and so on. Our argument is that although the authorities in Tiraspol undoubtedly influence the ways in which people express their political preferences, these are not reasons for leaving aside the question of the reality that is the experience of these people.

A pragmatist approach offers a fruitful way to study such questions because it is Realist and yet avoids the determinism of 'facts' and 'history'.[15] It offers analytical guidance for asking, for example, what it is that the Transnistrians and the Gagauz expect and reasonably can expect will be brought to them from their affiliation with either Russia or the EU, in terms of the things that matter in their lives. These are concrete things that symbolize some pattern or regularity in their habitual world (patterns of consumption, education, movement, etc., which are factual in their 'traces'). Some of these things have 'existential' value and 'make a difference' on a life-scale instead of only representing better or worse conditions.[16] The question concerning such qualitative difference in the experience of people instructs us to ask what it is that Transnistria or Gagauzia practically means for their residents in the patterns of life that are 'new' (and offered by the EU) against the 'old' (and represented by Russia)?

In a declaration in April, 2016, Gagauzia's Council of Elders expressed discontent with the growing influence of the 'unionists' who support Moldova's close cooperation or unification with Romania. Mikhail Kendigelean, the chairman of

---

[15]The realist point of departure means that the mind-independent world is a continuous challenge to our thinking and the concepts through which we make sense of it. However, to speak of a 'Realist ontology' is problematic because the mind-independent reality *(ens reale)* only gains its unity (becomes 'a world') in our interpretation.

[16]This means that 'reality' in human interpretation is 'experience' in three mutually interrelated dimensions. The existential dimension, the question of 'proof' in the habitual sense, and the concepts and discourses which are about the possibility of communication by using the symbolic practices of language correspond to what C.S. Peirce calls the Firstness, Secondness and Thirdness of experience. See, for example, Peirce (1992). The concepts and discourses agreed in the EU's institutional contexts are an example of the conventions of communication (Thirdness).

this council and former Chairman of the Gagauz parliament, argued that Romania has trained thousands of specialists in Moldova and that Romanian passport-holders are in leading positions in several governmental branches, including the Constitutional Court. His argument intertwines present experience with the past: 'In the Soviet time, unionists worked underground, training and preparing their agents over decades. It was in their plans to dissolve Moldova in Romania yet [*sic*] in 1990, but Transnistria and Gagauzia upset their plans' (cit. Infotag 2016). As the conflict about Moldova's European path becomes more severe the concerns of the Gagauz increase that their autonomy will lose its political support from the special relationship with Russia, which also has much economic significance in the region.[17] Mr. Kendigelean's statement is a warning that the EU brings along Romanization and that joining it will cause the separatist conflict to resurface. Because this is a political act and not a descriptive statement it makes little sense to count 'how many' Romanian passport-holders are in leading positions and to argue that the statement is exaggerated. The influence of Romania in the country is resisted because the experience of past events has such significance that it (through the abstractive processes of the mind) becomes the background against which new empirical encounters are interpreted.

When the Soviet Union was in the process of dissolution, Transnistria and Gagauzia both voted with an overwhelming majority in favor of maintaining the Union in the All-Union referendum in March 1991 (which was boycotted by the Chisinau-led regions). They also supported the failed coup in Moscow in August 1991 and in its wake reconfirmed their independence from Chisinau (Chinn and Roper 1998: 94–96; Katchanovski 2006, pp. 94–97). This was not so much to support the Soviet Union as it was to respond to the rising nationalist movement in Moldova. The present-day conflict in relation to the government in Chisinau was prompted during the last years of the Soviet Union by the language law, adopted by the Moldavian Soviet Socialist Republic (SSR) in August 1989, that made Moldovan the sole official language and reintroduced the Latin alphabet. The language issue strengthened the connection which had been made 70 years earlier when Moldova had joined Romania after the Bolshevik takeover in Russia. For Russian-speakers on both sides of the Dniestr the language law signaled a future that would leave them as second-rank citizens and a politically vague minority group in their own country.

The cultural divide that prevails under the mosaic of nationalities and instrumental citizenships has left a border dynamism that imbues issues of language and cultural belonging with much significance. In Transnistria Soviet-type multinational 'Moldavism' presents a counterforce to Romanian nationalism and is the basis for developing culture and identity in the self-declared *Pridnestrovskaia*

[17]In the present day, the special relationship with Moscow is manifested, for example, in the relatively speedy exemption of Gagauzian enterprises from the freeze on wine imports that Russian authorities implemented in autumn 2013 in relation to Moldovan producers (Bucataru 2015, 152). The Gagauz leadership emphasizes that the main problem of Gagauzia is economic development and that the main markets of the agricultural region are in Russia (Vlah 2016).

Moldovskaia Respublika (PMR) (Filippova 2012, pp. 42–47). The political border today is where it was set in 1924, when the western border of the Moldavian Autonomous SSR on the Dniestr River became the border of the Soviet Union. This was the area that the Russian Empire had controlled since the last years of the eighteenth century before it advanced further into Bessarabia ('right bank' Moldova) over the following decades. At the conclusion of World War II the Soviet Union rolled into regions that had existed in connection with Romania, and the Moldavian SSR, which now also included Transnistria, was set up with repressive measures including mass deportations.

Moldova is deeply cleaved and the experience of Russia is different among different parts of the population. Among the Russian-speakers, and especially on the 'left bank of the Dniestr' (roughly corresponding to the area of Transnistria), the experience of repression relates not only to the Soviet Union but also to the rule of Romania (1918–1940, 1941–1944), a period of time during which both ethnic Russians and Ukrainians and the Gagauz, the latter because of their historical loyalty to Russia, were exposed to severe treatment. Ukrainians and Russians, in addition to the Jews, were the main victims of the Holocaust in the region, and Transnistria under Nazi control became a territory of concentration camps, transit centers and killing fields. It was disconnected from the Soviet Union only during these war years, and when the Soviet Union ceased to exist it remained so closely connected with Russia that its residents barely have a common history without it. In Gagauzia, again, the experience of history is specific to what this ethnic population, which sees itself as a transboundary 'nation' with a 'national territory' in Moldova (Formuzal 2010), has gone through and how it has been treated by the majority population. Although the economic hardship of the Soviet decades even included famine, this period is considered as one of general hardship shared by the entire country's population. The historical experience of these different groups of people valorizes the question of why it is that the EU does not have the kind of appeal in these regions that it has when it also represents a reconnection with a course of developments (European integration) from which actors and agents see themselves to have been unrightfully disconnected by the Soviet decades. Understanding such 'existential' difference in the interpretation of developments such as the changes brought by association with the EU enables us to unfold the depth of borders and the sources of the conflict beyond contemporary geopolitical rivalries.

This point has relevance for epistemic attitudes. We cannot inquire about reality without genuine doubt, and in the pragmatist sense this means that the objects of our study are 'dynamic': they can resist our efforts to define and impose meaning on them. This, in our view, is the key point in studying borders as practices. It is overlooked when borders, for example the future borders of the EU, are approached as 'social construction', or examined with an eye to implementing a political model of a state or a concept of border management. 'Resistance' is thus more than the lasting effect of the action that embodies it in social processes (for instance, the movement for protest and non-compliance, evasion of rules and application of alternative practices): it is the quality that makes borders dynamic objects instead of being considered merely as objects of construction. The 'hard' reality of borders that leaves internationally recognized borders only apparent, void of real effect, is a highly relevant and yet neglected subject of study in the research of borders.

Resistance can be examined from an individualistic as well as a holistic perspective; for instance, it can be seen to be the result of the action and mobilization of groups of people as well as the force that structural entities and discourses demonstrate. For example, we can call Nagorno-Karabakh a region of Azerbaijan. However, a letter from Baku sent to an address in Khankendi (the Azeri equivalent for Stepanakert) will not arrive. Khankendi exists only as a name and does not have the intended practical implications. While this is an effect of institution, structure and discourse, the struggles of the conflict parties leave innumerable possibilities to study resistance as the result of the action of individuals and groups of people. Similarly, the efforts of the European Union Border Assistance Mission (EUBAM) to improve border control at the Moldova–Ukraine border, by assisting these two states in bringing their procedures and standards closer to those in EU member states, are resisted by the practices of people who evade the BCPs by using, for example, the many small, uncontrolled routes that have remained from the Soviet times when borders were non-existent. The communication networks built during the Soviet period of time are especially dense in the 'central segment' (the Transnistrian part of the borderline, 453 km) because Transnistria was part of Ukraine during 1924–1940, and the redrawing of Soviet administrative borders later brought little change at a local level. Today, when a state border is in the process of being established with border demarcation and border control institutions, the fact that this segment of the border is the part that remains beyond the control of the Moldovan constitutional authorities is the main structural and institutional obstacle for bringing a new level of control to the 985-km border between Moldova and Ukraine.[18] The more persistent the resistance is in spite of continuing efforts to implement new practices, the 'harder' is the reality of the border for implementing a concept, such as the model of border management proposed by EUBAM, FRONTEX and other EU agencies.

5 Conclusion

In Moldova the political gridlock over the status of Transnistria shows no signs of being loosened, and ultimately separation is the direction of the present course of developments. Simultaneously Gagauzia is becoming a more important issue in regards to the path that Moldova is taking. In neighboring Ukraine, the Maidan events proved that people there were unyielding in their opposition to the incumbent regime. They risked their lives for what was perceived as new hope and in this way set out an existential border. The idea of a new life, symbolized by the

[18] See the information platform of crossing the border of the Republic of Moldova (Government of the Republic of Moldova). See also the country reports by Olga Filippova (on Ukraine) and by Octavian Ţîcu (on Moldova) (University of Eastern Finland, no date).

prospects offered by the EU, provided a contrast to the experience with a corrupt regime supported by Russia. Soon after President Viktor Yanukovich had fled and the interim government was set up in February 2014, separatists in the eastern parts of the country demonstrated that they were not prepared to accept the rule of the new central government which, among its first measures, had initiated a process of abolishing the status of Russian as the second national language. They were not prepared to compromise their affiliation with Russia, which for large numbers of people takes the form of close ties of family and livelihood. Here, too, the deeper dividing lines can be unfolded by asking what it is that Russia and the EU represent for these people in relation to the opportunities that they have in their lives and the sense of belonging that gives them a history and a culture. This border has no fixed points on land but exists because it is sustained by some previous experience, both personal and stored in the memory of generations. It becomes actual when people in their 'new' encounters with the empirical world can recognize something with which they feel familiarity or what, contrarily, feels alien, and in its practical implications means discontinuity with their ways of existence.

Although slogans such as being 'closer to' or 'together with' Russia (Bucataru 2015, 152; Filippova 2012, 45–48) are politically motivated, they also have a meaning for the people that supports them on the political agenda. In other words, we cannot prejudge the political rhetoric about history and belonging as being merely manipulative; if it is so, it is uttering words not meant for an audience.[19] For example, although the multinational identity of the 'Pridnestrovian' is a Soviet-type ideal and clearly serves a political purpose, it also appeals to large numbers of people because it is coherent with their experience (see Chorba 2015). We also must take into account that words and images, which may seem like clichés, have meaning as symbols through which identity is consolidated when the threat appears that it may be degraded, for example in the situation where status is dependent on being granted recognition in terms of 'minority rights'. Although the residents of Transnistria, who have been able to benefit from the Autonomous Trade Preferences (ATP) introduced by the EU in 2007,[20] have demonstrated their willingness to trade in all geographic and political directions, this has not eased the political conflict with Chisinau. The crucial issue remains the autonomy that enables people to pursue their lives without feeling that their habitual ways and the culture which they recognize as their 'own' is not part of the national culture in their country.

---

[19]This point is common among philosophers of language and interpretation. It follows from speech act theory, which distinguishes the illocutionary force and the perlocutionary effect from the locutionary meaning of speech (Austin 1962).

[20]In spring 2014, more than 70 % of Transnistria's exports were to the 'right bank' of the Dniestr and to the member states of the European Union (Sobják 2014, p. 2). When Moldova's Association Agreement with the EU entered implementation in September 2014, the ATP for Transnistria was extended, and it was extended later until the end of 2015. In December that year, the Transnistrian authorities reversed their previous policy and agreed to implement, within the next two years, the reforms required by the region's inclusion in the Union's Deep and Comprehensive Free Trade Area (see, for example, Całus 2016).

We can term Moldova and Ukraine 'cleft countries' (Huntington 1996) or something else, but such framings (which are commonplace in IR) remain only conceptual stamps unless there is an interpretation that unfolds their practical meaning in the lives of people. While the history of 'cleft regions' has already received some attention in the study of politics (Katchanovski 2006), identification of borders in a comprehensive sense requires us to open our eyes to the practices that resist established concepts of borders. We have proposed a means of analysis and interpretation that considers resistance not only as a social movement but as a challenge to the repressive power of concepts, and that seeks to understand the deeper b/orders of existence from which it emerges. A better understanding of these borders remains a prerequisite for developing working solutions to these conflicts.

This chapter has been produced in the framework of the research project Proactive Conflict Management at Post-Soviet Deep Borders, funded by the Academy of Finland during 2012–2016.

References

Austin, J. L. (1962). *How to do things with words*. Cambridge, MA: Harvard University Press.

Bucataru, V. (2015). Moldova still at a cross-roads: Is the European path irreversible? In T. Rostoks & A. Spruds (Eds.), *The different faces of "soft power": The Baltic States and Eastern Neighborhood between Russia and the EU* (pp. 139–161). Riga: Latvian Institute of International Affairs.

Burton, J. (1979). *Deviance, terrorism & war: The process of solving unsolved social and political problems*. Oxford: Martin Robertson.

Całus, K. (2016, January 15). The DCFTA in Transnistria: Who gains? *New Eastern Europe*, Articles and Commentary. Retrieved from http://neweasterneurope.eu/articles-and-commentary/1861-the-dcfta-in-transnistria-who-gains

Carr, E. H. (1939). *The 20 years' crisis 1919-1939. An introduction to the study of international relations*. London: Macmillan.

Chinn, J., & Roper, S. D. (1998). Territorial autonomy in Gagauzia. *Nationalities Papers, The Journal of Nationalities and Ethnicity, 26*(1), 87–101.

Chorba, A. (2015, December 16). Pridnestrovian identity. *Novosti Pridnestrovya*. Retrieved from http://novostipmr.com/en/news/15-12-16/pridnestrovian-identity

Eurasianet. (2012, May 2). Can a flea market solve the Georgian-South Ossetian conflict? *Eurasianet.org*. Retrieved from http://www.eurasianet.org/node/65346

Ferguson, Y. H., & Mansbach, R. W. (1996). *Polities. Authority, identities, and change*. Columbia, SC: University of South Carolina Press.

Filippova, O. (2012). Dimensions of Transnistrian identity in present-day political developments. In H. Rytövuori-Apunen, H. Palu, S. Khatlamajyan, & N. Iskandaryan (Eds.), *Security and development in a complex policy environment: Perspectives from Moldova, Armenia, Tajikistan and Kazakhstan* (pp. 35–52). Tampere Peace Research Institute, University of Tampere (Finland), Caucasus Institute (Armenia), and the Institute for Civil Society and Regional Development (Armenia). Yerevan: Limush Printhouse.

Formuzal, M. (2010, April 9). Long live the free, democratic, prosperous and open to the world Gagauzia! Governor of Gagauzia [Speech]. Retrieved from http://gagauzia.md/newsview.php?l=en&idc=467&id=1255

Government of the Republic of Moldova. Information platform of crossing the border of the Republic of Moldova. Retrieved from http://www.frontiera.gov.md/en

Huntington, S. P. (1996). *The clash of civilizations and remaking of world order*. London: Simon & Shuster.
Infotag. (2016, April 22). Gagauzia elders condemn Moldovan unionists. *Infotag*. Retrieved from http://www.infotag.md/rebelion-en/222862/
Katchanovski, I. (2006). *Cleft countries: Regional political divisions and cultures in Post-Soviet Ukraine and Moldova*. Stuttgart: ibidem.
Marlin-Bennett, R. (Ed.). (2012). *Alker and IR: Global studies in an interconnected world*. London: Routledge.
Nye, J. S., Jr. (2004). *Soft power: The means to success in world politics*. New York: PublicAffairs.
Parham, S. (2016a). 'The problem with our borders in Batken': Local understandings of border control and sovereignty in Kyrgyzstan. In H. Rytövuori-Apunen (Ed.), *The regional security puzzle around Afghanistan. Bordering practices in Central Asia and beyond* (pp. 51–78). Opladen: Barbara Budrich.
Parham, S. (2016b). *China's Borderlands: Inside People and Borders in Central Asia*. London: I. B. Tauris.
Peirce, C. S. (1992/1878). How to make our ideas clear. In *Charles Sanders Peirce: Collected papers*. Charlottesville: InteLex. CD-ROM Databases. Also in Louis Menand (Ed.). (1997). *Pragmatism: A reader* (pp. 26–48). New York: Vintage Books.
RFE/RL. (2014, February 3). Gagauzia voters reject closer EU ties for Moldova. *Radio Free Europe/Radio Liberty*. Retrieved from http://www.rferl.org/content/moldova-gagauz-referendum-counting/25251251.html
Romashov, V. (2014). The nexus of linkage and leverage in Russia's policy toward the near abroad: The case of Moldova. *University of Tampere, School of Management, master's thesis in International Relations*. Retrieved from http://urn.fi/URN:NBN:fi:uta-201412092386
Rytövuori-Apunen, H. (2005). Forget 'Post-Positivist' IR! The legacy of IR theory as the locus for a pragmatist turn. *Cooperation and Conflict: Journal of the Nordic International Studies Association, 40*(2), 147–177.
Rytövuori-Apunen, H. (2016). Introduction: Bordering practices challenging state borders. In H. Rytövuori-Apunen (Ed.), *The regional security puzzle around Afghanistan. Bordering practices in Central Asia and beyond* (pp. 1–28). Opladen: Barbara Budrich.
Rytövuori-Apunen, H., & Usmonov, F. (2016). Tajikistan's unsettled security: Borderland dynamics of the outpost on Russia's Afghan frontier. In H. Rytövuori-Apunen (Ed.), *The regional security puzzle around Afghanistan. Bordering practices in Central Asia and beyond* (pp. 131–160). Opladen: Barbara Budrich.
Searle, J. R. (1995). *The construction of social reality*. London: Allen Lane, Penguin Press.
Sobják, A. (2014). Is Transnistria the next Crimea? *The Polish Institute of International Affairs. Bulletin 49* (644).
Toulmin, S. (1990). *Cosmopolis: The hidden agenda of modernity*. Chicago: University of Chicago Press.
University of Eastern Finland. Karelian Institute. Retrieved from http://www2.uef.fi/en/ktl/state-of-the-art-reports
Ursu, V., & Raileanu, D. (2014, February 2). Concerned about EU integration, Moldova's Gagauz region holds disputed referendum. *Radio Free Europe/Radio Liberty*. Retrieved from http://www.rferl.org/content/moldova-gagauzia-eu-referendum/25249087.html
USA Today. (2015, January 30). Ukraine to ask U.N. to call Russia a terrorism sponsor. *USA Today*. Retrieved from http://www.usatoday.com/story/news/world/2015/01/30/ukraine-russia-terror-sponsor/22593733/
Van Houtum, H., Oliver, K., & Wolfgang, Z. (Eds.). (2005). *B/ordering space*. Aldershot: Ashgate.
Vlah, I. (2016, March 21). 'Irina Vlah: Many identify themselves with the Russian world, the authorities don't like it'. *The Newspapers, News from Russia* [Interview]. Retrieved from http://the-newspapers.com/2016/03/21/irina-vlah-many-identify-themselves-with-the-russian-world-the-authorities-dont-like-it

Helena Rytövuori-Apunen holds a doctorate in Social Sciences (field International Relations) and is a University Researcher at the Tampere Peace Research Institute (TAPRI), University of Tampere, Finland. Her special areas of interest include the theory and methodology of Peace Research and International Relations, pragmatist and semiotic research, trust in international relations, Russian foreign and security policy, and the conflict processes and conflict management at post-Soviet borders. In geographical terms her current research concentrates on Central Asia and the so-called frozen conflicts (Transnistria, Abkhazia, South Ossetia, and Nagorno-Karabakh).

The Border Within: Immigration Policymaking in Europe and the Role of Science

Maren Borkert

Abstract While European countries differ in terms of migration histories, patterns and regimes, this chapter shows a common trend to link migration control with integration. The introduction of *compulsory integration courses for newcomers* before and after entry marks a clear shift from principally territorial control to more complex forms of regulating access to, and participation in, society. This establishment of '*a border within*' is accompanied by the re-definition of European territory along cultural-social lines (*Europeanism*), which translates into exclusionary mechanisms for specific groups of migrants, i.e. family migrants (women), particularly from Arab/Islamic countries. Analysing the role of science and knowledge in integration policymaking in Austria, the chapter illustrates how migrants are exempted from dialogues structures even in migration matters, highlighting mechanisms of *exclusion* in the *European knowledge society*. In this chapter, I argue that the area of 'integration' can be seen as Europe's new frontier in which related policies function as lines of demarcation and separation for what is deemed Europe's distinct 'spiritual-religious and moral heritage' (EU Charter of fundamental rights 2007). Evidence is based on two European comparative research projects conducted subsequently from 2009 to 2013.

Keywords Migration control • Compulsory integration measures • Exclusion • Europe

1 Introduction

Throughout history, migration and integration issues have been an important factor for all kinds of social transformations in Europe (Bade et al. 2007; Moch 1992). With an increase in migration movements, and their diversification since the 1990s, there has been a significant shift among European Member States' efforts to control

M. Borkert (✉)
Centre for Entrepreneurship, School of Economics and Management, Technical University Berlin, Berlin, Germany
e-mail: m.borkert@tu-berlin.de

C. Günay, N. Witjes (eds.), *Border Politics*, DOI 10.1007/978-3-319-46855-6_12

them. In consequence, migration and integration policies have been repeatedly changed, modified and heatedly debated (Borkert and Penninx 2011).

Some see these developments as a consequence of globalisation, which has led to the erosion of national sovereignty (Evans 1998; Keohane and Milner 1996) and thus the capacity of the state to control unwanted migration (Cornelius et al. 1994; Sassen 1999). Others hold that international norms have constrained national policy making (Goldstein and Keohane 1993; Katzenstein 1996) and that the emergence of an international human rights regime prevents nation-states from defining who is allowed to enter and leave their territory. In this vein, the absence of an explicit immigration scheme is explained by international value regimes (Jacobson 1996; Sassen 1996; Soysal 1994).

For Europe, both of these claims are contested by empirical evidence. Nor do European nation-states baulk at formulating whom they want to enter and whom they don't (by, for example, promoting highly qualified migration, while making family migration from 'less-developed' countries difficult), neither has the power of the nation-state to regulate migration *per se* ceased. But it has found new grounds. As this chapter will show, the demarcation of borders and the drawing of boundaries have significantly changed with the 2000s, moving from principally territorial control to more complex forms of regulating access to and participation in society. To reconstruct these shifts in the demarcation and drawing of borders and boundaries with regard to migration and migrant integration in Europe this chapter *firstly* shows the establishment of a link between migration and integration policies and thus between entry to a given territory and access to society. *Secondly*, it highlights (new) mechanisms of exclusion in the European knowledge society by analysing the changing role of knowledge and science in integration policymaking in the case of Austria. *Thirdly*, it will be discussed how the establishment of the European Single Market and the progressive elimination of border controls within the EU to promote the freedom of movement for EU citizens (Schengen Agreement) facilitated the emergence of new frontiers along cultural-social lines (Europeanism). Empirical evidence is drawn from two European comparative studies, 'Promoting Sustainable Policies for Integration (PROSINT)' and 'Science-Society Dialogues on Migrant Integration in Europe (DIAMINT)', which were carried out from 2009 to 2011 and from 2011 to 2013 respectively.[1]

In the following sections I hope to make three major contributions: First, to explore recent shifts of borders in the area of migrant integration including both formal-legal as well as social boundaries. Second, I will analyse the role of knowledge and science in integration policymaking, a topic only marginally dealt with in migration literature. Third, I will argue that despite migration regulations shifting from controlling external (territorial) borders to more latent forms of

[1]Both projects engaged with a wide range of research methods including the analysis of key documents, quantitative and qualitative media analysis, network analysis and well over 100 expert interviews. For Austria alone 30 expert interviews were conducted within the DIAMINT project. For more information on the PROSINT project please see: http://research.icmpd.org/1429.html. For more information on the DIAMINT project please visit: www.diamint.eu

internal social admission, space as a reference for inclusion/exclusion has not become obsolete.

2 Shifting Borders and Regulating Access: How Integration Policies in Europe Evolved into Lines of Demarcation

Although immigration issues, political structures, and policy making vary substantially among European countries (see Borkert and Penninx 2011; Zincone et al. 2011), some common features and trends in migration policies can be identified across EU Member States. One prominent trend and pattern is the establishment of a migration-integration nexus, i.e. the common practice among EU countries, since the beginning of the new millennium, to link access to and stay at national territorial level with the fulfilment of integration tasks. From the 2000s onwards, most EU countries have introduced post-admission integration measures such as civic integration programmes. These programmes vary from country to country according to their socio-economic or cultural focus, their voluntary or mandatory character, the request and type of post-entry tests, consequences in case these tests and programmes are not successfully completed, the presence and type of post-entry tests or the availability of state funding among other. Some countries such as the Netherlands, Germany and the UK have also introduced pre-entry language tests to assess the 'integrability' of international migrants *prior* to their arrival in the country of destination (in 2006, 2007 and 2010, respectively).

The linkage between migration control (entry permit) and integration policy (in the sense of admission to society) can be traced both in the political rhetoric of various European countries as well as their domestic legislation, and it has been implemented and institutionalised in related programmes. While it is often argued (by policymakers and in the mass media) that compulsory integration schemes are introduced to improve integration performances, from a scientific point of view such statements are questionable. On the one hand there is no empirical evidence on the (short or long-term) impact of integration courses on migrants' integration trajectories available at the national level in any of the chosen EU countries. On the other hand, the compulsory integration schemes introduced by EU member states are not applied to all newcomers or resident migrants alike. Highly qualified migrants e.g. from OECD countries such as Japan or Canada, as well as their families, are usually exempted from attending integration courses. In personal interviews conducted within the PROSINT project, policymakers explained this discrepancy not by referring to the proficiency of highly qualified migrants in the domestic language (which they mostly lack), but with their general 'integrability'. As will be shown in the following sections, the introduction of a migration-integration nexus in Europe is indeed very closely interwoven with (the reduction of) family migration from Arab countries and the 'well-intended' emancipation of potentially oppressed Muslim women. To better trace the increasing linkages between the areas of migration control and integration in Europe, the establishment of the migration-integration nexus is exemplified with regard to pre-entry policies, post-arrival policies as well as political debates.

Overall, the topics of admission and integration began to be linked in *political discourses* in 1966, when the later British Home Secretary Roy Hattersley, then Labour MP for the district of Birmingham-Sparkbrook, known for its 'race-related' problems, declared that 'Integration without control is impossible, but control without integration is indefensible' (Hansen 2000: 26; Kofman et al. 2012). It was not before the turn of the new millennium, however, that the linkage between migration and integration became prominent in European political rhetoric and became widespread across European Member States. The institutionalisation of the migration-integration nexus in political discourses started in the Netherlands, where labour market and civic integration demands initiated a major policy reform in 1998 (leading to the introduction of the Act on the Civic Integration of Newcomers). With the beginning of the 2000s, immigration in the Netherlands became increasingly politicised. Family migration of people with a Muslim background from countries such as Turkey or Morocco particularly raised major public and political concerns (Entzinger et al. 2011; Kofman et al. 2012). A policy memorandum on new pre-entry programmes argued that mandatory tests would be an effective instrument to enhance knowledge of Dutch, particularly amongst migrant women and eventually to facilitate their integration into Dutch society. Together with gender issues, and the educational performance of so-called second generation children, questions of radicalisation and security came to the fore with an explicit reference to Islamist terrorism as a potential threat posed by immigrants from non-Western countries (Entzinger et al. 2011).

In the late 1990s public debates in Germany had also begun to focus on the presumed 'failure of integration' as ultimately proven by the poor educational results of children with a migration background, the so-called second and third generation in various PISA-studies (OECD 2001, 2004, 2007). Political rhetoric was intensified by debates about religious and cultural differences, particularly with reference to Muslim migrants in Germany, which gained momentum after the destruction of the twin towers in the United States in 2001. Ethnic segregation, first and foremost of Turkish migrants and their descendants, in German metropolises was interpreted as a sign of the creation of 'parallel societies'. In this context, the honour killing of Hatun Sürücü, a Turkish woman of Kurdish origin, inflamed a public debate over forced marriages and equal rights for migrant women. In this climate consensus was evolving among political parties and in parliamentary debates that there was an increasing need 'to promote and to demand' integration (Süssmuth et al. 2001: 201). In particular, the connection between integration and the need to protect rights among migrant women, and to promote their emancipation, helped to secure support from the political left: Eventually, the introduction of mandatory pre-entry and post-arrival language programmes and tests was broadly supported by major political parties, trade unions as well as local governments (Deutscher Bundestag 2007a, b, 2009).

In line with the integration debates in the Netherlands and Germany, Austria and Switzerland also started to argue for the introduction of compulsory integration measures, in the late 1990s. Again socio-cultural and gender issues were at the forefront of these debates. With similar arguments, i.e. the rescue of migrant women from patriarchal oppression and their education, the Austrian government agreed on post-arrival integration courses and argued in favour of a mandatory German language test prior to immigration (Hollomey et al. 2011). In Switzerland, national debates stressed the issue of continuous numbers of children and women arriving through family reunification. In the context of a national referendum to introduce (more restrictive) asylum and migration policies in 2006, the linkage between integration and labour market as well as the importance of 'cultural closeness' figured prominently in Swiss debates (Borkert 2012).

In the UK, the term 'integration' was first used with reference to refugee services and began to spread into general migration discourses in the late 2000s. In the year 2000, the UK Home Office launched its first refugee integration report 'Full and Equal Citizens'. In 2005, a follow-up report entitled 'Integration Matters' was released. In the UK, from the early 2000s onwards, the concept of 'community cohesion' began to replace both 'multiculturalism' and 'integration'. The so-called Cantle report (2001), in response to disturbances in Northern towns, placed emphasis on newcomers and Muslims. The report accused minority groups of living a 'parallel life' and demanded from them that they make an effort to learn about and demonstrate 'common values'. Hence, a very specific issue linkage between language learning, everyday usage of English, inclusion and community cohesion was forged (Kofman et al. 2012).

Almost 10 years later, these integration debates were echoed in Italy, although assuming a slightly different shape. From a statistical point of view, Italy turned from being a country of emigration into a country of immigration in 1998, and thus is considered to be a relatively young immigration country compared to other European Member States. In Italy, the first link between migration control and integration was introduced by the Charter of the Values of Citizenship and Integration, which was enacted in 2007 by the Italian Ministry of Interior. In contrast with the original intention, the Charter was never used for the naturalisation of would-be citizens. Instead, the document later became part of the integration agreement that all regular migrants entering Italy on a valid visa must sign with the Italian authorities in order to receive a permit of stay. While the Charter was centred on Italian culture and values, particularly addressing issues of religion and social cohesion, and clearly inspired by a stereotypical and stigmatising vision of Islam, the so-called Security Law which followed it was dominated by security paradigms and concerns with combating undocumented migration. The Security Law (Law No. 94/2009) marked a clear shift in the definition of migrant integration, and formally established a link between the renewal of the residence permits and the meeting of specific post-arrival integration requirements, such as fulfilling an Integration Agreement (Caponio and Zincone 2011).

Besides political discourses, European countries also adopted a number of laws and policies fostering the link between migration control and integration. Many EU

Member States have, in fact, adopted a variety of mandatory integration measures, ranging from pre-entry tests to mandatory post-arrival integration courses. While pre-entry tests on civic culture and language have been designed to select the more 'integrable' migrants, and to withhold entry from others based on their knowledge of domestic rules, political institutions and the culture of the country they want to settle in, compulsory courses and tests make long-term residence status or naturalisation dependant on the degree of integration of the individual migrant.

In the Netherlands an obligation to attend civic integration courses was implemented in 1998, which included command of the domestic language at A2-level, according to the Common European Framework of Reference for Languages (CEFR) for third country nationals above the age of 18. A series of reforms toughened the requirements migrants needed to fulfil for their stay in the country, such as the introduction of a 120 % minimum wage level for family migration, and included the installation of pre-entry programmes in 2004 to help further decrease immigration into the country. The reform eventually resulted in an Integration Abroad Act in 2006 and a new Civic Integration Act in 2007 (Entzinger et al. 2011).

In Germany, the Independent Commission on Migration, installed by the then Minister of Interior, Otto Schilly, in September 2000, emphasised that migration and integration are not separate policy realms and in its final report clearly defined migration control and entry limitation as a precondition for integration. Following the commission's suggestions, a new Immigration Act was drawn up and entered into force in 2005. For the first time in German history, the Immigration Act combined both the restriction of migration and the definition of rules for integration in one single law. The 2005 Immigration Act installed compulsory post-arrival integration and orientation courses (run by the state) at B1-level CEFR for newcomers from so-called third countries who are eligible for permanent residency, ethnic German repatriates, as well as recipients of social benefits if their German proficiency is poor. In 2007 the Immigration Act was amended, extending the group of beneficiaries to EU-citizens and German nationals, and establishing compulsory language courses prior to arrival to the country (Bommes 2006: 70; Borkert and Bosswick 2011).

A similar development can be observed in Austria and Switzerland. In Austria, the Aliens Act (*Fremdengesetz*) of 2002 regulated the introduction of the 'integration agreement', i.e. the duty to attend a German language course of 100 h duration and to demonstrate a command of German at A1-level CEFR within a requested time period. In 2006, the level of German required to obtain a permanent residence permit was raised to A2 for all immigrants (with the exception of key personnel). In 2010, the minimum time period for proving a command of A2 was reduced from 5 to 2 years, while language proficiency for obtaining a permanent residence permit was raised to B1 (Hollomey et al. 2011). In Switzerland, integration became anchored to federal policy in the course of the revision of the Federal Law on Residence and Settlement of Foreigners (1999), which introduced the so-called 'integration article' (Art. 25a). The nexus between the admission of foreign nationals and the (potential) level of integration was formally anchored in Swiss migration policy with the new Federal Law on Foreigners (*Bundesgesetz über die*

Ausländerinnen und Ausländer—AUG) of 2005, which entered into force on 1 January 2008. According to article 54, the granting of a permanent or a short-term residence permit can be made under the condition that a language or orientation course (including on the Swiss way of life) is attended (Art. 54.1). This also applies to permits issued under the family reunification scheme (Arts. 43–45). The obligation to attend an integration or language course can be stated in an integration agreement (Art. 54.1). In addition, the degree of integration is taken into account when issuing a permanent residence permit (see Art. 34.4), and in discretional decisions ('Ermessungsausübung') by Swiss authorities, particularly regarding expulsions and denials of entry (see also Art. 96: 2005). These integration agreements found wide approval across the Swiss political spectrum (Prodolliet 2009: 50). Persons from third countries coming to Switzerland for family reunification are particularly emphasised as being the most important target group of integration agreements (Borkert 2012).

While clear-cut integration courses have been installed only in some European countries, others like the Czech Republic, UK and Italy have adopted more general ways of linking entry into their territory with integration requirements regarding a wide range of topics. With the accession to the European Union in 2004, the Czech Republic introduced knowledge of Czech language as well as economic self-sufficiency and orientation in the society as preconditions for obtaining a permanent residence permit. In 2009, proof of Czech language proficiency at A1-level CEFR in a written test became mandatory for all immigrants seeking a permanent residence permit (Babická 2011). In the UK, migrants seeking an indefinite leave to remain (permanent residence) are faced with a compulsory language test (ESOL3), and since 2007, a test on the British way of life (Kofman et al. 2012). According to the Italian Security Law of 2009, migrants should sign an integration agreement to commit him- or herself to acquire knowledge of spoken Italian corresponding to A2 as well as knowledge of the Italian constitution and civic life. The signee also agrees to fulfil his or her educational obligations towards minor children (Caponio and Zincone 2011). In contrast to mandatory integration and/or orientation courses in the previous countries, Spain and Sweden apply a different strategy. Instead of emphasising the demand side, both countries emphasise that *offering* language courses facilitates the migrants' individual integration process. In providing this offer local authorities play a key role.

Overall one might observe that in countries such as Austria, the Czech Republic, Germany, the Netherlands, (the German speaking part of) Switzerland and the UK both political rhetoric and domestic law are characterized by a rather strong nexus between migration control and integration. In comparison, in countries like Spain, Sweden but also Italy the nexus between entry control and integration is apparently weaker or more recent: In Spain and Sweden post-arrival integration programmes such as language courses are offered as an incentive to participate in the local labour market (Sweden), or seen as a means into welfare integration (Spain).

By combining entry control with integration, however, European Member states convert the policy of integration into an instrument of access control to both the territory (pre-entry tests) and society (post-arrival integration courses).

Interestingly, though, this rigid control of access to territory and society does not apply to all migrants and newcomers. Most highly qualified migrants are in fact exempted from these regulations. As most European countries seek to attract highly qualified so-called third country nationals, national legislation for entry and stay is eased. Take, for example, the right of family reunification recognized through the EU (Council Directive 2003/86/EC). In theory, the right to live in a family is inalienable and should be applied to all non-EU citizens alike. Recently, family reunification was hardened in Europe by the introduction of pre-entry language tests, minimum wage levels for family migrants and mandatory integration courses for long-term residence permits whose costs are (partially) borne by the migrants themselves. Due to the demand for (highly) qualified migrants in most European Member States, they and their families are usually exempted from compulsory integration measures (both pre-entry or post-arrival). This means, that in practice, it is people applying for entry on a family reunification scheme, often from so-called less-developed countries, who are affected by the more and more restrictive integration requirements (Perchinig 2012; Strik et al. 2010). As Kofman shows it is in fact mostly Muslim women from Arab countries who are targeted and affected by this new admission policy, based on the assumption that they have less 'integration potential'. Exceptions are only made for highly skilled migrants in reference to economic profitability and their positive impact on local and national economies (Kofman et al. 2012).

Overall, there has been a shift in formal-legal terms in the regulation of immigration into Europe by transforming integration policy into an instrument of migration control and, thus, moving external borders into the social realm. As has been shown, migration policies in Europe have evolved on various assumptions with regard to the integration process and the effectiveness of compulsory language and civic education courses. These assumptions are further fuelled by a stereotypical and stigmatising vision of Islam which eventually translates into mechanisms of exclusion for specific groups of migrants, particularly Muslim women seeking to enter Europe on a family reunification scheme. The question remains, however, what the source of this 'new knowledge' on mandatory integration measures is and how it ended-up in policy formulation and implementation. This is the topic of the following section focusing on the role of science and knowledge in Austrian migrant integration policymaking. In this context, the sole question of who is considered a valuable dialogue partner for migrant integration policy making, and what actors are excluded, will prove illustrative in this regard.

3 The Changing Role of Science-Society Dialogues: What Knowledge for Whose Integration?

According to current doctrine in the study of science, the late nineteenth and early twentieth century witnessed a gain in importance of expert knowledge for administrative and governing purposes and, subsequently, a change in the role of science in society. In consequence, social life became increasingly subjected to the process of 'scientification' (subjecting every aspect of social life to scientific investigation, i.e. the 'scientification of social life'), while the practice of science became more and more politicised (Raphael 1996; Weingart 1983). In that time, according to prominent scholars, knowledge and expertise were key resources for policy development and problem-solving, and a rational mode of government prevailed (Wildavsky 1979; Weingart 1999). In an attempt to analyse the (changing) relations between science and policy a number of ideal-type models have been identified in the literature, which have been successively applied to the area of migration research. Among these the most common are the *enlightenment model*, the *technocratic model*, the *bureaucratic model* and the *engineering model* (see Hoppe 2005; Scholten 2011). Operating with a clear-cut distinction between politics and science, these models run the risk of obscuring mutual relations, overlaps and impacts between science and politics. Numerous scholars have in fact argued that in post-modern or risk societies, boundaries between science and politics are increasingly blurred and scientific controversies become more and more debated in public through which the credibility of science is put at stake (Beck 1991; Weingart 1999).

The changing relation between science and politics obviously affects the dialogue structures between them provoking a substantial change. According to the literature, in the risk society dialogue structures between research and policy deinstitutionalise, and become more indirect, with media growing into a central arena for portraying (and mediating) discussions between knowledge producers and knowledge users. Furthermore, research-policy dialogues grow into science-society dialogues as their increased public nature offer opportunities for new and other actors such as NGOs, lobby groups or the 'well informed citizen' (Schütz 1972) to participate. Dialogue structures in the risk society also become more ad-hoc and changeable as their setup depends more on the perceived necessities and fast changing swings of a rather reactive mode of governance. Whereas previously research policy structures were dominated by one single, most likely governmental, actor and institutionalized, in the risk society multiple boundary organizations would rise brokering knowledge between a multitude of providers and users in multiple ways (Adam et al. 2000; Beck 1986, 1991; Lupton 1999; Taylor-Gooby and Zinn 2006).

While in general science as a source of truth and a key resource for policymaking becomes increasingly contested (Gieryn 1999; Weingart 1999; Wildavsky 1979), the role of social research in migrant policymaking is challenged by the perceived 'failure of integration' which shook many European countries in the late 1990s. On the one hand, this failure was to a certain extent blamed on the scientists involved in the formulation of integration policies. On the other hand, the effects of the close relations between migrant integration research and policymaking on the development of integration as a research field in itself was criticised as being problematic (Bommes and Morawska 2005; Lavenex 2005; Thränhardt and Bommes 2010).

In Austria, scholars started to become interested in migration and integration in the late 1960s and early 1970s, when the country attracted a large number of so-called guest workers and felt the need to regulate their influx and stay (Perchinig 2005). This initial phase was primarily marked by a handful of individual researchers focusing on either the movements of migrants or specific migrant groups or on the issue of 'guest workers' (Bauböck and Perchinig 2003). In the 1990s migration research in Austria increased, diversified and scattered. Contrary to most European countries, however, migration research in Austria remained a fragmented field of mostly small research groups and individual researchers. Migration scholars in Austria are in fact mostly embedded in institutions focusing on broader issues and often represent a minority in their institution (Fassmann et al. 2009: 13). Even though migration and integration research have gained relevance in the past decade in general, literature shows that this did not lead to better funding opportunities. Quite the contrary, migration research in Austria largely depends on political actors and institutions involved in migration and migrant integration policymaking, with substantial impacts on research agendas (Borkert 2015; Fassmann et al. 2009; Bauböck and Perchinig 2003; Stacher et al. 1997). The fragmented and politicised migration research landscape in Austria certainly affects both the production and the utilisation of knowledge in the area of migrant integration.

Overall, the two major structures for science-society dialogues are the Advisory Committee on Integration[2] and the Expert Council on Integration.[3] However, there is a certain division between scientific and non-scientific bodies and the 'knowledge' or 'expertise' they are able to provide. Qualitative face-to-face interviews conducted with more than 30 experts from politics, academia, media and civil society in the course of the DIAMINT project show that stakeholders see and make a great difference between 'scientific knowledge' and the knowledge provided by NGOs. Due to the fact that NGOs argue from a certain political position and mostly focus on the practical application of theoretical knowledge, their 'knowledge' or 'expertise' is perceived as being less objective. To be considered

[2]The Advisory Committee on Integration involves representatives from several federal ministries (e.g. the Ministry of Interior; Ministry of Labour, Social Affairs and Consumer Protection; Ministry of Science and Research), all federal state governments, the Austrian Association of Towns, the Austrian Association of Municipalities, the Austrian Chamber of Labour, the Austrian Chamber of Agriculture, the Austrian Chamber of Commerce, the Federation of Austrian Industries and the largest relief organizations in Austria (Caritas, Diakonie, Hilfswerk, Red Cross and Volkshilfe).

[3]The Expert Council on Integration involves established experts in the field of migration and integration from the sciences such as Heinz Fassmann, Ruth Wodak, Gudrun Biffl and Rainer Münz, and less well known journalists like Hans Winkler or businessmen such as Thomas Oliva from the Austrian Association of Branded Goods Industry.

an 'expert' by political institutions, scholars must be employed by a university or another research institution in Austria and work as scientists in their main occupation. According to the interviewees, however, the status of an 'expert' is not automatically granted to any scientist. Instead, most interviewees pointed out that being considered an 'expert' in the field of migration by political decision makers is very much dependent upon informal and personal networks, political courtesy and employment at one of the well-known and respected Austrian research institutions. This blend of political agenda-setting, state finance and expert recognition has an adverse impact on migrant associations which are often not included in these highly personalized networks of science-politics interaction in the field of migration. They are indeed exempted from both major dialogue structures on migrant integration in Austria.

If migrants are exempted from policymaking arenas, what is the basis of knowledge on which Austrian policymaking evolves? And what is the role of science in it? According to Boswell (2009) there are three ideal types of knowledge utilization in science-society interaction in the area of migration and integration policies: *instrumental knowledge utilization* (for policy development), *legitimizing knowledge utilization* (legitimizing one's own political role), and *substantiating knowledge utilization* (justifying decisions and orientations). In addition to this, a fourth type of knowledge utilisation was identified in Austria, for which we will distinguish between knowledge utilization (as an active way of appropriating knowledge for action), and knowledge consumption as a more passive attitude which implies the acquisition of knowledge, but no subsequent use. To the latter I will refer as *knowledge shelving* or *knowledge storing*.

In the Austrian case, there are indications of both *legitimizing* and *substantiating use of knowledge* in migration policymaking in Austria, but what is most striking is the use of *knowledge shelving*, i.e. when governmental actors commission research studies whose results are consumed and archived and, eventually, used for decision making at a later stage. Especially in the field of naturalisation, the interviewed stakeholders referred to a legitimising use of scientific knowledge, but it was also argued that (due to its overall primacy) there is little need for the Ministry of Interior (MoI) to legitimise its position from the field of science. The establishment of the Advisory Committee is regarded more as a legitimisation base for utilising civil society knowledge, for instance, in the development of the Integration Report.[4] Interviewed in the context of the DIAMINT project the two representatives of the MoI stated that the fact that several issues related to citizenship were included in the Integration Report is based on the decision of the Advisory Committee, thus indicating its use for substantiation. An example of *knowledge shelving* is given by the introduction of the so-called red-white-red card, a point-based immigration scheme introduced in Austria in 2011. Promoted particularly by the Industrialists Association, the idea was first suggested in a study by Heinz Fassmann and Rainer

[4]The *Integration Report, published since 2001*, provides statistical information on *integration* in *Austria*.

Munoz in 1992.[5] What proved to be most peculiar for the Austrian case, however, are the repeated attempts by governmental actors to influence the production of knowledge on migrant integration in Austria. To do so, a wide range of strategies was applied ranging from establishing own migration research facilities to openly claiming knowledge authority (as in the case of the MoI in naturalisation) and seeking direct influence on research findings (more indirectly through funding and directly by 'approving' results).

In summary one may observe that migration research in Austria is strongly politicised. The major shifts that mark the use of scientific knowledge and the establishment of somewhat exclusive dialogue structures in Austrian migrant integration research, however, cannot be explained by the changing role of science alone. As will be suggested in the conclusion, the recourse to scientific knowledge, and particularly the use of statistics, is also motivated by drawing a fine line between the inside and the outside world, and thus between the mainstream population and immigrants. In this regards, science is rather used as a tool to establish and legitimise new mechanisms of exclusion and inclusion. As the analysis of key dialogue structures on integration in Austria reveals, emphasis is placed on knowledge transfer between *science* and *politics*, while migrant or civil society organisations play only a marginal role in migrant integration decision-making. Only the Advisory Committee on Integration, in fact, explicitly involves non-scientific actors but the largest Austrian relief organisations that take part in it (Caritas, Diakonie, Hilfswerk, Red Cross and Volkshilfe) represent a minority (Borkert 2015).

4 Conclusion

The international mobility of people, as the summer of migration 2015, and the related political and administrative crisis illustrated, has become a test case for the EU. All sovereign states claim the right to control and limit immigration into their territory. Any expansion of the general movement of persons in transnational regions, as intended in the Schengen Agreement of 1985, means a gain in mobility and a loss of territorial sovereignty (Bauböck 2004; Bigo 1998; Ireland 1991; Huysmans 2000). In consequence, the development of migration policies in Europe is very closely interwoven with the development and design of the European Union itself. The project of the single market and the elimination of internal borders to facilitate the free movement of European goods, services, capital and persons created a common interest in the regulation of migration and external border control. This interest is the basis for the evolution of the EU's common approach on migration and asylum, which has gained increasing importance in recent years.

[5]Fore more information see Heinz Fassmann & Rainer Münz (1992), *Einwanderungsland Österreich? Gastarbeiter, Flüchtlinge, Immigranten*, Jugend & Volk: Vienna.

The communitarisation of asylum, refugee and gradually of migration policy, which began with the Treaty of Amsterdam, adopted in 1999 and subsequently concretized, is undoubtedly one of the most important expansions of the competency of the European Union in the past decade (Bendel 2009; Geddes 2003, 2005; Guiraudon 2000).

This silent Europeanisation of migration policies in Europe, the emergence of common trends and practices across the EU, has been accompanied by a shift towards more restrictive policies of entry and stay. By defining the goal of the EU as 'to maintain and develop the Union as an area of freedom, security and justice, in which, in conjunction with appropriate measures in relation to the external border controls, asylum, immigration and the prevention and combating of crime-free movement of persons is ensured' the Treaty of Amsterdam (1999) creates an imperative that runs through European migration policy like a red line: The Tampere program (1999–2004) still highlighted more liberal aspects of migration policy and emphasized immigration 'as a necessity and an enrichment of European societies'. But since 2001 the focus was placed back on migration control and security, as manifested in the Hague Programme 2004 (2004–2009) and the Stockholm manifest (2009–2014) (Bendel 2009; Geddes and Lazarou 2008; Guiraudon 2000).

In the European mobility area, analysis of these policy documents shows that the distribution of rights and obligations is fundamentally based on the self-perception of the EU as a common cultural space: In this sense the European migration policy distinguishes two classes of persons, EU citizens who have the right to free movement, and Non-EU citizens, so-called third-country nationals, who are subject to provisions for entry (visas) and stay, access to the labour market, family reunification, etc. The clearly restrictive and control-oriented imperatives for non-European citizens are manifested in a variety of regulatory practices, (political-media-academic) discourses, institutionalisation as well as legal and policy provisions. As was shown in this chapter, a number of laws and policies have been adopted in recent years fostering a link between migration control and integration. These new provisions include mandatory language and orientation courses and tests before and/or after entry as well as restrictive conditions for family reunification, converting the policy of integration into an instrument of access control to both the territory (pre-entry) and society (post-arrival). By definition, European measures for migrant integration should be applied to all non-EU citizens. In reality, however, this is not the case and the most highly-qualified migrants (as well as their families) from OECD countries such as Canada or Japan are exempted from these regulations. For the rest, the inalienable right to live in a family (based on Article 16.3 of the Universal Declaration of Human Rights 1948) has been gradually curtailed in view of the so-called 'integration potential' of those who intend to immigrate. As was highlighted, this policy mainly affects people from Muslim-Arab countries and particularly women who migrate under the family reunification schemes and are primarily affected by compulsory integration requirements. Exceptions are made only in terms of economic profitability and an expected positive impact on the local economy (Perchinig et al. 2012; Kofman et al. 2012; Strik et al. 2010).

In this overall framework scientific knowledge is used as an important tool to legitimise and substantiate new mechanisms of control and exclusion/inclusion. As the case study on Austria revealed, particularly quantitative data on migrant integration has a high reputation in society and is privileged by most parties as a source of neutrality and 'objectivity'. The practical everyday knowledge from migrants and civil society organisations active in the field is, instead, not considered as a source of knowledge and information. In this way migrants are de-constructed as knowledge experts even in migration matters, and are subjected to a system of public and social control. Their admission into society is only provisional, while their 'integration capacity' and contribution to making the EU 'the most competitive and dynamic knowledge-based economy in the world' (Lisbon Strategy 2000–2010) is tested pre- and post-arrival, and re-examined in case of an extension request for a residence permit (e.g. through the fulfilment of 'integration requirements' such as course certificates or proofs of income). The effects of this system of 'admission with reserve' on the individual and society as a whole are largely disregarded. As the PROSINT project revealed, evaluations at the national level of the (long-term) effects of newly introduced mandatory pre-entry and post-arrival integration programmes were either not conducted or not available in any of the European countries under investigation. Regardless of this, mandatory pre-entry and post-arrival integration measures and tests have spread across all over Europe and should be considered one of the main trends in European migration policy-making. In this vein, the area of migrant integration can be seen as Europe's new frontier, in which policies function as lines of demarcation and separation for Europe's distinct 'spiritual-religious and moral heritage' (EU Charter of fundamental rights 2007).

References

Adam, B., Beck, U., & Van Loon, J. (Eds.). (2000). *The risk society and beyond: Critical issues for social theory*. London: Sage.

Babická, K. (2011). The national policy frame for the integration of newcomers in the Czech Republic, PROSINT country report WP2. *ICMPD*. Retrieved from http://research.icmpd.org/fileadmin/Research-Website/Project_material/PROSINT/Reports/CZ_WP2_Final.pdf

Bade, K. J., Emmer, P., Lucassen, L., & Oltmer, J. (Eds.). (2007). *Enzyklopädie Migration in Europa vom 17. Jahrhundert bis zur Gegenwart*. Paderborn/München: Wilhelm Fink/Ferdinand-Schöningh.

Bauböck, R. (2004). Migration und innere Sicherheit: Komplexe Zusammenhänge, paradoxe Effekte und politische Simplifizierungen. *Österreichische Zeitschrift für Politikwissenschaft (ÖZP), 33*(1), 49–66.

Bauböck, R., & Perchinig, B. (2003). *Migrations- und Integrationsforschung in Österreich—Ansätze, Schnittstellen, Kooperationen: Ergebnisse des Workshops der Arbeitsgruppe EMIS vom 4. und 5. Juli 2003* (Kommission für Migrations- und Integrationsforschung Working Paper 1, 2004).

Beck, U. (1986). *Risikogesellschaft. Auf dem Weg in eine andere Moderne*. Frankfurt am Main: Suhrkamp.

Beck, U. (1991). *Politik in der Risikogesellschaft*. Frankfurt am Main: Suhrkamp.

Bendel, P. (2009). *Europäische Migrationspolitik. Bestandsaufnahme und Trends*. Bonn: Friedrich-Ebert-Stiftung, WISO-Diskurs.
Bigo, D. (1998). Europe passoire, Europe fortresse. La sécurisation et humanitarisation de l'immigration. In A. Rea (Ed.), *Immigration et racisme en Europe* (pp. 203–241). Brussels: Complexe.
Bommes, M. (2006). Integration durch Sprache als politisches Konzept. In U. Davy & A. Weber (Eds.), *Paradigmenwechsel in Einwanderungsfragen? Überlegungen zum neuen Zuwanderungsgesetz*. Baden-Baden: Nomos Verlagsgesellschaft. Retrieved from http://www.fes.de/GPI-NRW/forum/Bommes_IntegrationdurchSprachealspolitischesKonzept.pdf
Bommes, M., & Morawska, E. (2005). *International migration research: Constructions, omissions and the promises of interdisciplinarity*. Farnham, England: Ashgate.
Borkert, M. (2012). *The national policy frame for the integration of newcomers in Switzerland*. PROSINT country report WP2. *ICMPD*. Retrieved from http://research.icmpd.org/fileadmin/Research-Website/Project_material/PROSINT/Reports/CH_WP2_Final.pdf
Borkert, M. (2015). Research-policy dialogues in Austria. In P. Scholten, H. Entzinger, R. Penninx, & S. Verbeek (Eds.), *Integrating immigrants in Europe: Research-policy dialogues* (pp. 161–186). Dordrecht: Springer.
Borkert, M., & Bosswick, W. (2011). The case of Germany. In G. Zincone et al. (Eds.), *Migration policymaking in Europe: The dynamics of actors and contexts in past and present* (IMISCOE research series, pp. 95–128). Amsterdam: Amsterdam University Press.
Borkert, M., & Penninx, R. (2011). Policymaking in the field of migration and integration in Europe: An introduction. In G. Zincone et al. (Eds.), *Migration policymaking in Europe: The dynamics of actors and contexts in past and present* (IMISCOE research series, pp. 7–17). Amsterdam: Amsterdam University Press.
Boswell, C. (2009). *The political uses of expert knowledge. Immigration policy and social research*. Cambridge: Cambridge University Press.
Caponio, T., & Zincone, G. (2011). The national policy frame for the integration of newcomers in Italy, PROSINT country report WP2. *ICMPD*. Retrieved from http://research.icmpd.org/fileadmin/Research-Website/Project_material/PROSINT/Reports/IT_WP2_Final.pdf
Cornelius, W. A., Martin, P., & Hollifield, J. (1994). *Controlling immigration: A global perspective*. Stanford, CA: Stanford University Press.
Deutscher Bundestag. (2007a, March 28). *Plenarprotokoll 16/90. Stenographischer Bericht. 90. Sitzung*. Berlin. Retrieved from http://dip21.bundestag.de/dip21/btp/16/16090.pdf
Deutscher Bundestag. (2007b, April 23). *Entwurf eines Gesetzes zur Umsetzung aufenthalts- und asylrechtlicher Richtlinien der Europäischen Union* (BT-DS 5065, 173). Retrieved from http://dip21.bundestag.de/dip21/btd/16/050/1605065.pdf
Deutscher Bundestag. (2009). *Schriftliche Fragen mit den in der Woche vom 16. März 2009 eingegangenen Antworten der Bundesregierung* (Bundestags-Drucksache 16/12356). Berlin. Retrieved from http://dip21.bundestag.de/dip21/btd/16/123/1612356.pdf
Entzinger, H., Saharso, S., & Scholten, P. (2011). *Shaping immigration for integration? The Dutch migration-integration nexus in perspective*. Consolidated PROSINT country report for WP2. *ICMPD*. Retrieved from http://research.icmpd.org/fileadmin/Research-Website/Project_material/PROSINT/Reports/NL_WP2-3-4_Final.pdf
Evans, J. (1998). Economic globalisation: The need for a social dimension. In D. Foden & P. Morris (Eds.), *The search for equity: Welfare and security in the global economy*. London: Lawrence & Wishart.
Fassmann, H., Sievers, W., Buchl, S., & Kraus, V. (2009). *Migrations- und Integrationsforschung in Österreich: Institutionelle Verankerungen, Fragestellungen und Finanzierungen* (KMI-Working Paper No. 15. Kommission für Migrations- und Integrationsforschung). Vienna: Verlag der Österreichische Akademie der Wissenschaften.
Geddes, A. (2003). *Still beyond fortress Europe? Patterns and pathways in EU migration policy* (Queen's Papers on Europeanisation No. 4/2003). London: Transnational Press London.
Geddes, A. (2005). *The politics of migration and immigration in Europe*. London: Sage.
Geddes, A., & Lazarou, E. (2008). *Europeanization of migration policy and narratives of migration management: The case of Greece*. ESRC project Multi-Level Governance in

South-East Europe (SEE)—Institutional Innovation and Adaptation in Croatia, Greece, Macedonia and Slovenia. Centre for International Policy Research (CIPR) and South East European Research Centre (SEERC), University of Sheffield.

Gieryn, T. (1999). *Cultural boundaries of science: Credibility on the line*. Chicago: Chicago University Press.

Goldstein, J., & Keohane, R. (1993). *Ideas and foreign policy: Ideas and foreign policy: Beliefs, institutions, and political change*. Ithaca, NY: Cornell University Press.

Guiraudon, V. (2000). European integration and migration policy: Vertical policy-making as venue shopping. *Journal of Common Market Studies, 38*(2), 251–271.

Hansen, R. (2000). *Immigration and citizenship in Post-war Britain*. Oxford: Oxford University Press.

Hollomey, C., Wöger, A., & Kraler, A. (2011). The national policy frame for the integration of newcomers in Austria. PROSINT country report WP2. *ICMP*. Retrieved from http://research.icmpd.org/fileadmin/Research-Website/Project_material/PROSINT/Reports/AT_WP2_Final.pdf

Home Office. (2000). *Full and equal citizens. A strategy for the integration of refugees into the United Kingdom*. London: HMSO.

Home Office. (2005). *Integration matters: A national strategy for refugee integration*. London: IND Corporate Communications.

Hoppe, R. (2005). Rethinking the science-policy dialogue structure: From knowledge utilization and science technology studies to types of boundary arrangements. *Poiesis & Praxis: International Journal of Technology Assessment and Ethics of Science, 3*(3), 199–215.

Huysmans, J. (2000). The European Union and the securitization of migration. *Journal of Common Market Studies, 38*(5), 751–777.

Ireland, P. (1991). Facing the true 'Fortress Europe': Immigrants and politics in the EC. *Journal of Common Market Studies, 29*(5), 457–480.

Jacobson, D. (1996). *Rights across borders: Immigration and the decline of citizenship*. Baltimore: Johns Hopkins University Press.

Katzenstein, P. (1996). *The culture of national security: Norms and identity in world politics*. New York: Columbia University Press.

Keohane, R., & Milner, H. (Eds.). (1996). *Internationalization and domestic politics*. Cambridge: Cambridge University Press.

Kofman, E., Vacchelli, E., D'Angelo, A., & Lewis, H. (2012). National frame for the integration of newcomers in the United Kingdom, PROSINT country report WP2. *ICMPD*. Retrieved from http://research.icmpd.org/fileadmin/Research-Website/Project_material/PROSINT/Reports/UK_WP2_Policy_Analysis_Final.pdf

Lavenex, S. (2005). Politics of exclusion and inclusion in the wider Europe. In J. de Bardeleben (Ed.), *Soft or hard borders? Managing the divide in an enlarged Europe* (pp. 123–144). Aldershot, England: Ashgate.

Lupton, D. (1999). *Risk*. London: Routledge.

Moch, L. P. (1992). *Moving Europeans: Migration in Western Europe since 1650*. Bloomington, IN: Indiana University Press.

Organisation for Economic Cooperation and Development (OECD) (Ed.). (2001). *Programme for international student assessment (PISA), knowledge and skills for life: First results from PISA 2000*. Paris: OECD.

Organisation for Economic Cooperation and Development (OECD) (Ed.). (2004). *Programme for international student assessment (PISA), learning for tomorrow's world: First results from PISA 2003*. Paris: OECD.

Organisation for Economic Cooperation and Development (OECD) (Ed.). (2007). *Programme for international student assessment (PISA), science competencies for tomorrow's world: First results from PISA 2006*. Paris: OECD.

Perchinig, B. (2005). *Migration studies in Austria—Research at the margins* (KMI Working Paper 4/2005. Kommission für Migrations- und Integrationsforschung). Vienna: Verlag der Österreichische Akademie der Wissenschaften.

Perchinig, B. (2012). The national policy frame for the integration of newcomers. *Comparative Report*. Available online at www.icmpd.org

Perchinig, B., Hollomey, C., Kraler, A., Wöger, A., Babická, K., Güell, B., et al. (2012). *The national policy frames for the integration of newcomers. Comparative report*, PROSINT Comparative Reports WP2. ICMPD. Retrieved from http://research.icmpd.org/fileadmin/Research-Website/Project_material/PROSINT/Reports/WP2_CompRep_Final03052012.pdf

Prodolliet, S. (2009). Welche Integrationskultur? Zum gegenwärtigen Diskurs der Integrationsförderung. In E. Piñeiro, B. Isabelle, & K. Georg (Eds.), *Fördern und Fordern im Fokus* (Leerstellen des schweizerischen Integrationsdiskurses, pp. 48–60). Zürich und Genf: Seismo Verlag.

Raphael, L. (1996). Die Verwissenschaftlichung des Sozialen als methodische und konzeptionelle Herausforderung für eine Sozialgeschichte des 20. *Jahrhunderts. Geschichte und Gesellschaft, 22*(2), 165–193.

Sassen, S. (1996). *Losing control? Sovereignty in an age of globalization*. New York: Columbia University Press.

Sassen, S. (1999). Beyond sovereignty: De-facto transnationalism in immigration policy. *European Journal of Migration and Law, 1*(2), 177–198.

Scholten, P. (2011). Constructing Dutch immigrant policy. Research-policy relations and immigrant integration in the Netherlands. *British Journal of Politics and International Relations, 13*(1), 75–92.

Schütz, A. (1972). Der gut informierte Bürger. In A. Schütz (Ed.), *Gesammelte Aufsätze* (Vol. 2, pp. 85–101). Den Haag: Nijhoff.

Soysal, Y. (1994). *Limits of citizenship: Migrants and postnational membership in Europe*. Chicago, IL: University of Chicago Press.

Stacher, I., Demel, K., & Dostal, E. (1997). *Machbarkeitsstudie für ein österreichisches Forum für Migrationsstudien und Entwurf für die Organisation eines Forums für Migrationsstudien*. Vienna: Schlussbericht.

Strik, T., Böcker, A., Luiten, M., & van Oers, R. (2010). *The INTEC Project: Draft synthesis report, integration and naturalisation tests: The new way to European citizenship. A comparative study in nine member states on the national policies concerning integration and naturalisation tests and their effects on integration*. Nijmegen: Centre for Migration Law, Radboud University Nijmegen.

Süssmuth, R., Vogel, H.-J., Eylmann, H., Fücks, R., Hailbronner, K., Henkel, H.-O., et al. (2001). "Zuwanderung gestalten, Integration fördern", Bericht der unabhängigen Kommission "Zuwanderung". *Bundesministerium des Innern*. Retrieved from http://www.bmi.bund.de/cae/servlet/contentblob/123148/publicationFile/9076/Zuwanderungsbericht_pdf.pdf

Taylor-Gooby, P., & Zinn, J. O. (Eds.). (2006). *Risk in social science*. Oxford: Oxford University Press.

Thränhardt, D., & Bommes, M. (Eds.). (2010). *National paradigms of migration research*. Göttingen: V&R Unipress.

Weingart, P. (1983). Verwissenschaftlichung der Gesellschaft—Politisierung der Wissenschaft. *Zeitschrift für Soziologie, 12*, 225–241.

Weingart, P. (1999). Scientific expertise and political accountability: Paradoxes of science in politics. *Science and Public Policy, 26*(3), 151–161.

Wildavsky, A. (1979). *Speaking truth to power: The art and craft of policy analysis*. Boston: Little, Brown.

Zincone, G., Penninx, R., & Borkert, M. (Eds.). (2011). *Migration policymaking in Europe. The dynamics of actors and contexts in past and present* (IMISCOE research series). Amsterdam: Amsterdam University Press.

Maren Borkert holds a Doctorate in Sociology with a specialisation in migration and interethnic relations and works as a Marie Curie Experienced Researcher at the Chair of Entrepreneurship and Innovation, Technical University Berlin. As writer and editor Maren compiled and published numerous reports, studies and articles on the topic of migration and integration, diversity, ICT and social innovation/social change. Her main fields of research include migration and integration regimes in Europe; trans-nationalisation, development and social innovation; entrepreneurship, migrant women and the use of 'big/smart data' for scientific inquiries.

The manufacturer's authorised representative in the EU is Springer Nature Customer Service Centre GmbH, Europaplatz 3, 69115 Heidelberg, Germany. If you have any concerns regarding our products, please contact ProductSafety@springernature.com

Printed and bound by CPI Group (UK) Ltd, Croydon, CR0 4YY
25/09/2026
02222859-0012